CONTRABAND HEARTS

A CIVIIL WAR LOVE STORY

Calvin L. Osborne

Contraband Hearts
Copyright © 2025 Calvin L. Osborne

All rights reserved. No part of this publication may be reproduced, distributed, or transmitted in any form or by any means, including photocopying, recording or other electronic or mechanical methods, without the prior written permission of the author, except in the case of brief quotations embodied in reviews and certain other non-commercial uses permitted by copyright law.

Without in any way limiting the author's and publisher's exclusive rights under copyright, any use of this publication to "train" generative artificial intelligence (AI) technologies to generate text is expressly prohibited. The author reserves all rights to license uses of this work for generative AI training and development of machine learning language models.

Printed in the United States of America

Paperback ISBN: 978-1-965319-31-4
Hardback ISBN: 978-1-965319-33-8
eBook ISBN: 978-1-965319-32-1

Purpose Publishing LLC.
13194 US Highway 301 South
Suite 417
Riverview, Florida 33578

www.PurposePublishing.com

"All that you touch
You Change.
All that you Change
Changes you.
The only lasting truth
Is Change.

God
Is Change."

—Octavia E. Butler, *Parable of the Sower*

"She is a friend of my mind. She gather me, man. The pieces I am, she gather them and give them back to me in all the right order."

—Toni Morrison, *Beloved*

Praises for Contraband Hearts

A powerful Civil War-era love story rooted in real ancestry, honoring resilience, freedom, and legacy across generations. Based on true events.

"This work does a masterful job of filling in the blanks between the known facts of William Lacy's eventful life and, indeed, the author's quest to flesh out this important story. It's like the connecting mortar between the bricks of unit rosters, slave manifests and newspaper articles. It should inspire others to try to dig deeper into their ancestors' past."
— **Walter B. Sanderson, III. Retired HR Executive**

"Rich in ancestry, faith, and emotional truth. This is more than a love story, it's a powerful reclaiming of identity and legacy."
— **Angela Parks, Genealogy Researcher & Speaker**

"Empowered by baptism that the only true master of our lives is God. We adventure with William from the foundation of his enslaved status, to his escape for physical freedom, to him finding the love of his life Lucinda, to answering the call to fight for the exodus of his extended family, and to his constant struggle to be a citizen in this land of mislabeled doctrine."
— **Anthony G Jones, US Civil War Reenactor**

"Calvin Osborne displays his passion for his family history and Civil War History in particular with the compelling story of courage and triumph. It cannot be understated the challenges of 19th century African American boys, free and enslaved. Mr. Osborne guides the reader through the travails of his ancestor."
— **Bernie Siler, Lt Colonel, US Army Retired**

"A masterful blend of history and heart. Calvin Osborne revives the legacy of Black soldiers and love stories long left untold."
— **T. Harmon, Historical Fiction Author**

"A captivating, soul-stirring novel that brings the past to life through real people, real records, and real love."
— **J. Tate, Literary Reviewer & Book Blogger**

CONTENTS

Acknowledgments vii
Foreword xi
Chapter 1:   Baptism in Chains 1
Chapter 2:   The Unbroken Filly 11
Chapter 3:   Life on the Lacy Plantation 20
Chapter 4:   Journey to Arkansas 30
Chapter 5:   Rain and Wild Carrots 40
Chapter 6:   God Hears All Prayers 47
Chapter 7:   A Rumbling in Van Buren 58
Chapter 8:   Caught by Fate 67
Chapter 9:   The Civil War Begins 74
Chapter 10: The Winds of Change 85
Chapter 11: Whispers of Freedom 96
Chapter 12: A Promise Made 107
Chapter 13: A Midnight Flight 114
Chapter 14: The State of Freedom 123
Chapter 15: Welcome to Mound City 131
Chapter 16: The Meaning of War 141
Chapter 17: Sunlight in Quindaro 150
Chapter 18: Growing a Family 162
Chapter 19: The Kansas Militia 172
Chapter 20: Troubling the Waters 186
Chapter 21: The Battle of Westport 200

Chapter 22: What We Treasure 212
Chapter 23: Joining the 1st Kansas 223
Chapter 24: Endings More Bitter than Sweet 230
Chapter 25: A Parade Fit for Soldiers 239
Chapter 26: Peace and Family 251
Chapter 27: A Most Unusual Letter 261
Chapter 28: Storm for the Ages..266
Chapter 29: The Scars We Bear 274
Chapter 30: Passing the Torch..281
Chapter 31: Unearthing the Past...288

ACKNOWLEDGMENTS

First and foremost, I want to thank my wife, Tracy Osborne, for her steadfast support of this endeavor. Without her moral and spiritual support, this research, writing, and project would not have been possible. I cannot tell you how many books, papers, articles, internet searches, and hours focused on this project she has endured. It took a significant amount of funds and resources to explore the relevant geographical areas of the nation to conduct research for this book.

I want to thank the men of the 54th Massachusetts Civil War Reenactor, Company B, in Washington, D.C. Among these spectacular men, I found my Civil War purpose and voice. I thank them for their courage and keen interest in Black Civil War soldiers. I thank them for their drive to tell the true story of the glory and sacrifices that more than 200,000 Black men and 5,000 white officers made to make this nation freer than it was before the war—one of whom was my great-great-grandfather, William Lacy.

Through my involvement with Company B, I became interested and learned enough to speak to CNN with authority about Black soldiers in the Civil War. On several occasions, I almost quit the Company due to my other commitments. Yet something spiritual kept drawing me back in as if it were my expected place to be. I now know that the spirit of William Lacy would not allow me to walk away from my avocation.

Many of these men participated in the filming of the Tri-Star motion picture *Glory*. The filming of *Glory* turned out to be a golden calf for recruiting Civil War reenactors. The men of Company B stimulated my interest in research and writing about Black Civil War soldiers. They drove home the importance of preserving this part of Black American history for future generations. I thank them for accepting me into their fold and judging that my motivations and worthiness to move among them were sufficient.

Each month, for more than thirty years, someone from Company B has gone to a high school, library, college, government office, park, or national historical site somewhere across this nation to discuss the courage, involvement, and sacrifices that Black Civil War soldiers made on the altar of freedom—this cannot be measured. On a wall at the monument for African American soldiers and sailors in Washington, D.C., are the names of all of the Black Civil War soldiers and sailors and their white officers. There should be a wall somewhere in a museum for the men of Company B Civil War reenactors someday.

I thank John Allison and the Morgan County, Alabama, Archives for their support in locating the Lacy family wills and probate documents. It was there that I first saw on paper the names of my slave ancestors and the relative dollar value of each of them to their enslavers. While I have not had any contact yet with any of the Lacy family who owned my ancestors, just reading about their lives and the fullness of their effort to settle Alabama, North Carolina, and Virginia, it was clear to me that this was a fine and important family worthy of all the attention they received during their lives. The Archives opened their doors and allowed me to peruse their records, including 19th-century will and estate records.

I want to thank the CNN Network for their interest in my genealogical background, interview, and the media exposure they provided. I was surprised and puzzled when they reached out to me due to a comment I left on their electronic media. After exploring my Civil War interest in Black Civil War soldiers, CNN decided that I was interesting enough to have my genealogy researched.

CBS Morning News and Gayle King took an interest in a trip I planned to Oklahoma to replace the headstones of William and

Lucinda Lacy in the Thomas A. Smith Cemetery in Broken Arrow, Oklahoma. I thank CBS for sending a film crew and interviewing my cousin, James Hardman, and me. They felt that the story of William and Lucinda's headstone replacement would be interesting enough to share with the nation. Ancestry reached out to me to ask if I would be interested in sharing my story in a television commercial. I thank them for their support in highlighting the commitments of Black Civil War soldiers to America's history.

Todd Mildfelt is a resident of southeast Kansas. He is an author, historian, and perhaps the most knowledgeable historian regarding General James Montgomery. He has authored several books, including co-authoring his newest book, *Abolitionist of the Most Dangerous Kind*, about the life of fellow Kansan and Civil War General James Montgomery. Todd has shared a tremendous amount of information about Blacks in southeast Kansas and William Lacy and his family in particular. His support has been invaluable. I could not have done this without him.

I thank Ms. Ola Mae Ernest for her support at the Linn County, Kansas Historical Society in Pleasanton, Kansas. She has accumulated a tremendous amount of information about the people who lived, worked, and fought in and around Linn County. The county's collection of historical artifacts is in good hands with her.

When CNN aired the story of my military ancestors, James Z. Hardman was the first person to reach out to me and say, "Hello, Cuz." Because of our shared ancestry, we have become very close friends and shared research for future endeavors. I thank James for his steady support and interest. He is the only person who shares the same level of interest in William and Lucinda as I do.

I am thankful for the Kansas State Historical Society and Adam Hodge for his support. The KSHS has a wealth of information regarding the Civil War and Kansas history. It is well regarded as the leading institution for Kansas history.

I appreciate Gregory Schmidt's support from the National Archives at Kansas City. He has responded to each and every request I have made for information regarding William Lacy's involvement in the Civil War.

I want to thank Latez Ward and the Leavenworth Historical Society for their research and input regarding the 1st Kansas Colored Troop's parade.

Figure A – 1: The name of William Lacy—providing the start of a rewarding journey.

Figure A – 2: General Powell recognizing Black soldiers and dedicating the memorial

FOREWORD

The impetus for this book came to me in a most unlikely way. I was watching a sports telecast where they interviewed Drew Brees, the New Orleans Saints quarterback. As the team leader, he was asked a question by a reporter who wanted to know how the New Orleans Saints quarterback would handle it if one of his teammates knelt down on one knee while the national anthem was playing before a game. His response was abrupt, forceful, and sure.

"No one on my team will disrespect the American flag." Those were the words that came out of Drew Brees' mouth on the television I was watching that day. The tone of his voice made me believe that he would take any teammate to task if they chose to protest by taking to one knee while the song played. He was adamant about it because, as he said, his grandparents were World War II veterans. He seemed offended that anyone would not feel the same way he did about the American flag.

I also remember how it made me feel to hear him say those words. I felt shortchanged to listen to him take the position that he would personally see to it that football players on the Saints team had to pay the same respect to the national anthem or flag that he did. He should have known that people could have differing levels of patriotism.

When I hear the national anthem, I usually stand wherever I am, take my hat off if I'm wearing one, and place my hand over my heart. It's how I show my respect for those who have fought and died for the freedoms we all enjoy in the United States. It is the least I can do as a nonveteran.

I consciously leave room in my mind so that others may feel different. That difference is the freedom that we all enjoy and accept. However, Drew Brees's emphasis on the issues seemed out of place and misguided.

First, the national anthem protest goes back to the quarterback of the San Francisco 49ers, Colin Kaepernick, who started to take a seat whenever he heard the national anthem out of a protest of police brutality against Black men in the wake of the George Floyd murder. Colin was not protesting the flag or the actual anthem, but he used the anthem to make another point. Colin had initially determined that he would take a seat while the anthem was playing. Ironically, an army veteran persuaded him to take a knee instead of a seat because taking a knee was a more reverent and respectful position and would draw less attention, but it didn't. Colin agreed and took a knee each time he heard the anthem. The protest gained attention for most of the year, including the attention of team owners, politicians, and other famous folks.

Second, Drew acted as though he had power over the players because of his status as the team quarterback, and he could decide whether others could use the anthem to protest these issues. It seemed to me that Drew's tone indicated that he was planning to apply pressure on his team to punish anyone who dared to protest. The problem was the same for many people around the nation—they failed to separate what the kneeling was designed to protest. Drew Brees was caught up in the swarm of it all. He was guilty of thinking that all Americans should feel the same way he felt about the flag and the country. That may be understandable if America treated all of its citizens equally. Drew Brees misunderstood.

Watching Drew Brees discuss how he would feel about his teammates made me wonder out loud whether he had ever taken the time to think that others may feel differently and with legitimate reasons.

The next day, CNN had a story about Drew Brees' comment, placed it on their website, and asked for comments. So, I decided to offer my comment. Drew's respect for his grandparents made me think of my father, Jake Osborne. He, too, was a World War II veteran. He served in the United States Navy as a cook. He was drafted in 1943 and served on the USS Leon until 1945.

I mentioned in my comment that while Drew Brees was right to feel proud of his heritage and the valor of his grandparents, not everyone felt the same deep sense of pride. I knew my father was in the Navy, but we never discussed it. We did not spend much time together, but I felt that we spent enough time together for him to bring up his military service in a world war. He did not feel it was important enough to highlight it, or maybe he just wasn't especially proud of his service. Later, I realized that while he was drafted and fulfilled his duty, he was not as proud of his service as Drew Brees was of his grandparents' service.

As a "colored" man, which is how his Navy records describe him, he was not allowed to hold specific jobs in the Navy or on the ships. He had to endure a certain second-class citizenship even though he was risking his life for his country and for the freedom of other people whose culture, history, and pain he would never know. The United States military was still segregated by race in 1943.

My father's ship, the USS Leon, engaged the Japanese in four battles, winning them all and earning meritorious achievement awards for each battle when they returned home from the war.

But that was not all that my father earned when the war ended. He earned a seat on the back of the bus ride from Texas back home to Tulsa. It was still illegal for him to ride in the front of the bus.

He risked his life to do his duty and to earn freedom for people in Europe whom he would never see or know. The indignity of his "place" in society and even on the segregated ship stung him and stayed with him all of his life. Each time he felt these indignities, it was under the same stars and stripes as Drew Brees's grandparents.

I always considered Drew Brees an intelligent person and a spectacular athlete. However, that day, he sounded to me like every other snotty-nosed, entitled white kid who never worked hard for anything but felt that everything was owed to him. Fortunately, his teammates took him aside and explained the point of the whole protest to him so he wouldn't be caught off-guard again. As I suspected, Drew Brees was a class act of a person and listened to his teammates and how they felt about the protest.

A team of CNN producers reached out to me after reading my comments. They explored my reasoning for commenting and asked about my life in general. They were planning an article or segment on Black soldiers for their electronic media. I shared with them my love for studying Black Civil War soldiers and participating in a Civil War reenacting organization called Company B of the 54th Massachusetts Civil War Reenactors.

I also shared with the producers that the mission of my reenacting organization was to educate people about the role that Black Civil War soldiers played in the American Civil War and to instill a sense of pride in today's youth. I told them I had been involved for more than twenty-eight years, and it felt like a spiritual calling in some ways. They thought it a little strange to hear that but asked if studying my background would be okay. A month later, they asked for a video interview with me. We conducted it on my deck in my backyard in August 2021, during the second year of the COVID-19 pandemic.

What they uncovered in my ancestral background amazed me. The CNN producers employed Ancestry to assist them in searching my background. Their research revealed photos of my father's World War II ship, the USS Leon. They also showed that my great uncle was a member of the 365th during World War I, and he was a member of the only group of Black men to deploy to France during that war and fight at the famous Meuse-Argonne. However, what they told me next was the most shocking of all.

My great-great-grandfather, a man by the name of William Lacy, was a member of the 79th United States Colored Volunteers.

This organization was also known as the 1st Kansas Colored Volunteers, and they were the very first Black men to fight in the Civil War in 1862. I was floored! They showed me a small obituary for William Lacy that mentioned that he lived in Kansas for a while and had been a slave at some point in his life. I had been drawn to studying the Civil War and the antebellum period for most of my life. To learn now that one of my ancestors actually fought in the Civil War was breathtaking.

I felt a sense of pride and validation. Friends had inquired for years as to why I enjoyed Civil War reenacting. This revelation by the CNN producers and Ancestry made it clear to me that during all these years of reenacting, I was led by a spirit. I had been drawn to the Civil War by my ancestors.

An old African proverb says, "If you reach out for your ancestors, they will reach back." The time, energy, and financial resources required to honor these men were significant undertakings, but knowing I am reaching for my ancestors and they may have just reached back has made it all worthwhile.

Armed with the name of a Civil War soldier, I left for vacation the day after the CNN visit. My wife, Tracy Osborne, is from a small city called Decatur in Morgan County, Alabama. She had been gracious enough to let me delay our vacation a few days to do the CNN interview, which they did over two days.

Now we were in the car for a long drive. The whole way down, I felt the name of William Lacy rolling across my lips. This was a fascinating fact for me. I had known of the 1st Kansas Colored Volunteers, but I also knew there were not a lot of books about them.

So, armed with the knowledge that my great-great-grandfather was a soldier, I immediately ordered the book and had it sent to my wife's parents' house in Alabama. The day after we arrived, the book *Soldiers in the Army of Freedom* by Ian Michael Spurgeon arrived on the in-laws' porch. I immediately grabbed it and retired to a quiet place to read about William Lacy, turning to the back to look for his name, and—sure enough—it showed his name on the roll of soldiers who joined the war effort officially in 1865.

What was most interesting was where William Lacy told the military officers his original home was: Morgan County, Alabama.

So, I was at my wife's parents' home in Morgan County, Alabama, when I read that my soldier ancestor was also from the same county. What a huge coincidence! What are the chances that I would be visiting Morgan County when I discover in my new book that William Lacy was also from this county? Surely, this would be a spiritual journey.

A couple of hours later, my wife's cousin, Michelle, appeared, and I excitedly mentioned the news of my ancestor soldier and his county of origin. She then informed me that there was a town in the same county called Lacy Springs. Of course, we all wonder if his last name, Lacy, is related to the town of Lacy Springs.

After a few days, I visited the Morgan County Archives to see what they knew about Lacy Springs' history. There, I learned that there were three brothers named Lacy, and they owned slaves. The research at the archives uncovered the fact that one of the brothers' last will and testament showed a list of his slaves, their worth in dollars, and who the slaves would be willed to in case of death.

With this knowledge in hand, I drove to the town to see the land where the Lacys lived and discovered a small cemetery with the headstones of the Lacy family from the early 1800s. I knew then that this was the location of the plantation where my great-great-grandfather, William Lacy, was born and lived.

My research prompted trips to Arkansas, Oklahoma, and Kansas, searching for clues to the life of William Lacy. It is my hope that you will enjoy his story.

CHAPTER 1

Baptism in Chains

Lacy Springs, Alabama—July 1859

Barn doors burst open, and dust and hay flew by as William Lacy faced the other slaves. The boy ain't never had no sense—or so his daddy told him. His daddy said a lot of things that went over his head, just like the rope settling over his shoulders.

Before the boys crashed in, William had been feeding Buck. The dark brown horse pulled hay out of the bale in big mouthfuls, soulful eyes keeping tabs on the boy. At eight, he'd been left alone to tend to the horses since he "had a way with 'em," another thing his dad said. Henry Lacy, older by fifteen years, noticed him stroking Buck in a paddock, tiny as he was with the horse. That big gelding bit at everybody else, only accepting his touch. It might've been a scent thing, or it might've been luck. Either way, because of those words, their master entrusted him with the horses, and that was four years ago.

Today, William had to dive out of the way after the loud *bang*. Buck's eyes went wild, and he lashed out, kicking the bale across the stall. The kid barely had time to snatch his hat before a rope went over his head. In disbelief, William stared across the stall at his three friends, swiftly approaching him with angry looks.

"You comin' to get saved today. You old enough now, so cain't skip it no more," Catfish said. He was a head and a half bigger than William, going through a growth spurt as surely as he got his namesake. He was dragged at the Lacy River bottom, almost drowning, but came up covered in mud with a branch, like catfish whiskers, across his face.

"Yeah, you meetin' Jesus. We all did it when we turned twelve, and now *you* gotta," Billy hissed. "We been looking for you. All the slaves is waitin' outside down by the river. Ole Ben's there, and so's your daddy."

The two held the rope as the third boy, Matthew, walked over. William cursed his shaking legs. They all knew he'd freeze up like this. The same thing happened when they first met, when Catfish fell into the river, and when Matthew found a cottonmouth near the cow pens. William froze up like a lake in winter.

"I don't c-care," William forced out. "Ain't wanna m-m-m-eet no Jesus or g-g-get saved."

"G-g-guh," stammered Catfish, mocking the younger boy. "Cain't talk neither, stupid. You gettin' baptized today, and ain't nothin' you can do about it. Our parents did, we did, now you gon' do it too."

His limbs betraying him, William fell forward as the three boys overpowered him. A hot flush of panic washed through him as he flipped over, the coarse rope digging in under his arms as they dragged him out of the barn. Buck's wild eyes followed him as he rolled off. The horse couldn't help, but he called out anyway.

"Stupid, it's just a horse," Matthew said.

After a few minutes, William settled into the ride. It would be over soon, anyhow. This was just how things were at Lacy Springs.

"Waaaading in the water ..."

Soon, the ground turned from earthy gravel to a muddy riverbank. A chorus drifted in the air, getting louder as they approached. "Wading in the water, children ..."

"Waaaaaading in the water," Catfish sang along, grunting out the notes in harsh breaths.

Covered in moss, the banks sent cold rivulets down William's back as they dragged him the last ten feet. People's feet parted in the crowd to allow the boys entry to the river. The boy gave in, standing up as they slowed. One foot, then another, sank into the mud. Standing up, William walked the final few steps, passing his parents, the other boys, and community members. Ole Ben, his grandfather, welcomed him in the river with an open palm and smile, singing the last bit of "God's gonna trouble the water."

"William, you finally here," he chuckled, giving the other boys a half-joking stern look. "We not gon' have to drag ya down here every time we need ya, do we? 'Specially not for somethin' as important as meetin' Jesus."

Confused, the boy looked over at his parents. Nobody said anything about a "Jesus" coming to the plantation. Eliza, his stepmother, held close to Henry's side, grasping his hand. Was she holding him, or was he keeping her still? No Jesus around. Only the others. Catfish doubled over, and a coughing laughter broke ripples into the water as he pointed at William's perplexed expression.

"Jesus ain't a *person*. He God."

Ole Ben opened his arms and beckoned William to walk forward. Even though it was his grandfather, a cold thrill washed over William. Everyone around waited for him in the water while he was dragged there. If they stood around while it happened, how could he say no? *Maybe I'd better let it happen. Get it over with*, he thought. *Is this who I am?*

Going limp in the water, William floated along. Hands grabbed him, and he gazed at the faces of his family and his community, ferrying his body along toward his grandfather. Ole Ben drew the gaze naturally with his white hair and wise features. Ever since he could remember, William had heard Ole Ben's deep voice preaching calm over everyone. He held them together.

Even with all that, the fear beat his heart to a fierce pitch. Each loving gaze around him added to it—why was this happening? Small splashes cascaded outward as Henry left Eliza to hold his son. With two quick strokes, Henry had William by his arms, tightly held open, as Ole Ben placed a hand on his forehead, cold and wet from the river.

"William Lacy, I baptize you in the name of the Father …" started Ole Ben, but the words were muffled with a swift dunk into the river. More prayers sounded over the water, but William only felt the river rushing by and his own heart pounding.

It must've been a few seconds, but when he broke the surface, he sputtered, coughing. Snot and river water ran down his face. With the deed done, Henry released him. "We told you at church this morning, you gettin' baptized, boy. Why'd you go and make it so hard?"

Ole Ben shook his head. "Henry, it's fine. William's saved now. Don't matter how it happened. God sees him now, and he's baptized like all of us. He's accepted Jesus into his heart, like we did, like the massas did, and we all thankful for it. This is what brings us together."

"Accepted? He came fightin', and the boy still gotta learn he cain't fight when we tryna help," Henry said, delivering a sharp smack to William's head. This set off Catfish and the others giggling while adults whispered about violence at the ceremony. Ole Ben had to hold up his hands, but William wasn't being held down now. Free enough, he bolted for the shore.

William didn't know if Henry was done smacking him or if the deed was done, but in either case, no one stopped him as he fled. Nobody moved to block his path as he exited the water, struck out from the shore, and sprinted back toward the barn. Shameful tears blurred the path, but he made it into the barn. Safe there and alone again, he scurried up the steps and buried himself in the hay.

About an hour later, William collected himself and was back to his chores, mucking the stalls and keeping the horses fed. Wet hay still stuck to his clothes, and he hadn't bothered to wipe the river much off his face and neck. It took the better part of that hour brushing Buck to calm him down. As always, the horse provided a soothing warmth, neighing gently, bumping his hand, and looking for carrots.

He heard creaking behind him as the doors swung open, revealing his grandfather. Ole Ben limped in, more frail now than his powerful stature in the water, surrounded by the community. William saw the years on his grandfather's face. He took each confident stride, with the color in his hair, leaving only the strength in his voice.

"William, I know you in that stall, boy. Get over here so I can talk to you," he said.

Still shaken, he complied, exiting Buck's stall and joining his grandfather as he sat near the barn's big center.

"William, you twelve years old now. It's time for you to grow up. It's time for you to give your life to Jesus. You be a slave like the rest of us, and we must obey what the massa says. None of us like this life, but someday Jesus will lead us out of being slaves, just like he did with the Jews in the Bible."

Bending down to see William closer, Ole Ben continued. "The Bible says that slaves must obey their massas, and we be slaves with the Lacys our massas. We baptized you so that you will be free in your soul even if your body ain't never free. We don't want your soul to be a slave, too. Being baptized will make you a Christian, and that's the only way to save your soul. Someday, you'll be old and gray like me. Over time, you will come to understand. *You* could be the free one. Don't repeat none of this 'round any of the massas, so that's why I'm telling you here in this barn."

William looked up at his grandfather, wondering out loud, and said, "Then Catfish and Daddy draggin' me into it?"

Ole Ben chewed on nothing, bringing William closer in a tight hug. "Well, son, we don't have all day to convince you what's right. I'm just showing you what my own granddaddy showed me years ago before he died. He said we didn't always worship Jesus, but this is what the massa wanted us to do. They told us that you must obey your massa to go to Heaven. Someday, you will teach your own kids the same as I have taught you.

"Survivin' is what we have to pass on. This is why we showed you how Jesus works, how someday you may be so tired of this ole life that you may want it to end. And that you would never know what might happen to you or other slaves from one moment to the next. You must be prepared to meet Jesus anytime in your life."

William nodded in agreement but really still didn't understand what Ole Ben meant.

The doors opened again. This time, one slid to the side, admitting Theo Lacy. At nine himself, the youngest son of Master Thomas Lacy, the plantation owner, couldn't be more different from William. He walked upright, wore spotless clothes, and never had hay in his hair, even after riding all day. Jingling at his side was his bag of marbles. William, Theo, and some others would set the marbles up and play together at the end of summer days. This perked William up a bit. Playing marbles with the other boys felt right and was the only time the stress completely left.

"We playin' marbles, Theo?" William asked, setting the curry brush down.

"No, not today," Theo said. He looked William up and down, lip curling up. "Did you sleep in the barn? Why're you so dirty?"

Self-conscious and sorely disappointed, William brushed at the hay covering him. Buck even took a nibble at some on his shoulder. "No, I got under the hay earlier to get dry, though. Why no marbles?"

"Father says it ain't right to play with slaves," Theo responded. "I came over here to learn how to ride Buck, and you're gonna teach me."

It ain't right to play with us? The words tumbled over themselves in William's head. "You cain't ride him," was all he got out. Buck wasn't like the other horses. He never let anyone ride him, and that included even Master Thomas. He bought him a while back, and William had been gentling him down, but Buck only recently let him place a saddle on his back—actually riding him would be dangerous.

"You don't tell me what I can and can't do," Theo said, walking forward. "How did you get that horse to let you stand so near anyhow?"

William held up one hand, keeping the other on Buck's flank. "Nothin'. I just gave him an apple."

Years ago, when they first brought Buck to the plantation, the Lacys let him loose in a paddock nearby to show him off. The horse was wild, kicking, and vicious, making dealing with him difficult.

For days, William just stood near the paddock, watching the horse. It took about a week for him not to lash out when William refilled his water trough and another week to allow a hay bale to be rolled in. In the third week, William brought a fresh green apple. He seldom got fruit like this, but an extra one rolled out of a basket, and no one seemed to notice when he picked it up. Apparently, the harvest was so big that they had to jar most of the sweet, crisp fruit. He ate it slowly, relishing the sweetness, something he barely got. So when Buck approached, he was half-scared.

However, the horse didn't rear back. His eyes were calm and alert, sniffing gently through the paddock's wooden fence. He'd already eaten half, so he offered the other half with a flat hand to the horse. Since Buck took that half an apple, he'd allowed William to brush and lead him around. That day, Henry suggested he care for all the horses.

"I just gave him an apple, is all," William said.

"I don't *have* an apple right now. So you saddle him up and get him ready."

Sensing something wrong, Buck shied backward, eyes rolling. William rushed out of his stall, almost knocking into Theo as the horse reared back. "Get down," he motioned to Theo.

The other boy stopped, staring upward in fear at the horse, before realizing what had happened. He put his shoulders back and stared down his nose at William, something he'd never done before, even when he won at marbles. "You get that horse under control, you hear me? I'm gonna be riding him by summer. Papa said he was *my* horse, and a Lacy has to have his horses under control if he's gonna be a man."

With that, the boy turned and huffed out of the barn.

Since his baptism, William walked around the plantation differently. Everyone seemed like a threat. Was this what meeting Jesus meant? Or what growing up meant? He wished he'd never been "saved."

The best he could piece out was to work hard and keep out of sight. Longer days and longer hours in the barn meant less time around the others, but this kept more incidents from happening.

Still, whenever he spotted Theo or the Lacys walking from the big house toward their plaza, he knew it was a day closer to passing Buck over to the other boy.

He still faithfully tacked and saddled the other horses: Chip, Toni, and Buttermilk. They'd all been around for a while and knickered softly when he approached. Slow and steady, they each allowed him to prepare them for the day's ride or to be hitched to a plow. Slow and steady, the days passed by at Lacy Springs.

The plantation comprised rolling hills that hugged the bend of the Tennessee River. The land was lush and rich for hunting, and the dirt was fertile for farming. Being next to the river gave it a prime location for growing food for the plantation and even enough for selling to others around Lacy Springs. The plantation also had a small spring that flowed northward to the Tennessee River. It was used to fetch water and where the slaves washed clothes. Maybe there'd be answers on the other side of the plantation.

William allowed curiosity to pull him away from his usual chores one afternoon after the Lacys had ridden away for the day. Theo had called back to him, calling him "horseboy" now instead of his given name. Well, maybe he was "*horseboy.*" Who was he to say differently?

That Sunday, William wandered to the property's other side, past the big house, across the plaza, and toward the sprawling fields. Lazy cotton drifts moved through the air, stirred by the chillier fall wind, now blowing across the red and orange trees. Summer had left before he knew it.

Ten minutes in, and he'd arrived at the fields. More than twenty slaves bent over their spots amongst the cotton, picking at the fluffy plants and placing their harvest in a large sack. Sweaty brows and gnarled hands marked each one, singing songs about a drinking gourd. Like the lyrics to the baptism song, only a few reached his ears enough to catch what they said. One slave looked up at a tall man at the river: Sam Lacy. He was a distant cousin, but William seldom saw him since he worked the fields.

"Well, if it ain't the sinner," he laughed, pointing at William. Other pickers stopped to see what Sam was pointing at. "We saw you fightin' not to get saved. Might as well call you what you is, sinner. You ain't gon' to church neither like us. You think you different, huh?

"Little nigga, you looking at us like you ain't know what's comin'. Soon as you get a little bigger, you gon' be right next to us, cuttin' your fingas on cotton like us too. Jus' 'cause massa likes you with the horses now don't mean it ain't gon' happen."

Angry, Sam finished his speech with a hand wave as if dismissing William. With the others, he turned back to picking cotton. A few other slaves looked him up and down but said nothing as they returned to work.

The bitter words washed over William. Was he really going to be taken from the horses? But they said he was good with them. That was the best place in all the world.

Sinner? Horseboy? Which one was it? All this time, he thought he was William, but if that ain't the case, these people all be calling him different names.

Who was he?

Serena	age 12	to James L. Kolb	valued	$350
Milly	age 48	to Nancy Thompson	valued	$325
Christiana (not in Inventory)		to Rachel K. Kolb	valued	$200

In 1838 Joseph Kolb paid Jesse Wright $9.00 to make 18 pairs of shoes.
In 1840 he paid Jesse Wright $10.50 to make 21 pairs of shoes.
In 1842 he paid Edmond Toney for 10 pairs of course shoes and paid $10.20 for 6 Negro blankets.

LACY, JOHN   3/28/1831

Sam - man	from Inventory list dated 1827		
Pleasant	from Inventory list dated 1827		
Dabney	from Inventory list dated 1827		
Billy	from Inventory list dated 1827		
Burnet - boy	from Inventory list dated 1827		
Joshua - boy	from Inventory list dated 1827		
Young Lucy & child Elizabeth	from Inventory list dated 1827		
Elisa - girl	from Inventory list dated 1827		
Priss - girl	from Inventory list dated 1827		
Mary & 2 children	from Inventory list dated 1827		
George &	from Inventory list dated 1827	to Theophilas Lacy	
Aaron	from Inventory list dated 1827	to Theophilas Lacy	
Catoe - boy	from Inventory list dated 1827	to Theophilas Lacy	
Alex (Alic) - boy	from Inventory list dated 1827	sold in sale	$500
Katy, age 17 & child Rachel, age 1 ½	to Thomas G. Lacy	hired for 1828	$128
Ole Lucy	from Inventory list dated 1827		
Silvia	from Inventory list dated 1827		

LACY, THEOPHILAS   8/80/1831

Old Ben	age 45	to Thomas H. Lacy	$350
Henry, son of Old Ben & Milly Jefferson, age 23		to Thomas H. Lacy	$525
son of Old Ben & Milly age 20		bequeathed to Theo. Lacy, Jr.	
Alfred, son of Old Ben & Milly age 14		bequeathed to Wm. Henry Lacy	$400
Ben, son of Old Ben & Milly	age 12	bequeathed to Theo. Lacy, Jr.	$375
Pleasant, son of Old Ben & Milly age 10		bequeathed to Alexander H. Lacy	$312.50
Caty, child of Old Ben & Milly		bequeathed to Rebecca E. Lacy	
Polly, child of Old Ben & Milly		bequeathed to Thomas H. Lacy	$500
Milly, child of Polly		bequeathed to Thomas H. Lacy	
Polly Creasy & child Lucinda	age 33	bequeathed to Martha Lacy	$427.50
Eliza, child Creasy	age 15	bequeathed to Martha Lacy	$400
Abram, son of Creasy & York	age 5	bequeathed to Alexander H. Lacy	$215
Jenny (Ginny) & child Washington		bequeathed to Theo. Lacy, Jr.	$500
John Calvin child of Jenny	age 2	bequeathed to Theo. Lacy, Jr.	$110
James Henry, child of Jenny	age 3	bequeathed to Theo. Lacy, Jr.	$162.50

Figure 1 – 1: "Property" list of slave names for the Lacy family and their assigned value

CHAPTER 2

The Unbroken Filly

Lacy Springs, AL—November 1859

A chilly dawn broke over Lacy Springs when news of Harper's Ferry reached the plantation. Whispers leaked like raindrops down the gutters—people talking about a man, John Brown. While talk was happening, just as fast as the whispers leaked, they got all stopped up.

"Don't go spreading anything more, 'Liza," Henry said. "Just sayin' his name makes everybody nervous. We got to a nice spot this year with how good the beans came in. Don't spoil it repeating nonsense in this house."

William's father and stepmother were up before dawn, preparing what they needed to for the day, but his brothers had already left for their duties. Sometimes, they even slept in the big house since their work took them late into the night.

The name "John Brown" floated through the plantation in a hush for two days, but no matter how much he asked, questions went unanswered for the boy.

"It ain't nonsense, Henry. It's hope," Eliza said, lowering her eyes from Henry to William. "We need hope more than ever now. My boys and yours could use some."

"Ain't no hope here," Henry whispered.

Eliza had gotten William some dry clothes after his baptism. Even with the new "Christian" title, he still felt the same. Nothing changed besides people stopped bothering him about it. Church would come later in the day without more questions about baptism.

Warm but distant, William's stepmother cared for him like a pet. She maintained a dutiful presence, but beyond that, she saved any familial warmth for Rufus and Joe Wheeler, sons she bore from her own body. She had them with their father on a different plantation years ago in Morgan County. William barely remembered the day they arrived, besides lots of confusion with new people showing up in their little cabin. Henry explained later that even though William's mother had died when he was two years old, and he had promised never to love another woman, Master Thomas had different plans.

He had called Henry up to the big house, introducing him to Eliza and her boys.

"Henry, you've been a good slave, so as a present, I bought you a new wife from a friend, Joe Wheeler. He never was a good card player. She already got two boys, but she'll still make you a good wife," he chuckled. "May even *more* boys."

After that, the trio returned to their family's cabin, a wattle-and-daub shack grouped with others on the eastern side of the plantation. Their place had enough space for more people, but that was lucky. Most families were cramped with three or four in one spot.

"Henry," Eliza said as she entered his shack. "I know you ain't want this, and I don't either. But we gotta do what Master Thomas wants us to do. Now, I was a slave to Mr. Joe Wheeler, and he was a soldier in a war from a while back. Everyone celebrated him like he was some kind of God or something. So, I reckon being called Wheeler was a good thang for us. But now I'm your wife, and I will call myself Lacy, like I seen on that sign at the end of the road."

Henry nodded in agreement, even though his eyes were far away, his chest sunken in. As he looked at his son, William saw a deep sadness take hold.

"You might be a good woman, Eliza. I'll do right by you in this house. As long as we together, we'll get food, blankets, whatever our boys need. But I ain't never jumpin' no broom, ya hear? Best I can do is be a good daddy for your boys and keep all y'all safe. Best I can do is give my boy more of a choice than we have in all this—if that day ever comes."

That'd been eight years ago. Eliza and Henry got to know each other as William grew up, settling into a calm, steady friendship. They respected each other—except on some matters.

"Ain't no hope but to survive."

Eliza shook her head. "We got more than that."

The morning dragged on, and William went to work.

The barn's calm refuge only lasted so long. On another cooling afternoon, William dozed in the hay, ignoring the scratchy pieces poking into his shirt. Its sweet smell and the soft noises the contented horses made lulled him from standing and mucking the stalls to taking a short break to rest his eyes a moment behind the wooden doors.

"William? William!"

William startled awake. That was Master Thomas' loud baritone.

Jumping to his feet, the boy rushed to the door, throwing both his arms into it to slide the barn open. Master Thomas stood outside, glancing from the sky to the barn. Impatience reddened his face. "Now, why do I gotta call for you, horseboy? Why aren't you outside and ready to attend when it's time to ride?"

William usually had the horses ready, but it wasn't their riding day. "Yessuh, I'm sorry. Who you need saddled and ready?"

"I'm breaking Buck today."

William swallowed hard. Master Thomas had broken many horses before, but Buck wouldn't stand anyone on him for longer than a minute. Still, he did what he was told and had the brown horse ready to go. Even with his gentle strokes, Buck rolled his eyes and shied away from the white man. Master Thomas grabbed the horse's reins firmly and led him from the barn. When Buck shied away or tried to run the last time this happened, he lashed the horse soundly—a lesson both the boy and horse learned and carried the scars from.

Worried but without much to do, William stood nearby while Master Thomas led Buck to the paddock. Behind them, a manservant headed toward them from the big house: William's adopted brother, Rufus.

Rufus Wheeler was about five years his senior and already running mail back and forth from the house. He approached nervously, eyes flicking from William to the white man on the horse.

Master Thomas rode Buck hard, lather and sweat already forming as his firm hand took him around the paddock. Rufus stood nearby with an envelope in hand and made toward the paddock. William moved forward.

Earlier that year, Rufus had shown William the southern dirt road leading from the river to the western towns. Directly across the dirt road was a cadre of small businesses serving all who traveled down the road to the west. The Lacy brothers had led the way with the United States government in establishing a small post office at the corner of the dirt road some years earlier. Everyone in Lacy Springs and the nearby towns to the west, including Hartselle, used it for mailing. The postmaster was a close friend of the Lacy family, and years earlier, one of the Lacy family members had served as the actual postmaster. Rufus himself carried the letters back and forth.

"Wait, you can't interrupt. It's dangerous. Buck isn't full broke, and he might throw 'im if you get too close," he said.

Rufus turned to him and nodded. "Thanks. I don't want to deliver this news anyhow."

"What's in it?" William nodded at the envelope curiously.

"It's about Harper's Ferry. Something bad happened over there. All the talk in the big house was about it this morning. Best you keep quiet about it, though. Ain't no good news for us. Ain't no good news for anybody."

William's ears perked up with the song floating through the air.

"John Brown's body lies a molding in his grave ... John Brown's body lies a molding in his grave ... John Brown's body lies a molding in his grave, but his truth is marching on."

They only sang it toward the end of the day when the white folk went inside. William asked his father about it as he was near their house, but Henry only shook his head.

"Don't worry about it none and grab that sack over there. We tradin' in town today."

His father's clipped speech signaled a bad morning. Past him, Eliza, his stepmother, cleaned dishes over a tub, eyes kept forward and on her work. Since the baptism, a sizzling tension thrummed between William's parents. Eliza said only once that she thought it was a bad idea before the uncomfortable silence grew like mold into the cracks in their house and family.

While Eliza didn't sing the words, she hummed the John Brown tune and scraped plates into the soapy water.

Grabbing the wheelbarrow nearby and filling it with burlap, the boy seesawed it back and forth out of the mud. Overuse made the wheel sticky, so it always took a minute and some oil to warm it up. Soon, he said goodbye to Eliza and was out the door, following Henry on the path leading out of the Lacy property.

Fall held a spicy tinge in the air in Lacy Springs. No more cicadas sounding. Now, the air turned to sleepier animals nestling amongst the fallen leaves. The squeaky wheel kept the two of them company, only marred by William's panting as he struggled to keep up with Henry's long-legged steps.

"Gimme that, boy," said Henry. While he sounded exasperated, the man switched out with William, easily pushing the wheelbarrow twice as fast as they headed toward the nearby plaza.

Word had reached the plantation earlier that a Creek Nation caravan was passing through. Some folks spread rumors that they were bringing maize, baskets, deer skins, dried medicines, and special pipe tobacco. Henry loved their pipe tobacco and rarely had the chance to trade for it. An exceptional harvest afforded Henry and Eliza extra time to grow more beans this week. Their tiny gardens were usually left alone by the Lacys since they ate less of the plantation's main food crop.

Soon enough, the two rounded the forest edge to the trading plaza. Most white folks got there first, making good use of their money and reputation to get the best from the Muscogee people, but Henry knew where to go to find the surplus.

A man sat whittling behind a wagon train. These wagons had tattered canvas, edges waving in the brisk wind. As they approached, William fell behind his father. Something about the man set him on edge. The Creek's legs were longer than his daddy's, fierce eyes slowly rose from his whittling to lock onto them, and a dangerous smile cracked his mouth.

"Well, the local farm force, what're you boys bringing me today?"

"Nice to meet ya," William's father began, removing his hat and making a quick bow. "I'm Henry Lacy from the Lacy plantation, back that way a bit. This is my boy, William."

"Postoak," was all the man replied with.

"Pleasure meetin' you, Mister Postoak. We got some fine beans in our crop this year. Reckon this would be good to trade if you had some extra tobacco and deer skin. We could use the stronger leather here."

"Not sure if beans is all I can take," Postoak said, turning his gaze from Henry to William. "Seeing as what's happened at Harper's Ferry. Doesn't bode well to make a trade with slaves right now."

"What happened at the ferry?" William asked.

Henry hissed. "Shut it, boy, men are talking."

The two engaged in trade banter, and William tried to make heads or tails out of the ferry comment. Was that what Rufus hinted at earlier? What was in the letter he brought to Master Thomas?

A muted scream, between sand thrown and struggling gasps, sounded from behind the wagon. Neither Henry nor Postoak motioned like they heard anything, absorbed in their tense exchange. William wouldn't be missed, would he?

Taking one last look at this father's back, the boy inched away slowly, like molasses out of a jar. As long as it wasn't sudden, the men wouldn't know he was gone. Adults seldom did when they talked like this.

The angry whispers died off behind him as he rounded the wagon. His bare feet left imprints in the dusty sand, and the canvas rustled by them as a gust picked up. The boy shielded his eyes with a hand as he rounded the edge.

Three boys dragged a girl about his age. Each wore a wooden cross. Two had her legs while another flailed to secure her arms. It was eerily similar; the biggest of them even carried himself the way Catfish did, lumbering around like his size gave him the right. Coughing, the girl spat a wad of grit out.

"Get off me *now*!" Her clipped syllables and strange speech stopped the boys momentarily. Two of them looked at each other before the biggest one shook his head.

"Don't worry 'bout nothin' she sayin'. She a sinner, and we gotta take her to get saved. Everybody got to get saved today. Is what the pastor told us," he said, even winded himself from holding the girl's legs.

"I thought your Jesus only saves people in they heart," she hissed out, sending another wave of struggle through them with a vicious kick. "Drop me now! Or I'll send my gods after you in your sleep. Raven and Owl will never let you rest another night again."

She talks so loud, William thought. Her words carried weight with them. Stock still and frightened, the boy wished he could run up and help her. He knew what would happen if he caused a fuss, though. She was caravan folk, and they had to look out for themselves. If his father found him tussling there instead of where he was supposed to be ...

Still ...

He couldn't let this happen to her. Meeting Jesus was so scary, and he had to do *something*.

A rock lay nearby. Hands moving faster than his thoughts, William had it up behind him and sailing in an arc in seconds. The sharp rock collided with the biggest boy's head, knocking him over as a red spray coated a line in the dust.

Blood? Oh no ...

Adrenaline flooded into him, and the boy ducked behind the wagon, praying hard that the caravaner wasn't dead. One shriek and a hard thud sounded before he hazarded a glance, peeking his head around the wagon edge.

The girl must've knocked over one of the other boys because the last one fled, kicking up dirt with how hard his feet hit the ground. She called out an ululating cry after him, grabbing another handful of dirt and throwing it into the smaller boy's face on the ground.

"See? My gods hear my cries, and where does that leave you?" She stomped toward the smaller boy, who was holding his knee. Another red spot, matching the biggest boy's forehead, spread, soaking his pants with blood. The last crimson splash was the sharp rock in the girl's hands. She raised it above her head.

"Damnit, girl!"

Postoak, the Creek they talked to, rushed from the other side of the wagon. William didn't notice before, but they had the same straight back, clear eyes, and matching armbands. Where the girl stood proud like a she-wolf, the man stalked toward her like some predatory bird.

"I *told* you not to wander off. Now look at all this mess. What the hell happened?"

William wanted to run out there and tell him what he saw—that they were dragging her to the river and being unnecessarily cruel with it, and she was only defending herself. The fear kept him rooted. He couldn't involve himself with the caravan folks.

The girl met his eyes.

He drew in a breath. She was so beautiful—more beautiful than any girl in the whole world. She was also madder than Buck when he didn't get hay for a day.

William froze like a deer. Would she turn him in? Did she know he'd thrown that rock? It didn't matter. The man laid her down in the dirt with a powerful backhand.

"Get your ass back into the camp and find your mama. If I ever catch you messin' around like this, I'll make sure you can't never walk or wander again."

Standing up and holding her face, the girl marched behind him. "Yes, Papa," she whispered, almost out of hearing level. While the words came out calm, she glared daggers at his back. With only one backward glance to cement the fact that she saw William, the girl disappeared with Postoak.

"William!"

His father's voice rang out.

Turning quickly, the boy hightailed it back to where his father waited, at the archways leading into the campsite.

CHAPTER 3

Life on the Lacy Plantation

Lacy Springs, AL—March 1860

William turned in his cot, the straw scratching into his arm, before getting up for the day. He left with Eliza to gather some biscuits and semi-cold eggs for breakfast. Their sausage supplies ran out last week, and no traders came by to resupply the town. Creaking wooden doors slammed as each person prepared for the day: backbreaking work, toiling in the fields.

William walked alongside Henry after breakfast. Since winter was over, their work shifted from harvesting and preserving to cleaning and planting for spring. The girls he walked past were already hard at work, some barely older than him at 15, preparing meals and moving the crop preserves. Eliza wove between them, guiding a hand here and there when a mistake happened. These crops ranged from greens like spinach to carrots, tomatoes, and watermelons,

Henry took William under his wing since last summer's baptism. As he moved into adolescence, Henry allocated more responsibility to him. The fields would've been his new home. Joe had even mentioned how carpentry might be good to take up besides horse handling.

The plantation folks barely kept the tobacco and cotton; more was shipped off to make money. Beyond that, William noticed these two specific products were shipped out by wagon more than the others. People spoke of the caravans heading north and west and even as far as overseas. His brothers would boast about seeing the map in the big house with their trade routes, displaying lines stretching way down the Tennessee River to foreign lands. The Lacys kept this route and grew it, over sixty years' worth of growth, beginning with the exit from the Revolutionary War.

Henry explained that these products were valuable. They couldn't grow any themselves because the Lacys would take it away from them. Beans were fine. Beans and other cheap plants could be grown in their little garden. Even that would be gone now with the imminent move.

All through this, William's thoughts turned to that beautiful girl near Postoak's caravan.

Rufus turned to William as they set the trays down in the study. The Lacys needed extra help getting more paper and maps out of storage. The big house stirred, a flurry of activity, as folks rushed to and fro. Both the Lacys and their slaves rushed more than usual for wintertime. William couldn't remember this much fuss when it was cold.

"Our home is special," Alexander said angrily. He was one of the Lacy brothers, older than the others. They argued often, but with tempers especially strained, the brothers frequently raised their voices at each other. Only Master Thomas could quiet them down when they got like this. Rufus told William to stay out of sight during these outbursts. William crouched to make himself smaller, continuing to move boxes into place.

"We've built a reputation around here. Everyone knows to treat us with respect, from Lacy Springs to Huntsville. Hell, even the slaves get preferential treatment when they got our name attached to them."

"Don't matter if we're dead," John, the other brother, sneered back. "You know what *they're* up to."

William knew he was talking about the other Black folks around. He paused before lowering another box onto the desk, wincing at the change. He should've ignored what they were talking about, but now, his pause caught their attention.

"Get out of this study!" John yelled.

"Hey," Alexander put a hand on his shoulder. The other white man shrugged it off, angry eyes darting back and forth from William to his brother. Rufus set his box down in the hallway and stayed outside, freezing.

"We need all these boxes in here to get our paperwork in order. Do you want to do it yourself?"

John shook. His rage centered on William. "It's *your damn fault* we have to move, you know. Because of all this bullshit, a war is stirring up. We Alabamians have to save and scrape by now with trade slowing down. They say some places have *freed* their slaves. We lost another contract with our French trading company because of this—say they don't wanna risk trading with the losing side. We're losing *everthing* 'cause of this.

"You dumb negroes need to stay where you're put. John Brown found out the hard way what happens when you try to act stupid."

Rufus came around the corner and slowly tugged at William's shirt, pulling him back toward the door. "C'mon, Will, we gotta wait till they cool down."

The boy, caught in a frozen state, allowed himself to be led away, not breaking the angry eye contact from John Lacy.

"Stop scaring the little ones. We still need boxes moved, and we can't do that if you yell at them like that. The bigger ones take to it easier. Just slap one around a bit, but don't hurt 'em too bad. Ask Overseer O'Toole which ones need the fear o' God put in them." Alexander's voice floated like mad wasps after the brothers into the hallway.

O'Toole, the Irish overseer, was a constant, fear-inducing presence in their midst. William learned early on not to do much with him in sight but to keep his eyes focused and his hands busy. O'Toole had freckled skin and reddish hair like the other Lacys. That must've been why they hired overseers like him. All William knew about him was that the trip when the Lacys went to hire him was the same trip his birth mother was never seen again.

Master Thomas' familiar heavy boot steps sounded from outside the barn. He had a slight limp, so William could tell the *clunk, drag, clunk, drag* of the master's gait. If you listened carefully, everything had a special gait— horses, cows, people.

William dug the last tangle out of Buck's mane, a careful unknotting, when Master Thomas opened the creaky barn door. Buck shied, a nervous tic he'd developed since the breaking day, and William stilled him with a warm hand against the beast's neck.

"Willie? You in here, boy?"

"Yes, Massa," William said, keeping his tone even near Buck.

"You're doing a superb job with these horses, Willie," Master Thomas said. "Never seen these creatures so shiny. Toni and Buttermilk'll fetch a good price at the market. Take them out of their stalls. We need to get them ready today."

He gon' sell 'em soon? William thought but exited Buck's stall to do as he was commanded. Buck would stay with them—he knew that. The horse was too wild to fetch a different price, even now that he'd been broken. But why sell the others?

"Thank you, Massa," said William before continuing, half-distracted by this news and the yelling from earlier. "Henry says I'm doin' a gooder job than anyone he seen, even gooder than the white boys. Gooder than Theo."

Master Thomas dropped his hands off his hips and motioned for William to come closer. The boy set down the bridle he'd grabbed and jogged over to his motioning gesture. In a quick switch, Master Thomas snagged a strap off the wall and struck the boy across the face. The force sent him reeling into the wall as a fierce *crack* echoed through the barn.

He screamed, collapsing into a hay bale. Angry welts popped up along his cheek, and blood welled up where the skin broke. His frightened shriek caused the horses to buck and rear in their stalls.

Buck burst through, sprinting past Master Thomas and knocking him over, carrying the momentum outside. Following his lead, the other horses also neighed loudly and crashed outward as William and Master Thomas crouched out of the way.

For a moment, William and Master Thomas lay on the barn floor looking at each other. William's mind reeled. Should he run? Why did this happen? His head and neck stung from the blow. His knee was quickly swelling up. When Buck ran by, he'd grazed his knee, an afterthought as the scene pieced itself back together. Through it all, the questions buzzed around why he was punished. A crushing stone sank in his chest, moving down as quickly as his pride swelled earlier. He *was* better. So why?

Footsteps approached—Henry, his father.

"What happened? Why're the horses loose?"

"Doesn't matter," Master Thomas lurched to his feet as a slight red trickle ran down his face. "Catch those horses, Henry."

Henry looked from Master Thomas to his son. "You both bleedin'." He said it simply, a statement of fact, but a thread of anger kept him rooted to the spot despite the order. "You good? Why you bleedin', Massa?"

Tears poured freely down William's face, blurring the world. Fear kept his mouth closed. *Whatever happened was because he spoke, so he wouldn't do that no more.* A sob bubbled up, the pain coursing upward when he tried to put weight on his hurt knee.

"Never mind, *boy*, don't make me repeat myself." Master Thomas pointed his finger. "And don't you *ever* fill this little shit's head with any more talk about being better than whites. You hear me? None of y'all will *never* be as good as white folks. No matter what you do, where you go, or how many government papers come this way. Now get those damn beasts corralled back in here. Now!"

Henry walked over to William and tilted his head toward the barn floor, pressing the boy's hurt leg against his own. Strong hands held his shoulders up while Henry steered him outside. It took long, agonizing seconds to get outside the barn before the man waved a free hand back and leveled a flat "Yessa, Massa" behind him.

Out of earshot, Henry put William under a tree outside, spotting the horses who were, fortunately, only grazing nearby in the vegetable garden.

"William, you cain't be sayin' things like that," Henry said, giving the boy a stick to grind his teeth into. He examined his leg. "No matter if it's true, cain't say it out loud. I shouldn't have done it neither. These white folk get mighty sore like Massa Thomas did."

William swallowed another yell as Henry tested his leg. "Nothin' broken, just smarts real fierce. You'll walk again in a few. Just sit tight, and I'll get the horses."

"I … I was happy he said it," William gasped.

Henry turned around. "He said what?"

"I was gooder with horses. I only said it 'cause he did."

Henry nodded. "I know, Will. Don't be sayin' nothin' to white folk, 'cept 'Yes, Massa,' or 'No, Massa,' if it needs a no. Don't share nothin' else. You got off lucky today, son. Promise me this, alright? Promise me you won't go sharin' nothin' else. They might sell you off just like …" Henry stopped, catching a sob himself.

"I'm sorry, Daddy. I promise."

"We're heading northwest."

Master Thomas Lacy announced, his tired voice carrying through the still air. The entire plantation had gathered in the spring air. There was no snow last season, but enough frost to make up for it. The slave population stood in family groups of seven or ten, huddled together and deathly silent as the weight of the news settled on them.

"Y'all know I'm not one for speeches, but this one gotta be said. I won't brook nary an angry glance about this move. It's all been settled already, so you have a week to gather what's needed for the trip. Say what you need to say, and then be ready by next week for the travel."

William turned to Henry and Eliza, but both kept a calm mask on, staring at Lacy. There wasn't much to their cabin, but those cozy walls couldn't come with them. They would be hard-pressed to find space in their packs for their harvest, preserved on shelves.

"This is because the United States might be outlawing slavery soon," Henry spoke in a hushed whisper to Eliza. "This, and what happened down at Harper's Ferry. Mark my words. We ain't moving for whatever reason they say it is. Massa Lacy's scared. They all scared if things change too fast around here."

"How do you know so much about Harper's Ferry?" Eliza asked.

"Becca, from the big house, passin' on the news. The folks at Hartselle wear shirts with the words disguised. They only talk about it at night, between the grapevines or the weeds growing past the fields. Becca hangs shirts upside down outside the house when it's time for us to meet over there. We stay quiet and hidden.

"We had to meet now. Been too long between without news, but I saw the upside-down pants this morning and went over to see. Big John and Alexander from Hartselle came by to give us the news. Brown had a few slaves with him when he killed them white folks. They all came down from a place called Kansas, far away. We don't know if John Brown won that battle in Virginia, but a war must be coming. I can't think of no other reason why everybody be so upset. We gotta stay watchful."

That night, William opened the door to their cabin and found his family standing around with a few strange girls. Each carried a small sack and looked around nervously at the cabin. O'Toole stroked the shoulder of one as he nodded to Henry.

"You know what to tell them," he said in his funny, musical accent. "Make sure each of your boys knows what's expected. All these are women now, childbearing age, and we need to make sure they're with child before the move. They'll be ready by the time we get to the new place."

Eliza stirred a pot silently in the background. The fire crackled as Henry rounded up Joe, Rufus, and William, pointing to each girl who was approximately their height and age. "Alrighty, now listen, we showed you what the horses did outside come springtime, and we do it, too." He rambled on again for a bit while O'Toole watched. The topic turned to God and the fruitfulness of the people, which caused him to sneer and quickly dip out the front door. Henry's tone changed as soon as he was gone, and Eliza stopped stirring her pot.

"Now, listen, y'all need to keep quiet," Eliza said. Her face turned serious, looking at each girl in turn. "Now I know y'all want to be married and settled in before having babies, right?"

The three of them looked confused at each other, then back at Eliza. The youngest one piped up. "Babies? You mean that's what them horses were doin'?"

"Yes, honey, they wantin' you to get yourself some babies. Means more family to help in the fields and the house," Henry added. "You gon' need to do your duty if you want to keep eating. 'Liza did it too over at the Wheeler plantation, and you gotta learn to make some good food. We needin' two meals a day around here: one in the morning before we hit the fields and one in the evening when all the work's done. Eliza'll show ya how to haul water and vegetables from the fields to the big house and leave enough for us after ya done making the full meals for the Lacys."

She glared at Henry. "Let me explain all that. Also, I was married. Now how you gon' tell them to do this when you won't do the same? William's mama been gone o'er ten years now."

William looked from Eliza to Henry. "Gone? Isn't she dead, Daddy?"

Henry shook his head. "Don't worry about that. And you, 'Liza, it's different for me and you. These girls just turned into women. The Lacys expect 'em to have at least two more kids to add to us. I wish it didn't have to be this way, but it does."

He nodded to his and Eliza's sons. "You boys watch over them, and if anybody asks, you say you be layin' with them every night and while we travelin'. In this house, ain't nobody forcin' anyone to do what God gave us. You hear me, boys?"

Joe and Rufus nodded.

"And if the time comes, you decide you want to marry, then you can bring more babies in. Maybe they won't notice with all the packin', and travelin', and walkin' around.

Without a word, each brother nodded to the girls before heading over to their cots. William stared at the girl closest to his age. She gave her name in a scared whisper after he asked: Mary.

Feeling more awkward by the second, William held her hand gently and introduced himself before heading to his sleeping pallet. He knew what the horses did come springtime, but Mary's large, fearful eyes only filled him with sadness. He didn't want that for Mary and was happy Henry didn't make him and his brothers do such a thing.

He wondered if the Creek girl from the caravan had done it, too, and that thought struck a match inside his chest—a fire too dangerous to let smolder.

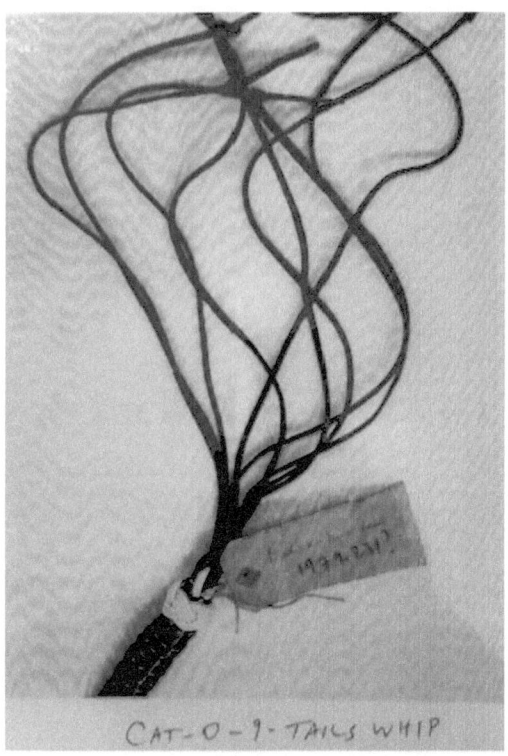

Figure 3 – 1: A cat-o-nine-tails whip used by overseers to terrorize their captives

Figure 3 – 2: A photograph of the Lacy Springs cemetery

CHAPTER 4

Journey to Arkansas

Lacy Springs, Alabama—April 1860

An unseasonable chill settled over Lacy Springs in the morning. The entire Lacy clan, from Master Thomas himself down to the slave babes nestled in their mamas' arms, set out for Arkansas. Henry, Eliza, Joe Rufus, William, Mary, and her sisters hefted their burlap sacks, each stuffed to the brim with their lives. Anything that wasn't sold had to be carried. The most prominent equipment was tools. Precious wagon space held their meager livelihood as they finished packing in the wee hours of that spring morning. Henry and his sons had worked all night to prepare for the trip.

William hooked Buck to the wagon. While he wasn't a good wagon horse, the Lacys couldn't sell him, so William and his family had to care for the half-wild horse. The beast stilled under William's careful hands and allowed himself to be tied to the wagon. With the others in the caravan, the boy prepared Toni and Buttermilk, the only horses left after the sale. He checked their hooves for loose rocks and cleaned their shoes, readying them for the journey.

By now, the sun crested the trees surrounding the plantation, tinting the greenery with flecks of gold and filtering through the low fog. The entire populace gathered, placing their sacks in the wagons.

The Lacy family hugged and cried together, knowing this would be a long journey and that this might be the last time they'd see each other for years, if ever.

Each Lacy offered a parting gift, exchanged with the ones near the wagon. Even distant cousins of the white folk had come to see them off. Mementos to remember their kinfolk passed hands as the entire clan split. Toiling together throughout the years couldn't keep them together as the times grew rough.

On the other side, near the shacks, the Lacy slaves held a similar ritual near their place of worship. The tiny church sheltered only three benches, each row consisting of a ten-by-twelve-foot tree log split by hands as old as Ole Ben's. The elder used this area to give spiritual comfort and guidance to his people, and the place now held steady for the memory of those parting. Ole Ben passed his hands over each member, offering only prayers as a gift for the road. The folks left here at the plantation knew what the white folks did: this might be the last time they saw those leaving in this Lacy split.

While life at Lacy Springs had grown difficult to bear with the unrest, at least they were all together. With Rufus and Joe gone, William wondered who would deliver mail and take care of the carpentry. Who would handle the ironwork with Henry gone? When they got new horses, someone else's hands would steady them—not William's.

Other families would be in the fields alone now. Without Eliza and the girls, breakfast would be changing hands too.

Now? Now, the whispered prayers held a fervent wish for safety and better lives out west. These muttered out as people passed each other— no time for emotional goodbyes, with even more work to be done.

William's chest sank heavily as his community broke apart. At Lacy Springs, people disappeared overnight, some between noon and dinner, with no word except Rufus overhearing the Lacys talk of selling another slave that day. The gossip passed through from the big house to the rest. Even in the years he'd watched and come to accept the uncertainty plantation life held, with close friends and family sold at a moment's notice, the knowledge brought no comfort or eased a creeping dread.

A line to Ole Ben formed, each slave coming to receive a blessing from him before joining the caravan or heading to the fields for the day. William knew people could leave at any point, but somehow, knowing and watching this happen in motion was worse. William sprinted down to the church, reaching his grandfather, his heart beating loudly.

"Why cain't you come, Ben?" he cried, tears pouring down his face. He knew these things happened, so why did it hurt so much? People disappeared, but how do you handle it when you leave them behind?

The words came tumbling out, even though he could feel the Lacys' gaze drawn by the scene. It didn't matter at this point if he got a whipping. He had to try. "We can all live in the new place. You can walk some and ride some. I'll carry you if I gotta—massa gotta let me try! Who gonna give me advice and tell me what to do? I don't know who gonna show me how to live, Grandpa." The word slipped out. William never called him that, but this could be the last time he saw him.

Ole Ben held him close, giving him a quick hug before holding up William's chin. "My boy, my William." His eyes shone, and his voice broke. "I wasn't chosen for the new life, but that's okay. I lived mine here, and I'm thankful for all the time I got with you and your daddy. I'll see y'all again soon. If it ain't in Arkansas, it'll be in Heaven above. Remember who God is." He leaned in close. "You be yourself, William. Don't never let them take it from you. I cain't remember who I was at your age, and I regret it. Don't let them make you like me. Listen to ya daddy. Keep ya head down. Live a better life."

One last time, William returned to the empty stables and barn area, checking to make sure nothing was left behind. A creaking smash rang out as a door slammed into the side, pushed by the wind. Besides that, the entire place was as empty as William's chest, hollowed out by long, dry tears. No snorting or neighing by horses or swishing tails sounded in their stalls. The barn was half empty now, and the caravan was fully loaded.

William walked around the barn for what seemed like an hour. Rich, grassy hay filled his nose. The walls would be lost, but he'd carry the skills picked up within them. And while he'd never dozed safely hidden in the hay, he could find new places in the next spot. The fear and dread earlier cut away the sadness. Without the barn, he didn't know where he belonged anymore. Would he still be William without afternoons in the barn?

William sighed and shook himself out before heading back to the wagon train. Henry helped him up and settled him next to the younger kids, with their feet dangling from the wagon. With a sharp whistle and a quick jerk, the clan set out on their journey.

The post office was long gone behind the caravan as they set out westward. Lacy Springs, then Hartselle, and the outskirts of both settled into memory. Half the Lacy clan wound their careful way from their ancestral home toward the wilds of Arkansas.

Creaking along gently, the first wagon sheltered all ten Lacy kids and a newborn baby, only six months old at the journey's start. Master Thomas and his wife, Mary, walked alongside the wagon, giving up the room to their children.

Close behind, the second wagon drifted. William walked alongside this one while his step-brothers kept watch. Joe and Rufus followed the Lacy boys' lead by scanning the horizon. So far, they had passed a few folks coming toward them. Everyone seemed to be either settling into their farms or heading out west.

William tired quickly walking along the road; the travel was different from toiling back at the plantation. Where the farm took your energy in sweat, dripping down into the soil, here, it fed off it, pulling you down. The road was different. It sapped you in small ways, wearing you down till you were too tired to keep going. Thankfully, between driving the wagon and walking themselves, Henry and Eliza allowed him and the others brief respites riding the wagon, often when it felt like William's knees would fall right off. Blisters formed over calluses he'd had for years.

He bounced along, alternating between this spot, staring at the final wagon, or trying not to move too slowly and get hit by the oxen pulling it. Behind, Alexander and John Lacy drove the last wagon, saved for supplies only, like corn, rice, sugar, potatoes, meat, eggs, and tools for wagon repair. With these crates, they'd make it all the way to Memphis, Tennessee. The older boys stalked around the clan heads, keeping an eye out for anything approaching their caravan, each one swinging a rifle. Alexander shared his grimace at the road ahead and then looked back to William and his brothers, watching them as closely as their surroundings.

Theo rode in the first wagon, cooing at the baby, before wandering back to walk alongside his brothers. He motioned for them to join the first wagon, where Master Thomas handed out ammunition.

"Outlaws ahead. From now on, you keep your rifles loaded and the extra ammunition dry and nearby. We aren't in friendly territory anymore, and we don't have the strength of our name and history protecting us. Bandits don't care where you're from or who your mama is. They'll take everything: the shirt off your back, our daughters, crops, and leave you to starve, crawling back to the nearest town. If you don't struggle." Master Thomas' voice floated back through the quiet wind, and William listened. He'd impart some new wisdom to Alexander, John, and Theo every day.

Once Master Thomas quieted down, William hopped off the wagon and found his father staring off into the woods nearby. Henry studied the treetops, pointing a finger at them. "Massa Thomas don't know this," Henry said, leaning in close to William. "This route is a Creek trail. Postoak told me about it during our trade before you made a damn fool of yourself. Creek Indians took this route earlier, 'bout thirty years ago when they moved west and gave up their lands to the white folk."

"Sorry," William muttered. He wanted to ask more about the girl and her father, but he'd get smacked if he tried. "Why'd they give up their land and move?"

Henry nodded at the hills behind them. "United States Army. We followin' this route too, but it's been traveled before. We know how they found a way across the Tennessee River. Same as we doin' now. We ain't doin' it blind, though. Made these wagons so we can float 'em across. It's called 'fordin'' a river."

"Fordin'," William repeated. He waited a moment, taking a breath. "You think Postoak be out there ready to trade more?"

"Maybe."

"I hope so," William said. Henry gave me a sidelong look but didn't press any further.

Soon enough, the Lacy clan met the riverside, traversing the road alongside it to cross before it turned southward. The river, only a tributary south of Decatur, Alabama, became their next challenge.

Once they found the shallow ford area, Master Thomas called for the preparations to move everyone across. Working together, Henry, Eliza, and all the siblings placed the wagons, one at a time, on a series of canoes and flat boards offered by the operator nearby to cross the river. They had to pack down their belongings, too, and then reset once they completed the fording, keeping the Tennessee River on the right for as long as possible. Master Thomas conferred with his sons in earshot when they stopped to make plans, and William overheard them discussing the need to stay south of the Tennessee River the whole way to Mississippi.

Dusk arrived each day, and the tiny wagon train would tighten up and pull off the dirt road for the night. Making a half-circle like the wagons at the market plaza, William helped them stretch out canvas from the wagon sides to block off the wind and shelter everything inside.

Sharing her daily chores with the younger girls, Eliza would prepare food after the boys set up the fire. Winter was gone, but the chill followed them into the spring nights, so they huddled together for warmth around the fire.

After dinner, they bedded down separately. The men took spots around in the soft Alabama grass while all the women slept in the wagons, swaddled together with the Lacy kids. John, Alex, and Theo Lacy frequently snuck out to sleep under the stars with William and the other boys. It was strange but welcome to William, who was happy for the camaraderie under the darkness and the stars. Out here, on the road, it seemed like they were all together, all one family.

"What do you think is over the next ridge?" Theo whispered. They played this game night after night, wondering what new discovery the next day would bring. William guessed they'd see bears, farms, hills, and sometimes, he was right.

"More bears, probably," William said.

"You guessed that *last* night," Theo said. "You gotta guess something different now."

A fire crackled as it died down to embers. William thought about this, his belly full and his back comfy against the sweet-smelling grass. "I hope it's more Creek people," William confessed. "We do good trades with 'em."

Theo looked at him strangely. "Maybe we'll see them."

Fifteen long days proved otherwise, but the lonely, short wagon trail finally reached Memphis.

Camping outside of Memphis, Henry roused William in the early morning hours. "We gotta restock," Henry said, pulling on a coat. "Provisions held out all the way here, but now, we need more. Stay here with your mama and watch over the wagons."

When Thomas and Henry returned from the stores, they both wore grim looks—Thomas more angry and Henry more tired.

"They want *fifty* cents a bushel for corn." Henry shook his head. "Was only twenty back in Lacy Springs."

"Why they askin' for all that?" Eliza settled a blanket down and brought Henry some water.

"Feed and everythin' else been bought up already. Settlers been comin' through here movin' out west now. So they buyin' all the supplies, mean prices goin' up."

Master Thomas went back into town and returned to the wagons with all the necessary goods. William helped load the crates and sacks, but the supply wagon was only half full when he was done.

Henry mentioned this was temporary, and they'd need to go into the city all together to bargain for supplies to make it all the way to Fort Smith, Arkansas.

The next day, William accompanied Master Thomas, Alexander, Joe, and Henry into Memphis. They rode through the streets westward. The cluster of buildings, all up against each other with barely any room, shocked William.

"How they all live like this? They all up against each other with no room to move," he asked.

Master Thomas laughed at him, and his sons followed suit. "Never seen a city before. They're all like this, too, so get used to it. Can't have you gawking like a halfwit the whole time."

So many people walked, sang, hurried, and yelled around William. He'd never seen so many folks together in his life, coming *out* of the buildings and buzzing around into others. The city had an aliveness to it. People leaned up against walls and each other, laughing and carrying on as they conducted business.

More buildings than he could count had women hanging out of them, waving and calling at the men as they passed. Henry whispered to ignore them, even if the Lacy boys waved back.

They passed signs declaring "Main Street" and "Beale Avenue." William observed how mighty fine they looked and thought he'd want a sign like that for his home someday. Along Main Street, he found many shops, businesses, hotels, restaurants, and even places called theaters. It all made his head spin.

While he didn't see it elsewhere, he and Henry walked alongside Master Thomas and the Lacy boys. They sometimes pulled ahead slightly to make some distance when they walked past certain businesses. William learned not to keep up with Theo when that happened.

As they walked, cotton bales sat stacked to the ceilings behind open doors, and William wondered if any of it got picked back at Lacy Springs. The spiffiest horses trotted by on carriages, but they weren't like the ones back home. Beautiful paintings decorated their sides, and bold, gold letters were painted too.

Similar to their group, other slaves moved throughout the city on their errands. Something was different about them, though. These slaves wore clothes like those of Master Thomas. Why were they dressing like white folks?

Passing right through Victorian Village, then to the western edge of the Mississippi River, he saw it wasn't just the men but women, too. Other slaves wore the same things Ms. Mary wore: long hair, skirts, corsets, gloves, and parasols.

Familiar lilting Irish accents floated over the rumbling crowds, directing those other, better-dressed slaves through Memphis. The Mississippi River stretched out in front of William, more water than he had ever seen before

Finally, they broke through the city to the river banks. So many people gathered around the docks and the boats. Behind them, the water stretched out almost to the horizon. He stared, gobsmacked at it, wondering how in the world they would ford such a huge space.

"No, no, no!" Master Thomas cursed, wringing his hands. "Just look at that damn line of people."

William refocused on the throngs of people and their wagons by the ferries. So many people clustered around, waiting to be taken across the river. It must've been those big ships that would do it instead of them fording like they did with the Tennessee.

These "ferries" steered across the vast river and returned with travelers from the other side. While Master Thomas went to argue about the heavy fees, William turned to his father, who was now alone.

"Henry, why did those slaves in the city wear clothes like white folks?"

"Some men be different than us. Livin' different lives than we do. Don't know why, but I think they be free. No massa like we got."

No massa? William thought, looking at Master Thomas as he argued.

After the day dripped into the next, the Lacy clan finally crossed the Mississippi into Arkansas. The whole time, William steered clear of Master Thomas, jumping to obey any of the Lacy boys as they fumed at the expensive delay. The master was eager to get a good

day of travel, putting the "sinful" city of Memphis behind them. William caught him more than once conferring with Alexander and John about keeping the wagons outside as much as possible.

However, now, on the other side, the Lacy clan butted up against a different situation. Many other travelers and their wagons were moving west after ferrying across, and following these well-worn tracks made it much easier. No longer alone, the travelers often passed other caravans moving at different paces or settling into their campsites. All of them headed west together.

After each day, Henry marked another fifteen miles on their traveling log. He maintained this with Joe to keep track of provisions for their journey. Now, in Arkansas, William counted campfires in the distance with Theo at night, guessing who was at each one. Were they soldiers? Heroes? Or plantation folk like them?

Sometimes, they'd visit other trains, confirming the boys' guesses made at night or giving wildly different answers. Men whispered between trades of raiding Indian tribes nearby, but Master Thomas' only concern was ensuring no one got more than their fair share from their trades.

Over the next two days, the Lacys rolled along steadily, passing through Crittenden County, Arkansas, and losing sight of the smoky trails Memphis laced into this sky. William wondered about the "sin" the city committed and how a city could even do such a thing. He kept his eyes trained behind him, picturing the "masterless" slaves of Memphis.

Eight more suns and moons rolled overhead before the Lacy family followed alongside the brand-new Memphis and Littlerock Railroad line. Henry told William that another wagon train hinted that the railroad went the entire way down to central Arkansas, closer to Fort Smith. A steam locomotive would occasionally scream past them, blowing its whistle and startling the horses. Eventually, the railroad ended right outside their next destination: Little Rock, Arkansas.

CHAPTER 5

Rain and Wild Carrots

Little Rock, Arkansas—May 1860

Three wagons, one with a sagging canopy, pulled in close to Little Rock before bedding down for the night. The exhausted Lacy clan popped out, setting their usual camp up, but now with less energy than before crossing the two rivers. Even Buck had less spirit as William brought him feed for the night.

The dwindling provisions came down to just about scraping the bottom of the barrels. Master Thomas announced they'd need another supply run into Little Rock to secure them. Even with the good time, he fussed over keeping everyone well-fed and ready for anything, stopping often to kiss baby Rebecca in Mary's arms.

William followed Henry and Master Thomas again, excited to see another city. However, Little Rock held little of the same zeal as Memphis. No bright paint adorned storefronts or carriages, nor were goods packed neatly out of display. Here, no Black folks paraded in their fancy clothes and top hats like in Memphis. Just the same people here, reminding him of Lacy Springs, but now, hundreds were milling around.

"Did you know it's been since 1860 when that first railroad was built?" Master Thomas said, pointing at the one that led them here.

Alexander and John both looked with varying degrees of interest. "Little Rock blossomed just for that reason—railroads. They brought cotton, oil mills, factories, and all kinds of industry to the area. This place is full of saloons, gambling, and criminals because of it. So y'all stay close by."

"Yes, Daddy," they said in unison.

"Wait out here while I negotiate more supplies for the wagons. Need to check the price of corn and flour."

Master Thomas headed into a store. As his heavy boots clomped across the store's wooden planks outside, Henry and his boys settled in to wait. When Master Thomas got to negotiating, he could whittle at a storekeeper for hours.

Sure enough, the sun sank a little while they waited outside. Enough time passed, and a white man with long whiskers and a round belly walked briskly into the store, followed by two slave boys. One turned to stare at the group. He could've been a lost brother, sharing William's hair, age, and even a familiar tan shirt.

Must be goin' in to fetch provisions, too, William thought, but they stopped at a few sacks before heading into the shop. The white man pointed at them, indicating that the boys should check them. Before they could check, the door opened, and Master Thomas leaned out. "Alright, c'mon, grain is bought and paid for. Let's get all of it back to the wagons."

The sharp opening startled the other white man and the two boys, who quickly moved away from the door. Irritated, the bearded white man stood right in the way as William and the others moved onto the porch to collect. Master Thomas let the door slam shut behind him when he ducked back inside.

"Y'all wait your turn," the white man said, spitting at them. "We already bought all the grain this morning. See that label? Has my name on it: Barling. Them sacks belong to me."

Henry moved in front of William while he stood in indecision. His eyes darted to the other slave boys, his lookalike, and then back to Barling. Pulling up his hands, he showed his palms to the bearded man. "Now, we ain't here to cause no trouble, but our massa says we gotta start loadin' up these sacks."

"These *ain't* your sacks. Or are you niggas too dumb to read?"

Henry stared at him but didn't reply. After some seconds passed, Barling smacked his side and cackled. "You are too dumb. Hah! I figured. Get off this porch." His hands went to his belt, undoing the buckle. "Before I tan your hides. And you two, don't make me say it again."

Henry moved over to the sacks and grabbed one side as the two boys went for the others. William stood rooted to the floor as the tension escalated. Joe and Rufus moved to go with Henry but gave Barling a wide berth.

Similarly, Barling's boys alternated between moving to the nearest sack, picking it up, and then trying to move out of the Lacy boys' path. All the while, Barling seethed until he unslung his belt in one quick movement and struck it to itself, sending a lightning crack across the storefront. The sound stopped everyone, and William's heart jumped in his throat.

He was suddenly back in the barn. His heart pounded, and a deep ache sank into his knee. A cold sweat broke out across his forehead.

Barling rounded on Henry, raising the belt higher. William swallowed hard, wanting to reach out or yell something. Anything.

The door opened again with a crack, and Master Thomas leaned out. His face carried irritation as he took in the scene on the porch.

"What the hell is going on here that's taking so long?"

Surprised again, Barling let the belt down, cracking Henry across the shoulder. He winced but kept his grip on the sack, throwing a sharp glare at the man.

"You best tell them to let go of my property and get the hell off this porch," Barling spat.

"Don't be crackin' at my folks," Master Thomas said, stepping out onto the porch between Henry and Barling. "They ain't no better than what I said. Now, what do you mean, 'your' property?"

"Thems *my* sacks," Barling said. "My name's on the side of them. I bought 'em this morning, and we comin' by to pick up. What I was tellin' these idiots 'fore you came out."

Master Thomas gave him a sidelong glance before moving over to the sacks. He examined one of the labels before huffing and pointing at the door. "Henry, you and the boys go in and ask the shopkeep for more grain. Seems he's trying to cause more problems than this shitkicker town is worth. Alexander and John are in there. Tell them I said they need to move the provisions out now."

Henry nodded, and William let out a long exhale. Shaking, the boy followed his father behind the group. Behind them, Master Thomas apologized to the man for the misunderstanding. Far from diffused, Barling turned his shouting to the two boys, who had ripped open a bag of flour in the shuffle.

Before the door swung back shut, William caught sight of them scraping their dusty hands across the floor, frantically putting the spilled flour back in the bag.

"You lazy niggas is always messin' up something," Barling yelled, lashing them across their heads and backs. "Only trouble for white folk. Worse than nothin'. Good for nothin'!"

William and the others made it back to camp with sweat dried to their backs in the hot sun after carrying the sacks. In Memphis, the shops had equipment to help them bring supplies back. In Little Rock, they only had their own backs.

Henry sank down against the wagon once it was all loaded up. With everything secure, the man wiped at his face and closed his eyes. Eliza came by with a wooden cup filled with cool river water.

Eliza wiped her hands on her apron as Henry drank. The man could feel her eyes on him, so he peeked one eye open, hands across his knees. "You got somethin' to say?"

"Henry, we gotta be leavin' soon. I know ya tired, but ain't nothin' for us here. Mary got the animals all ready to move, and we packed up. Little Rock don't look friendly, and Fort Smith right around the corner now."

Henry sighed and waved at William to come closer. When he did, he placed a hand on the boy's shoulder and groaned as he got to his feet. "You right, 'Liza. We better shove off. Need to put some miles between us and this place. Everything ready?"

She nodded.

"A'ight."

With the oxen lowing, the Lacy clan brushed past the outskirts of Little Rock on the road once again. *Three thousand seven hundred people*, William thought. *Little Rock. Memphis. Both places so different. What will Forth Smith be like?*

Lush greenery and rolling hills wrapped the travelers in beauty. The Arkansas Valley spread around them, with the Ouachita Mountains cresting the southern horizon and the Ozark hills to the north. However, William discovered the lush greenery had a reason: rainfall.

Each day, it seemed, another drizzle hit as the rainy season swirled around the valley, turning the trails into mud. Mornings arrived fair, sunlight glinting off dew and streams as they prepared the muddy animals for the next day's trail. Then, once afternoon hit, like clockwork, a downpour started, drenching the three wagons. While the people could manage, the rough terrain strained the horses and oxen, their breaths puffing out streams while they strained to pull the wagons through muddy channels.

Henry urged them each time, jumping off to help William coax them through muddier passages. Their trip would soon be over, and this sense of urgency spread through the crew from Henry's coaxing to Master Thomas when he roused his sons to help. One broken axle caused a mild uproar as Mary screamed at Joe and Rufus to hurry up and fix it. They moved to comply, and she soon apologized for losing her temper, cradling baby Rebecca under the wagon's roof. Despite the pressure, Henry slowed how hard he pushed the animals, checking the wagon's bearing with the Lacy boys at each stop.

William couldn't remember being so wet and muddy before, even back at Lacy Springs, during the rainy season. He could always dry off in the sun. Here, it was like water was a constant.

Besides this, the trail made progress easier. Like earlier, Master Thomas stuck with the railroad to Little Rock. On his map, he showed John and Alexander a curling blue line that led to Fort Smith. When they moved again, William spotted the Arkansas River through the trees and learned to predict where the wagons would turn based on its curves.

"Henry? Why do we always follow these rivers? What's so important about 'em?" During a lull, William questioned his father while lunch was passed out: hard traveling tack. At least the rain softened it before they got their mouthful.

Eliza handed him the biscuit before passing out more to Rufus and Joe nearby. "I can answer that," she said. "My daddy told me these rivers is what makes Indian Territory so rich. We farm, hunt, and fish on account o' these rivers. Where the Arkansas here meets up with the Mississippi is what's called a 'tributary.' That's a small branch of a river, kind of like a tree, and these all flow up as far north as Colorado. It comes from headwaters in the Sawatch and Mosquito Mountains."

William, his stepbrothers, and the girls sat by, chewing thoughtfully as she drew the rivers' pathway in the mud, beaming with pride at her explanations. "My daddy, your granddaddy," she motioned to Joe and Rufus. "He always said the land takes care of ya if you take care of it. Gotta know your land, so ya know how to care for it."

After lunch, the clan packed up, rolling northward past Conway before turning westward to Russellville. Trudging through muddy roads, the spring rains remained a constant companion. The resilient group had to adapt their nighttime camping grounds, stopping near thicker copses or cresting hills to combat the downpour. Their pace slowed from the fifteen-mile treks earlier to ten-mile treks now, with special care to keep their wagons safe. Slower progress meant more days on the road, and this caught up as Master Thomas reduced their rations to half. Although William understood why, it didn't stop his stomach from growling because of the all-day grueling trek.

As if their prayers were answered, the rain eased up on the next journey leg as the clan progressed toward Arkansas' western border. The daily wagon routine, now done automatically, allowed William to daydream about summer days in the barn back on the plantation. The wagons circled up again for camp. While Eliza and the girls worked on preparing food for the group, William went with Rufus and Joe to search for the driest wood they could find. The animals were tended to by the Lacy boys while William looked on. He'd care for them at least once a week, but now Buck's care was solidly in Theo's hands. He'd sneak Buck extra wild carrots some afternoons if he could forage them quickly enough.

"Why're you feeding my horse?" Theo said from behind him.

William turned and shrugged at the other boy. "He's hungry and likes carrots. Didn't mean anythin' by it."

"Stop," Theo said coldly, walking to put himself between Buck and William. "He's *my* horse. I don't ride him now because we need him for the wagon, but I don't want him coming to you when we get set up in Fort Smith. Got it?"

William said nothing while Buck knickered and kicked nervously behind him.

"Horses gotta eat," the words tumbled out. "If you don't want me feedin' him, fine, but he likes his carrots and apples. Gotta feed him somethin', or he gets wild." William said his part and backed off, even though his heart screamed at him to protect the horse.

"I'll feed him whatever I want," Theo mumbled. "And he better be grateful."

CHAPTER 6

God Hears All Prayers

West Arkansas—June 1860

Master Thomas strode back into the campsite, a cluster of dead fowl tied to his back from his hunts. The game bag bounced heavily, meaning the forest held many animals nearby. The game kept the clan provisioned while their supplies dwindled, boosting everyone's spirits. William felt a tug toward this. If he could also provide for the family, maybe this could be a path forward. No one could call him "horseboy" if he brought in supplies. Not that anyone did anymore. The thought brought a spark of fear. Horseboy, even if it irritated him, was at least something that made him valuable. If he wasn't that, what was he?

"Massa Thomas, I wanna go on a hunt," he said one afternoon. "Lemme be useful. I can carry the bag or set traps."

The man sighed but allowed him to tag along, giving him his extra ammunition, ropes, and other supplies.

Together, they moved toward the treeline in search of birds. Master Thomas whispered stark orders for him to be quiet, watch, and listen. Birds were sharp, and you had to be silent to sneak up on them. William nodded, slowing his footsteps to mimic the white man's.

Bringing a finger to his lips, Master Thomas pointed to the east. An Eastern Wild Turkey sat where he showed him. Master Thomas motioned for William to stay put while he crept closer to the bird, swinging up his 1855 Springfield musket and firing a precision shot. Without a squeak, the bird went down in a puff of feathers.

Proudly, he grabbed the bird, refusing to let William carry his prize back to camp. While he didn't learn as much as he wanted to, he paid extra attention to Master Thomas' movements through the brush. The man stepped carefully, watching for loose branches, and avoided the brush to minimize any sound. Much smaller, William could sneak just as well in that afternoon.

That night, the family ate heartily; the turkey provided enough meat for everyone to at least have a taste. In the blazing fire, without rain and with fresh meat, the travel seemed to ease for a moment. Tensions leaked away, and friendly conversation flowed through the camp.

Riding this high, the next few days found William setting traps for pigeons. Master Thomas brusquely offered a few tips when pressed, especially when William promised he was catching them to feed other slaves. However, the simple traps set on the wagons and nearby camps proved fruitless, as each morning resulted in no trapped pigeons. While it frustrated William, he resolved to pull his weight somehow, even if hunting or trapping wasn't his path.

A few more days of travel brought the wagon train through the sleepy town of Clarksville. Besides a town square with a few stalls and its strange number of brick buildings, not much marked the tiny place.

Master Thomas made snide comments about Clarksville when the sight of the town dipped beyond some hills. Supposedly, cousins back home warned him of the area. While Clarksville was the county seat, its influence only stemmed from the judges that resided there, making the town politically important, regardless of its size. The same could be said of the area they traveled through as the Lacy clan passed westward through more sleepy hamlets nestled in the valley. The entire county boasted only six thousand people, and Master Thomas admitted that nine hundred of those didn't count because they were slaves.

A cold morning dawned, and Master Thomas declared that he'd keep the Sabbath that day, ordering everyone to stay put. They'd made good time, and that day could be reserved to rest the animals and safeguard their souls. After caring for the caravan and doing the chores, the children played in the morning light, cherishing the easy day after the wet slog from earlier. William's knee had swollen again, so he stayed off it as long as possible.

Mary, shouldering baby Rebecca, produced a Bible and gathered the entire clan around to read verses aloud. Both slaves and the Lacy family sat together in the sunshine to hear the Word and enjoy being off their feet. Mary Lacy's height gave her an advantage, which worked well when ordering people and shouldering the weight of her life on those tall, unbent shoulders.

"You know, she's from North Carolina, Ms. Mary," Eliza said to William when the readings were over. They all called her "Ms. Mary."

"She's like me. We both came from somewhere off the plantation. I think Ms. Mary knows what it's like to tend to men." She looked slyly at Henry. "We both gave our husbands strong boys, and other folks introduced us to our now families. Maybe in another life, we woulda been friends."

When supper time came around, Ms. Mary stretched out several blankets, dusted them off, and instructed the girls to fetch drinks for the Sabbath.

"We're having a discussion this holy day," Mary said. "After we finish reading, it's only proper we talk about the Bible as well. We just read the story of David and Goliath today and how David defeated the mighty Goliath with a mere slingshot. He was fearsome. Everybody knew him as the strongest, largest man in the entire world. It just affirms what we know to be true: through God, all is possible. You can overcome anything, even as an underdog. Through faith, we can move mountains."

William listened to her preach, surprised at the places where she said exactly what Ole Ben did and other places where the words differed. However, he could not understand how a small boy like himself could ever defeat a giant with only small stones and God's favor.

Their next stop marked Ozark, a small town that capped another multi-day trip. At least it had more than just a few brick structures, unlike the previous town. Unlike the others, this one hid a strange group of buildings William had never seen before. A scaffold covered the top of an actual hole in the mountainside, sheltering people with completely Black faces, darker than William's skin and powdery.

Henry explained it was a coal mine. The mines here powered the locomotives that raced between Little Rock and Fort Smith, moving the state's industry forward. Master Thomas pulled them to a stop here to load more provisions before beating a path ever westward.

That evening, William resolved he'd catch a pigeon. After watering the animals, he moved to try setting up a trap farther away from the campsite. Some hundred yards away, he posted his pigeon trap: a box held up a foot and a half stick. The boy carefully set leftover bread under the box. He put all this together with a string tied to the stick, stretching to where he hid nearby.

Hours ticked by, and he got itchy to move. Reminding himself of Master Thomas' lessons, he wiggled his fingers to get some restlessness out before quieting down. Several pigeons noted the bread, flying down from their perch and hopping nearer. His heart beat faster, fingers tightening on the string.

His world narrowed down to the pigeon hopping closer to the box. One hop. Another. Almost there. *C'mon,* he thought.

The pigeon bobbed its head under the box's lid, pecking at the crumbs near the bread. One more hop, and he'd pull the string. He'd be a hunter. Maybe this meant he could bring it back, and Master Thomas would teach him how to hunt turkey! William braced himself with one hand behind him, ready to pull.

A powerful, pinching pain lanced up his hand into his arm, and he screamed. The pigeons took off in a flurry. Whirling around, he pulled his hand back and leaped to his feet. Twin gashes oozed blood on his hand. Slinking away between the grass, a spotted snake's tail disappeared, slithering quickly into the brush. *A Water Moccasin?* Mortal danger surged through him as William raced back to camp. *Snake bites kill people!*

Joe rushed to meet him, closest to the edge, but others stopped and wandered closer as he broke camp, clutching his burning arm to his chest. "Pa! 'Liza! Snake got me!" he kept repeating. Joe curled an arm around his shoulder and brought him into the camp. Henry dropped the rabbit he was skinning and strode over, his eyes sharp.

"Hold him steady. Joe—whiskey. Now," Henry ordered.

Joe grabbed the nearest bottle of corn liquor from the camp and brought it by, but Henry didn't let William drink any. Instead, he poured it over the bite. William hissed in pain.

"Goddamn it, hold still!" Henry growled. "Joe, pass my knife. Gotta cut it now."

William jerked back, eyes wide. "No! Don't cut my hand. I need it! Won't that make it worse?"

Henry hesitated, knife poised nearby. Joe looked over to Eliza and little Mary, the slave girl. She came over with another whiskey bottle, staring at the wound with large eyes.

"Ole Ben back home said cutting spreads the poison faster," Joe said.

Henry scowled but didn't answer. Instead, he tied a strip of leather above William's wrist, tight enough to bruise. "Better 'en lettin' it crawl up your arm."

"Need tobacco. Anyone got any?" Henry yelled the question out to the camp, but nobody moved.

"That's fool's work, Henry," Eliza said, her eyes growing colder. With a few quick steps, she took a knife and held it in the fire. "Saw men die at my old place, even with tobacco, from the rot. We gotta set fire to the wound … and pray."

William tried to stay calm, but panic caused him to thrash and jerk while Eliza brought the hot knife to his skin. Wincing, the boy shrieked piteously into the night as his family wrapped around him, holding him in place.

Behind them, the Lacy clan gathered to watch but kept their distance as the slaves took turns tending to the boy. Eliza took the knife away, inspecting the cauterized wound, and prayed over it. "God, please, please, don't take our boy away. Please."

Henry called Rufus over, and they prepared his sleeping pallet near the fire. William's breathing became labored, and his vision faded in and out, the world swimming between light and dark.

"He gonna lose that arm, ain't he?" Rufus' voice sounded like it came through cotton pressed into his ears.

"God willing, he won't," Henry answered.

It was a long, tense vigil. The family took turns watching William throughout the night. Come dawn, William still burned with fever, but he was alive. Bleary-eyed and exhausted from staying awake the entire night, Henry loosened the tourniquet on his arm. Blood flowed out, but dark, not black—a good sign. He exhaled in relief.

"Reckon he'll make it now."

Master Thomas walked by to check on the family. He placed breakfast nearby himself and shared a glance with Henry. "Make sure to watch for rot. He won't die, but he'll carry a scar on that hand for life."

Two suns spun overhead and then two moons, but William's arm continued to heal. Eliza gave thanks in her morning prayers. The boy favored his wounded hand, still purple and swollen, but could manage his chores through the aches. His fever also dissipated.

The Lacy wagons crept toward Crawford County, low on rations and exhausted from the month-long trip west. Fort Smith seemed so close on the map, but moving through these days after coming from Alabama had taken their toll. Their morning chores dragged, even though they became routine. By late afternoon, the sun shifted to shine directly into their faces while they walked, riding into the hot air. For a while, the sun blocked all sight of the road ahead, masking the approach of two men on horseback until they trotted right in front of the wagons.

The two men drew rifles, trained at Master Thomas and Ms. Mary in the lead wagon.

"Get down off the wagon, or we'll blast you to pieces," the man on the right said. He waved the gun forward, both threatening them and motioning for where he wanted them to move. Master Thoms climbed off the riding box, placing one hand slowly after the other before hitting the ground. He showed them his palms.

"What do y'all have back there in the wagon?" the man on the left said, jerking his head at the group.

"A little food and more mouths to feed," Master Thomas said. "Mostly children," he added, a dry dig at the outlaws.

Before they could move closer, Alexander and John stepped out from behind the first wagon with their smoothbore muskets trained on each man. Master Thomas, following the outlaw's surprised gaze, continued to speak as the situation flipped. "… but I don't think you want to take food out of children's mouths, do you? My grown sons might take issue with it."

William cradled his hand nearby, watching the outlaws weigh their options. While the seconds ticked by, Henry and Eliza motioned for the other slaves to stay low and quiet. William calculated how fast he could run and if he could grab a knife before they started shooting, for all the good it would do. He hated feeling this helpless.

"Y'all have a nice day now," the right outlaw said, tipping his hat. "Just friendly advice, since y'all ain't from around here: stay outta the roads. Folks be less nice around here than us, and we just came by to make sure you was ready for it."

With that, the two kicked their horses and rode back in the opposite direction. Sighing in relief, Ms. Mary placed a hand on Alexander's shoulder. "Don't know what would've happened if you boys weren't here. Thank you for acting quickly." At the same time, Master Thomas hugged John. "Keeping watch helped, my son. Thank you. Don't know what I'd do without my family here with me." They tucked closer together, hugging closely with baby Rebecca in the center.

The last day of travel set the group abuzz with daydreams, plans, and whispers. Fort Smith, their destination, got closer and closer with every step, and it renewed the Lacy clan's vigor with their new home so close. William still struggled with his chores using only one arm, but the sense of accomplishment buoyed him, and he worked through stretching his wrist and fingers through the dull aches.

Unfolding in front of them was their last hurdle: the Arkansas River. The tiny wagon train lined up, and like before, they waited for the ferry operator to help them across. Henry and Eliza tucked everything into the wagons while William, Rufus, Joe, and the other children prepared the animals. When the ferry operator returned with patrons going eastward, the Lacys were ready to board.

The wooden planks creaked under the wagons as they trundled onto the boat. All three settled into place, and the families took up spots near them. Two wagons from another group already stood in place. The strangers shared friendly nods toward Master Thomas and Ms. Mary, and they even struck up a pleasant conversation. Ms. Mary beamed, showing off baby Rebecca as the boat shoved off, and the talk turned to Fort Smith and hopes for settling in.

About fifty yards from the opposite shore, the ferry swayed, growing in strength from a gentle rock to something more violent. Water rushed over the sides, soaking William's boots and socks and causing the horses to rear up. Buck's eyes rolled, and William shared his fear.

With the oxen and horses attached, the wagons backslid, first an inch and then faster as the river water turned the deck slick. Shocked into stillness again, William watched, wide-eyed, as the two wagons ahead of their group tumbled into the river. The folks they belonged to tumbled in after or jumped in to save what and who they could.

More screams erupted around him as the world tilted at a sickening angle. Lightning quick, the boy's good arms shot out to grab the wagon, even though half of him realized it wouldn't help, as it would surely pull him down with it. A creak. A splinter. The ferry trembled with fresh waves pulling it under.

Around him, the Lacy clan either crouched in place or staggered to the side, securing their belongings. Ms. Mary wobbled back and forth, clutching baby Rebecca to her chest while she fought to regain her balance. Dropping a sack, Master Thomas cried out and rushed forward, swiping his hand to catch them but narrowly missing. Shrieking, the woman fell into the water while her husband wrung his hands together before diving in after her.

The cold, muddy water rose to claim the rest of them.

William swam in long, awkward strokes, his painful arm dragging through the water. People thrashed around him, catching onto debris that bobbed up around them. Henry, calling out, swam toward William.

"You okay, boy? You okay?" he yelled, clasping William's face to get his attention. Still in shock, William nodded wordlessly at his father.

"A'ight, you get to shore now," Henry said before swimming away, calling out to Master Thomas.

The next few minutes happened in a confusing swirl. William felt the Arkansas River pulling at him, tugging him down into the river's cold swirl until a large, powerful body churned the water white around him. Buck!

The horse came back for him, and William grabbed onto his mane. The water frothed beneath the horse's powerful legs as he propelled them toward the shore. William coughed out the earthy river water before rolling across the bank. He'd made it to dry ground.

Buck shook himself off and trotted over to the grass nearby to feed. William lay panting on the shore for a moment. His chest rose and fell before he could get his breathing under control. He sat shivering, watching as more of the Lacy clan made it to shore. Joe and Rufus stood nearby, hovering over the girls. Even Little Mary had made it. She clung to her sisters, sobbing, her eyes just as wide as William's.

The boy cast about, looking for others. Eliza was there. She pointed at a pile of wood, talking to the Lacy boys, Alexander and

John, as they paced back and forth, looking at the river. Eventually, she snatched the flint and steel from their hands to start a fire.

People clambered out of the river, coughing and sputtering like William did. More Lacy workers. Theo, Master Thomas, but where was Henry?

An hour passed. William got dry near the fire while Alexander, John, and Master Thomas yelled hoarse curses at each other, the ferrymen, and the waters themselves, threatening to kill them if they didn't get a boat. Finally, they found one and hit the river, searching and calling Ms. Mary's name.

The boy settled into a numb mockery of his earlier chores. The oxen and other horses, all besides Toni, had swum to shore. He patted them dry with blankets warm from the fire, tied them, and settled nearby where the grass was green, farther down the shoreline. Quieter here, the animals were still in sight but less prone to spook with all the commotion near the recovery effort. The tasks absorbed him, pulling his focus so much that it took a few times before he realized someone was calling his name out behind him.

"William ..." a hoarse voice came from the water behind the reeds.

Scared, the boy froze again, not recognizing the grating, desperate voice. When he inched forward, pulling the reeds aside, he spied Henry, clutching an unconscious Ms. Mary to his chest in the shallows.

"Pa!" He rushed forward, hugging his father. "You alive, and you got Ms. Mary ashore. Where's the baby?"

Henry shook his head. "Didn't see her. They still lookin' for her out on the river."

With the boy's help, the two staggered back to the campsite, towing Ms. Mary while she blinked back to consciousness.

Eliza immediately took her from the two and placed her near the fire. "Shhh, shhh," she said when she came to completely. The woman clutched at her empty chest, a bundle now missing.

"Where ...?"

"Shhh, Ms. Mary, just rest up," Eliza said, patting her brow. "Ain't nothin' to do but wait for the men to come back. They lookin' now."

Toward the end of the day, Master Thomas and the boys did return, but empty-handed. They'd searched miles downriver for any sight but couldn't find baby Rebecca. When their silent faces met Ms. Mary's, she fell to the ground, keening and rocking back and forth.

"Why?" she yelled into the sand before rounding on Eliza. The woman was mid-reach to comfort her before the Lacy matriarch's fury turned on her. She smacked Eliza across the face. Surprised, the slave woman fell over, the hot bowl of soup splashing into the soil.

"God saved *your* boy!" Ms. Mary shrieked. "And took *my baby*?!" Her fury cast a bloodshot rage to her features, spittle dripping from her mouth. Eliza backpedaled away, but before she could rear back again, her husband and sons caught her, and she collapsed into them, screaming into the night.

"What kind of God does this?"

CHAPTER 7

A Rumbling in Van Buren

Fort Smith, Arkansas—May 1860

Drenched, sore, and eyes red from crying, the Lacy clan arrived at Fort Smith, each carrying their share of a terrible burden. The wagons rolled to a stop outside the fort's brick wall, leaving Henry and William enough space to care for the horses while Master Thomas, sons in tow, broke from the group. The man hadn't spoken to his wife since the river, and she retreated into herself, huddled in the wagon's riding box, refusing food and care. Hands shaking, the man stood in a silent battle behind her until the silence won, and he dragged himself away to business in the city. The land nearby wouldn't buy itself.

William counted the rooftops he could see, and the number ended up far smaller than Memphis or even Little Rock. The fort sprawled out inside walls, about three blocks long and wide. While protected, the wall ended at head height for the Lacys, meaning Henry could see clear over it, and William had to stand on a crate. Inside, six three-story buildings, each boasting a chimney that spat out thick smoke, held the local Arkansans. From the smell, the smoke was from cookfires.

Henry pulled William aside near them, pointing surreptitiously at a group of passing men in uniforms. "Soldiers," he hissed at the boy, even though they were well out of earshot. "Don't talk to none of them, you hear me? Gray or blue. They all bad news. Only gonna get your hide tanned if you get caught up. If they say anythin', just say 'yes, suh' or 'no, suh' and go on your way."

William looked after the trio as they cavorted down the main thoroughfare, glancing now and then at their tiny wagon train, mostly at Ms. Mary and the girls. One said something that caused an uproar of laughter from the other two before they walked into the fields nearby.

"This fort's been here since 1817. It ain't just a post for the United States military or a fur tradin' post," one soldier called out to the group as they waited. "Y'all better respect this place's authority. We been protectin' the settlers around here as we move westward across this beautiful country."

"White settlers," another added, with a pointed look at the slaves.

"By Thomas Adams Smith's name, we established this place here on the Arkansas River to clean out them Injuns, and put 'em where they supposed to be. Over there in Indian Territory."

Inside, more soldiers wandered. *How'm I gonna miss 'em if they everywhere?* William thought, watching Master Thomas and his sons edge past more clumps in the main thoroughfare. The blue-uniformed men had created a parade of tents in line to make streets inside the fort. While the town of Fort Smith surrounded the military base, it looked like the places they passed on the way over, with around 2,000 people living there.

"It's smarter to live closer to this fort, for better or worse," Henry said, keeping watchful eyes on the blue-uniformed men. "For all the trouble of talkin' to 'em, they keep those ruffians away from robbin' us and maintain trade so we can get salt and tobacco if we need it. They keep some semblance of law and order in case Indians attack."

The sun rose high in the sky and sank close to the horizon before Master Thomas returned to the wagons. He called his family around him, unrolling a piece of paper onto the wagon's driving box.

"We got some land nearby now. Traveling is over, and we can start settling down in a new home. It won't be within sight of this town. We're going to a place called Van Buren. The land is much better over there, a little farther from Fort Smith," he said.

"Much cheaper, more likely," Ms. Mary added, bitterness edged her words these days.

Master Thomas gave her a placating look before continuing. "It is more affordable to live there as well. We can have about the same life we had at Lacy Springs. At Van Buren, we have sixty acres on the north side of the Arkansas River. It isn't that far now. We got the deed here, and it's ours. Let's go home."

With that, everyone gratefully packed back into the wagon for the final leg of their trip. Trundling along, not a few minutes into this leg, the ground rumbled beneath them. Growing louder and louder, William wondered if the earth would erupt around them and jumped off the wagon, preparing to run. Down the road, a blue column of men on horseback approached the fort. A large red, white, and blue flag whipped in the wind as the bannermen sped along.

William sat, mesmerized, as the column passed. Others around him hid in the wagon or sat, looking around, but no one from the Lacy party interacted with the troops. Even Master Thomas kept to himself. The boy, however, had never seen such coordination before: horses, weapons, carts, and hundreds of men walking in unison. No longer afraid, he used his good arm to clamber up on top of the wagon to see better. William thought, *Maybe if I ain't a hunter, I could be a soldier. Bet they ain't never been dunked in a river or beat on the porch before.*

At the new homestead in Van Buren, Master Thomas paced with the deed in hand, surveying the land while addressing his sons. John, James, and Theo listened nearby while he strategized the workload, how it'd be divvied up, and who would lead each section.

Afterward, Theo called William over to care for the horses. Now that roots were being laid down again, the white master's son fell back into step with who he was before the journey started. He even joked with William about playing a game after this had all wrapped up. Nervous, William agreed but kept an eye on him while they brushed Buck and Buttermilk.

They rushed to join their fathers in the fields when they finished. William noticed the game promise was quickly forgotten in Theo's fervor to prove himself useful to his father. On the way, they passed Eliza and the girls, ever a flock around her like baby chicks, preparing a large soup. A more permanent kitchen was built with a deeper fire pit lined with stone.

Days passed in the new spot. Henry led a team of builders to construct a big new house while William split his time between the horses and the field. Now old enough, with his arm improving by the day, the boy picked up how field labor worked, using the plow to break earth and make it ready for seed. Many more days swung by, and William contended with a soreness pulsing in his knee alongside his healing snakebite. The Lacys needed the field plowed and tilled quickly to prepare for a harvest. William pressed forward with his own need to eat, joining his family in prayer at night that God would grow the plants fast enough that they'd survive the winter in their new home.

By summer, Master Thomas had brought neighbors over to break bread and build community. He talked with them about Lacy Springs and why they'd come all this way. Each of them had stories to tell about the Van Buren area, assuring Master Thomas he'd made the right decision to save his livelihood. They'd speak more softly when walking by the fields, discussing trouble brewing from the fort.

Out of those visitors, shopkeepers and feed store owners also visited the burgeoning plantation. While this happened, William, Henry, Joe, and Rufus had to step up their efforts—not just in building the houses and tending to the land. They also played a crucial role in helping Master Thomas establish himself as a new power here in Arkansas. While Master Thomas had a large family, the amount of work needed to build a new reputation called for many hands. Endless tasks stretched as far as the sun did in the long summer days and even pushed long into the night with lanterns lit and moths fluttering around them.

Rufus carried letters again back to Fort Smith so they'd be on their way to Lacy Springs, sharing the good news of their home in Van Buren. William wished he could send a letter that would somehow get to Ole Ben. The exhaustion of traveling, surviving, and then the endless work caught up to the boy, who stumbled across his sleeping sack at the end of each day, collapsing into it.

Henry carried on through construction, taking breaks by running errands to the general store. The walk there was his only reprieve. He'd insist William needed to accompany him, even though he could make it himself. William studied him, picking up from Master Thomas' lesson in the woods: watch people to learn what they know. Henry would make his routine trips to the stores, waiting outside for the whites to finish their shopping before he approached, making minimum polite speech, and mentioning the Lacy name for the supplies he bought. He'd knock on the back door, careful to stay out of sight. He and William would rest behind the store in silent companionship, sweating in the quiet afternoons, before heading back to join the rest for dinner. Everyone, from Henry to Little Mary, worked to the bone setting up their new place, and they barely spoke to one another between rushed bites of food or sips of water. A deep weariness settled into William.

By fall, William hit thirteen, marking him ready to harvest the cornfields. He learned which corn needed harvesting and which ears needed more time on the stalks.

"Corn matures top down," Joe said. His stepbrother held an ear to demonstrate, pulling the stalk forward. William nodded but was barely present, his mind wandering back to Lacy Springs and his old barn. The sadness from summer had grown to a dark pit in his chest, something more to carry through each day. It was easier to keep his secret when he spent his days in the cornfield, protecting it from vermin. All kinds of mice, raccoons, and hawks lived in the field. Snakes, too, but he had learned to give any of them a wide berth. The hawks in nearby trees provided conversation when other slaves turned in, leaving him to keep watch. He even named a few of the birds, half-heartedly speaking to them about his travels and surviving the snakebite. They weren't good listeners like Buck was.

November rolled around, and Master Thomas' visitors became more tense, telling stories of unwelcome changes spilling out from Forth Smith and into Van Buren.

"Some man from the neighboring state is running for President of the United States," one shopkeeper spat. "Your letters are right from back in Alabama. They ain't doing so well over there with all the laws. You got out when you should've."

Master Thomas nodded safely before he said, "I had a feeling it'd come to this. My family has always been involved in politics, you know. I'm not getting involved quite yet until we have a good home and everything settled here, but you can bet as soon as things are quiet, I'll be making some noise in Fort Smith. They can't be doing this to us. We've always had things this way, and we always will. I don't care what this 'Abraham Lincoln' fellow thinks."

"Don't even say that man's name around me," the shopkeeper said, shaking his fist angrily. "That devil is excitin' people all up and down the north about his candidacy, if you can call it that. Them damn Republicans nominated him from Illinois, and he's saying we can't exist as a country with half-slave and half-free. Well, he's half-right. We can't. They need to stop this nonsense while we still have our businesses intact. There's a reason they're enslaved, and we're free, and it ain't hard to see why. Now, we need to rally behind this Stephen Douglass. He's also from Illinois."

"Popular place," Master Thomas replied. "I want to know all my options."

"He's pushing that the states decide whether or not they want slavery. The Southern Democrats are wantin' John Breckinridge of Kentucky. The Constitutional Union Convention hopes to avoid this altogether, which is plum dumb in my opinion, but they're behind John Bell from Tennessee."

Still, Master Thomas read letters aloud to Ms. Mary and the boys—news from Lacy Springs that Eliza would bring back after attending as Ms. Mary's maid. But each letter became more dire, and soon, they barred her and other maids from the room when they read them. "Whatever is in them," Eliza said to Henry one night, "they ain't want us hearin' it."

More nights passed, with fewer slaves allowed in the big house's freshly built den. Almost as soon as Henry put the finishing touches on it, he and the others were rushed off by Master Thomas. Visibly, the man grew more suspicious and fearful of his slaves by the week. Each talk with the people of Van Buren and Fort Smith dripped a slow toxin into his ears that trickled out to his sons.

"Don't know what we gonna do, Henry," Eliza said in their shack. They'd put a lean-to together during the fall, just in time for the autumn chill rolling in. "They have us in for breakfast but shoo us out soon after. Then, we gotta just wait till they call us back in. Lord, the way we gotta wait in between ain't right when we got so much to do."

"Just clean somethin' nearby," Henry said, easing himself down onto his sleeping pallet. The man had grown skinny and gray from labor, his bones and cheeks jutting out. "I don't know, 'Liza. This ain't what I thought neither. Lacy Springs wasn't great, but we had peace. Here, it ain't nothin' but war or talk o' war. Rufus brought more news from the town."

William lay on his sleeping pallet, too exhausted to move. A tear slid down his cheek while he listened. They were never going back to Lacy Springs again and were now stuck in this hellhole in Arkansas. He didn't know what growing up meant, but he couldn't see past the end of the day now. *I wish I could've asked that girl her name*, he thought, his mind drifting back to the girl from the caravan. *Doesn't matter, I guess. She probably dead now. I wish I was.*

"What'd Rufus say?" Henry's voice interrupted his thoughts.

"This Lincoln man is winnin'. He got into the race for the presidency in May, enough to corral all the Republican's together here in November. He ain't gon' be takin' office till March next year, but we got somethin' to hope for."

William heard the word, but hope didn't feel like something real anymore.

More letters poured in, from Fort Smith to Rufus' hands to Master Thomas. They came not just from Lacy Springs but from Huntsville and farther reaches, all from Master Thomas' family, mostly asking for his opinion on whether the state should secede from the United States. Thomas conferred with his sons, talking loud enough and sometimes yelling angrily, while Rufus waited for his replies outside the door.

In all his bluster, the plantation owner didn't know what to think or believe about the nation's cataclysmic choices. However, Rufus knew without him saying it and passed it along to the others: the Lacy family wouldn't survive without Henry, Eliza, William, Rufus, and Joe.

Throughout the winter, more echoes of Lincoln's election rumbled around Van Buren. Saloons, taverns, candy shops, and feed stores buzzed with talk. Visitors had the same concerns. Anywhere William and Henry went for supplies, the questions surrounded them. Even in all the letters Rufus brought to the new big house, everyone wondered what would happen with slavery when the man took office.

Despite the dull ache weighing on William, he found strength in the hushed talk and whispered warnings amongst his community. Abraham Lincoln ran on a platform that slavery would not exist in the territories, and Master Thomas had moved them all to Arkansas, in part to be closer to Indian Territory. These conversations had to happen in bursts around the darkening faces of the white slave owners, some now openly hostile to William and his family. Beatings happened once a week instead of once a month. Because of the beatings, the yelling, the errands, and the persistent dread, William worked the cornfields to produce enough to survive, even selling some to get more money. Passing his knowledge to William, Henry crafted small items to use as tools or art.

It'd become clearer through the tense air that a war was brewing: one that'd end slavery. Master Thomas uprooted their entire lives and worked them to the bone in the soils of Van Buren to cling to them. In between the work, it became harder to serve them as Master Thomas' irritated yelling roused the plantation visitors. All of them cursed Lincoln's name on the cold winter nights. They cursed "Congress." William didn't know some words thrown about but clung to a distant, flickering hope that this nightmare would end. That was enough to keep him going through another winter, shivering in their shack.

CHAPTER 8

Caught by Fate

Coweta, Creek Nation—December 1860

"The Creeks are nearby. They've got many items unavailable in Fort Smith. We need to establish a trading system with them, too. Daddy John traded with Creeks in Alabama. Now we have to bring that tradition here," Master Thomas told Henry and William on the veranda. The two helped him place empty crates in neat rows in the cart. When William stayed quiet, they acted differently, like he wasn't there.

The Creeks? Maybe she's there. William felt his heart beat faster. It's a big world, way bigger than he ever thought before traveling. He had seen the maps. It was impossible for that girl to be in the same place Henry and Master Thomas were heading toward. Still …

"Can I come?" he whispered. The words didn't go far, and Master Thomas' voice drowned them out before anybody heard him.

"Now, what were those words again? I need to practice," Master Thomas said, glancing at Henry before shaking his head. "Never taught you any. Nor my boys. Didn't seem worth it at the time." Alone, Master Thomas often used softer words with Henry. This would be the first time they took an extended trip away from their new home. It'd take two days to reach Indian Territory, and trade could take longer before the return trip. Henry had to ensure things would still be taken care of while they were gone.

"Can I come?" he asked, louder this time. The two men turned to him.

"Now, why you wanna come on this trip? We'll be gone a week, and there's way too much to get done here," Henry jumped ahead of Master Thomas, quickly denying it before the other man could.

"Theo's takin' care of the horses now, and the cornfields are bare. 'Sides, I be much more helpful on the road than here."

Henry settled another crate in place, working until it fit. William did the same, following his father's movements to prove his worth. "Y'all need to move all these crates when you trade and then come back with more. I can hunt and carry things and help watch. I need to learn, too." He finished the speech and kept packing more as he did so.

Master Thomas looked at Henry before waving his hands. "If it means saving our backs some, then sure, you can come too, boy."

"*Vnokeckes cv. Vnokeckv vkerrickvn eskerkv,*" Henry said.

"What?"

"It means, 'I'm here to trade and bring gifts,'" Henry replied in a measured imitation of Master Thomas' speech. During the packing and loading, Henry made sure to bring an extra case of rum, tapping the alcohol with a toe as he addressed Master Thomas.

"Better to start on a good foot if ya want to make friends with the Creeks. Sure thinkin' they ain't want more to do with us settlers now. 'Specially with the fort marchin' around and makin' trouble." He gave Master Thomas a pointed look.

"*Vnokeckes cv,*" Master Thomas repeated, snapping his fingers. William and Henry climbed into the cart, sitting down between the crates. "It does sound familiar. Well, these supplies won't trade themselves. Let's get to it."

The three set off that cold winter morning. William and Henry kept the crates from rattling around. They packed clothes, carvings, and things made of iron that the Creeks didn't have much access to. The metal kettles clanked against other assorted tools. When William shifted to a more comfortable position, his foot knocked over the blanket covering the bottom, revealing at least twenty rifles. Henry kicked the blanket back over them, tucking the corner in before sharing a look with William. *Why's he got so many guns?* William thought. *And why's he givin' them to Creeks if they just gonna use 'em on the fort and white folk? They were forced out of their home. I'd want a gun, too.*

The two-day ride ended as they reached a town in the Creek Nation called Coweta. Master Thomas laughed, folding up the map he got from the general store's shopkeeper. Scrawled across it were directions to this more friendly village. Coweta was known for a few Indians who were more openly ready to trade with the settlers.

Master Thomas reined in the horses to slow their approach. Henry sat up straighter in the back but maintained a cautious watch over the town. The nerves were infectious, and William caught himself glancing around at the houses while his foot rested on the rifle barrels under them.

The houses in Coweta huddled together, made of wooden logs strung together to form walls. The roofs completed the rustic structures with thinner wood, blending them into the nearby forest. The same wood went from trunk to saw to house. Dried prairie grass joined the trees, stuffed into the cracks to seal them, while branches, twigs, and mud kept out—William guessed—insects, vermin, and sunlight. A well stood between the houses with several buckets resting against it.

Some had folks resting on porches right outside their home, held up by wooden beams and facing each other. Coweta was built with twenty houses clustered like this, facing each other, different from the ordered streets of Fort Smith or Little Rock. While not as impressive as the settlers' brick houses, they looked cozy and inviting. William hoped the trade talks would take a while so he could stay in one. Maybe someone knew about Postoak and his daughter here.

The thought raised hope in his chest, but he shook his head—better not to hope for that. It was better to accept life was like this—whatever this was. Hard work and pain. Even though he came all this way, William decided he'd let the dream of meeting that girl again die on the way into Coweta. It'd hurt more if she weren't there, and the hope was unrealistic.

Master Thomas pulled to a stop in front of a quaint house. A garden spilled out around it, and a fair-skinned Black woman worked the soil. Even in winter, there were things to prepare for. She set her tools down and strode over to the fence, giving Master Thomas a shy smile and studying the crates in their cart.

"If y'all gon' sell that stuff, might as well turn right around now 'cause we ain't got no money here," she said. Wiping her hands on her apron, brown earth fell about her feet. "Not to be rude, y'all welcome to get supper nearby if ya can pay. Jus' lots o' poor folk here."

William stared off. The woman looked familiar, but he just wished the trip was over. No trade meant they'd have to try a different place.

"Now, now, that doesn't have to be settled so fast," Master Thomas said. "We don't want to sell anything. We're more than happy to start trading supplies. That's why we're here: to see if your people want to trade with mine. We're over near Van Buren."

"Luvinia, what'd I say about talkin' to strangers?" a gruff voice called out from the doorway. "Get back in the house. Now."

The woman, Luvinia, faltered mid-speech, her smile dropping. She turned and lowered her head, walking back into the house. Henry perked up at the voice, sliding out of the cart.

"Vnokeckes cv. Vnokecky vkerrickvn eskerkv," Henry called out.

"Well, if it ain't the Lacys of Lacy Springs. Y'all far from Alabama, ain't ya?" Billy Postoak said, heavy boot steps hitting his porch. The tall man watched Luvinia close and latch the door before he joined Henry and Master Thomas near his gate. "My wife, Luvinia. What brings y'all so far west?"

"We moved out here," Master Thomas replied. "Much easier to keep your livelihood out near the territories."

Postoak laughed. Some of it echoed off the house, and some was directed at Henry. "Now you ain't kiddin' there. Welcome to the territory, then. Good to see some familiar faces. Like my wife said, we ain't got much money, but we do have space for more friends to trade with, depending on what those friends bring."

Master Thomas walked around the cart and popped open the rum, removing a bottle before handing it to Postoak. The man grinned widely. "Now, there's that gift you were talkin' about. Was waitin' on it. You can put some over in that bin." He nodded at a space near his house. "We'll take it in when we need it. You're gettin' fur, deerskin, and corn, but that's about it. Call it a 'good faith' exchange, and I'll make sure you stay welcome in Coweta."

Henry waved his hands at William, who was staring, thunderstruck, at Postoak. "C'mon, let's go, boy." He had to snap in front of him to get him moving. William jumped off the cart and grabbed a crate, unloading it to move it to the bin. As he walked, he searched Postoak's property, spying the same wagon he had hidden behind a year earlier.

"'Cinda, get out here and come help." Postoak clapped his hands and leaned against the fence as the door opened again. He chatted lazily with Master Thomas while Henry and William unloaded more crates, moving back and forth.

Then, she came out.

It was her! William's heart nearly leaped from his chest when he saw her, almost exactly like she was so long ago. The girl was just as traffic-stopping beautiful, with her proud, determined expression, strong strides, and that unmistakable aura of someone who knew she was meant to be there. Her caramel-colored skin marked her as half Indian, with the single, long braid down her back. It didn't matter what Postoak said. This girl was helping because she wanted to.

"That's my daughter, Lucinda. She takes after me, which makes her hard to deal with," he laughed with Master Thomas. "Girl's got more spirit 'n a filly. Just needs more time to get broken. Lucinda, we tradin' the skins for corn and squash. Make sure to count while you unloadin'."

Her suede dress swished, and William stared, slack-jawed, at the ground her tweed and leather shoes walked across. She was here. Alive. After everything, he stood before her again. She came up right beside him at the cart.

Behind, while he stood frozen, Master Thomas waved Henry over to help with things in the house, using a smattering of Muscogee to impress his friendlier host. Now that Postoak was warmed up, he was ready to talk trade deals. Henry needed to balance out Master Thomas' knowledge of what their home needed, not just now, but when spring, summer, and the whole year rolled around. This left William alone with the girl. Mostly ignoring him, she unloaded first one, then two crates, and as she returned for the third, she rounded on him.

"You gon' help or just stand there lookin' silly?"

Even her voice was musical up close. William swallowed.

"What do they call you?"

"Jus' William."

"'Jus' William,' huh? I'm Lucinda Postoak. I'm sorry if you're dumb or somethin'. Know you can't help that, but this is gon' go much faster if you help. So don't just stand there like some big ol' stone. Then you and your family can get on down the road back wherever you're from."

She don't remember me, William thought sadly. *Why would she, though? You jus' standin' here, dumb and quiet as ever*. It took him a moment, but he got his feet moving, turning around to the cart before he grabbed one and followed her to the bin.

She smiled, encouraging him. "That's it. Put 'em all right in a line, so it'll make it easier for me to count. Take the lids off, too, when they're settled."

William needed her to know who he was. But what could he say that'd remind her without making him look bad? "I know you was tradin' with your daddy near Lacy Springs last year."

"Oh?" she said simply, counting the items.

"Yeah, we traded with your daddy back in Alabama."

She didn't react to the news, and he didn't want to press further. Now that they had an easy conversation going, one that meandered between the differences between Alabama and Indian Territory, he never wanted it to end. He never wanted to talk about anything but what she liked, what made her laugh. Luckily, they finished their work, moving to an oak tree nearby.

Inside the house, the adults argued, drank, and debated specifics, much like they did. Three hours flew by while they alternated between listening to the adults and sharing their own conversation. They shared stories of Coweta and Fort Smith, things happening here that Lucinda didn't know about. He whispered about Abraham Lincoln and other things the adults told him never to speak about, but Lucinda was different. William had never felt so light. So carefree. Lucinda's eyes drank in all his pain, and he felt lighter in his chest—a feeling not there since he left Ole Ben at Lacy Springs.

Lucinda shared something big with him: she was Postoak's daughter but also his slave, just like her mama, Luvinia. Billy inherited Luvinia when his father died, even though he was also born in Indian Territory, and ended up marrying her. She talked so candidly about their ownership. It sparked a feeling in William that maybe it wasn't right. She spoke about it like she knew it could be different somehow.

By the time the adults came out, it was time to leave. They promised to come back and visit, as this was a "most fruitful" agreement, or so Master Thomas said. He had them all packed up into the wagon and on the road faster than he could say a proper goodbye. Lucinda gave a short wave before following Billy and Luvinia back into the cabin.

No matter what, William would be on every trade trip to Coweta now. He'd make sure that he'd be invaluable, so Master Thomas had to take him. *Lucinda*—that was her name. She was alive, and well, and nearby. Next time, he'd tell her who he was.

CHAPTER 9

The Civil War Begins

Van Buren, Arkansas—Spring 1861

A happy period enveloped William. It crept up behind him like someone playing hide-and-seek, catching him with two hands over his eyes. The world faded away—his worries, his aches—in those visits to the Postoak house in Coweta.

While that first visit concerned a simple connection between Master Thomas' household and the Postoaks, subsequent trips had the white man introduced to other villagers via the satisfied tradesman. These meetings swam in rum, the full crate used for trade quickly disappearing down their throats before any agreement was facilitated.

All of this worked out just fine for William. While Master Thomas cozied up to other Creek tradesmen in Coweta, he spent more time with Lucinda, each trip blessing him with a few more hours of her company.

William eagerly awaited the next trip. Henry made excuses that morning, saying he needed to finish something up, giving his boy a slight smirk at his excited reaction. The man noticed a cheerful change in William over the last month, and he knew the trips would last that much longer if it were just William and Master Thomas.

Exiting the house with a quiet door closing behind him, the plantation master sauntered off the porch, letter in hand, absorbed in reading it.

Theo rushed over from his side of the porch. "Is that from home, Daddy?"

"Yes, some news from our cousins," Master Thomas said. "War's getting worse now. People are enlisting in the effort. They're asking me if I'll be joining too."

"You're not leaving, are you?"

"Never gave it much thought," Master Thomas said, patting the boy's head. "Your daddy ain't young anymore. I'm fifty-six now. Battle's a thing for young men. Maybe it's better if I don't get too involved." His head turned toward Forth Smith, and Theo's eyes followed curiously. "Things are getting worse and worse every day, though. Shopkeepers and even the milder tradesmen ain't bringing any more good news from back east. This letter from your cousin makes it even clearer. I don't think I should leave, son, but I may have no choice soon."

As April rolled by, Master Thomas grew increasingly agitated, muttering to himself on the trips and at home. William listened as the man soured. His spirits, lifted for a few months by the happier times in Coweta, were back to before with the shopkeepers and others from Fort Smith. Those folks, plus the letters from home, brought an acidic unease to his mind, dripping out once more into his family and across the growing plantation.

Copies of the Thirty-Fifth Parallel, a local Fort Smith newspaper, appeared in the big house, usually starting in Master Thomas' hands before moving to John, James, and finally, Theo. They spoke at length, gathering together around the newspaper and discussing its contents, as well as the character of the editor, a military man: General A.G. Mayers. They grew to rely on the paper, as it brought reliable information about national and local news. Master Thomas remarked that it was a piece of their old home showing up in Arkansas.

Receiving their paper meant the Lacys would sit in the parlor, eating, drinking, and discussing how this news affected their home. He especially brought in Theo, now considered a man of the plantation, and would be expected to consider the news when he did his chores.

The talk hearkened back to simpler times at Lacy Springs, where politicians were discussed, but in a lazy manner, more as gossip than anything serious. Master Thomas would read stories from Washington about Senate battles. Mostly, these involved the issue of slavery, an institution so ingrained in the American economy that it seemed unthinkable to Master Thomas that it could change. His family's fortune was built on the backs of slaves. With the growing realization this could change, his survival instincts kicked in, and he clenched at each publication, ravenously devouring the news, before disseminating "plans" with his sons—plans to keep a level of fear, like the fear of God, thrumming through the community he held under his thumb.

The newspaper's information brought critical news for the Lacys, such as farming advances, entertainment, political shifts, and government decisions. Each of his boys took a different piece to focus on, forming a mini council for the farm. The most concerning news, seldom shared beyond whispers, was the slave revolts. This only reached William when Master Thomas let it slip on their rides to Coweta. Before they reached the town, Master Thomas would hide the newspaper beneath the seat, and William would covertly bring this news to Lucinda, her face grim as she accepted it.

Back in Van Buren, Master Thomas kept his family updated, but the Lacys pulled back more from the slave community working the spring planting. More than ever, it was vital to set new growth in place, as this would be the first full year they'd be living there, and the master wanted his children to be cared for. This wouldn't be possible without maintaining his slaves and broadening their horizons of living. They'd already moved through three states—Virginia, North Carolina, and Alabama—seeking to fortify their family's legacy. Here in Arkansas, it felt like they'd reached a limit.

"The nation is expanding westward, but I don't know if we can expand with it any further," James said to the group. The Lacy men sat around the table while Ms. Mary crocheted in the corner.

"You right, son. We can't. This is the last leg of our journey for a long while. People are grabbing land left and right, pushing farther west, and building more political power. There's more reasons why I chose this place for our home besides being cheap," Master Thomas said, shooting a look at Ms. Mary, who continued to crochet in silence. "We got neighbors here who believe the same as us. That amplifies our political power. Settlers like us keep moving farther west, meaning more folks like us can apply for statehood in the union. We can push to keep the things we need to survive. People in the north want to take our livelihoods from us, claiming this issue is a 'spread' that needs to be stopped. We're only spreading and moving to keep our families fed. Keep our roofs up. This is our way of life, and we ain't givin' it up."

A chorus of "yays" and nods sounded from around the table. Outside, after delivering the mail, Rufus crouched right below the salon window to listen.

"Northerners are moving west, too. It ain't just us," James said. "I know you planned on using the territories nearby as a safeguard in case the slavery issue came up again, and I know the westward expansion is a good thing, but more people are moving around."

"I know, James, we just have to hold tight. This was an enormous step for us. We lost so much on the way here …" Master Thomas' voice broke, and the family sat in prayer. "… So, we're here for now. Arkansas has good, trustworthy neighbors. We're holding out here for our family back at Lacy Springs. This is why we send letters back and forth. To bolster them with hope. This is why we read them together."

Rufus waited as their talk meandered from gossip about Lacy Springs before he was called back in. The little news from other slaves was handed out last to him. Any letter from back home, even those several pages long, usually contained only a few sentences of updates from the slaves' family members they were separated from. Ms. Mary called Rufus back in, and he rushed back inside the house, sitting near the front door like he was there the whole time.

"Boy, there ain't no more news from Lacy Springs for you this week," Ms. Mary said. She stood in the doorway while the Lacy men got up from their council meeting, alternating between staring suspiciously at Rufus before heading off to work.

"Uh … yes, ma'am, you sure there ain't no more talk of the weather?" Rufus asked carefully. For no news to come, that meant they were hiding something. The Lacys didn't want them to know about what was going on. Every week, they would at least talk about the weather, the Tennessee River, the post office, Huntsville stores, and other everyday happenings—small, cherished connections to their loved ones back in Alabama.

"No, nothing this week," Ms. Mary said again, impatiently.

"Oh, I see. Thank you, ma'am," Rufus said and bowed. He knew better than to press the woman when her lips drew into a tight line. As quickly as he could, he disappeared from the big house, making his way back to the slave quarters.

In their shack, Rufus waved his mother and stepfather over to share more news from the "council" meetings Master Thomas had. Barred from the house, Rufus took to sneaking around to the side window to listen after delivering the mail. He knew every time the Thirty-Fifth Parallel appeared, the Lacys would talk, and things would immediately worsen for him and his family. To counter this, Eliza had Rufus bring any news to her so that she and Henry could warn the other slaves and provide some comfort and stability. In the new plantation, the community felt more unified by their journey.

"A senator's been attacked," Rufus whispered to Eliza. She set down her washing and rubbed one aching elbow.

"What happened?"

"Seems like a northern senator got beaten with a cane by a southerner. The Yankee's name was Charles Sumner, from Massachusetts, and it was after the Senate been talkin' about writin' some laws to help the smaller fights around the region. Didn't know what some other words meant, but I gather they be hoppin' mad 'bout the revolts 'round them parts. South Carolina folks been talkin' loud. Alabama folks, too. They say slavery might be goin', and they gon' be forced to free us."

"Shhh," Eliza hissed at him. "Don't say that part too loud, now."

Henry put a calming hand on her shoulder. "We been talkin' here for weeks without the massa hearin'. Rufus, you thinkin' the same thing as me?"

"Yes, Massa Thomas done picked up and moved us here 'cause he afraid he gonna have to set us free."

The family sat silently, the ramifications of this information settling around them.

"We cain't be tellin' other folks this," Eliza said. "Word gon' travel, and it's gon' come right back to us that we be spyin' on Massa Thomas' meetin's. They ain't no comin' back from that. He already lookin' at us sideways."

"But we can be free."

The three turned to look as William spoke up for the first time.

"Son," Henry said and knelt to speak to him, eye-to-eye. "'Liza's right. We ain't gon' be free. Them white folk can talk all they want up in the gov'ment, but we ain't seein' nothin' 'round here 'cept pain and misery. We gotta s'vive. That's our lot. I keep a watch for you, and you keep a watch for me, but we ain't movin' further than that."

He got up and nodded at Rufus. "You keep listenin' for news, and we'll let the others know when it's another bad day. Keep they heads down, work a little harder, and don't say nothin' to them 'bout anythin'. We s'vive another day."

Dear Thomas,

At the time of my writing, Alabama has fully seceded from the Union. It started back in January, but now we are seeing the ramifications of this decision as the Confederacy forms. We must do this since they think they can push anything through now that Lincoln is in office. The travesty! We Southerners must band together as the war approaches.

I am writing to let you know I will be joining the war effort and ask you to do the same. Virginia has just seceded, and several other states have followed the secession: South Carolina, Mississippi, Florida, Georgia, Louisiana, and Texas. Hopefully, Arkansas will join soon, and so will you.

War is upon us, and we need to take appropriate action. Please stay safe, cousin.

Regards,
James Lacy

Dear James,

Thank you for keeping my family up to date with the news. We have a newspaper nearby, but sometimes it comes late. We rely on our family during these times to keep everyone safe. I see that the newly formed Confederate States of America are here now. This is good news.

While it does not gladden my heart that we are in the midst of war, I have faith that our integrity as Southerners will hold the line. We are farmers, simple men of the land, and I do not believe we want this war. In my opinion, we will fight with all our power if it comes down to it. At this time, I cannot ascertain the intentions of my state in these efforts.

We are strong! We are the backbone of this country, and if those Northerners are stupid enough to press us fully into this war, they will not last long.

Stay strong, cousin,
Thomas Lacy

William and Henry walked a few paces back while they were in Fort Smith, wheeling a handcart behind Master Thomas. The man approached the general store, picking up a copy of the Thirty-Fifth Parallel from a stack near the door. Men near him were discussing the events reported.

Master Thomas stood quietly, reading the paper as a steady stream of men came, growing around the store and passing around the news. A deep uneasiness threaded through the crowd. Questions flew about what would happen, and predictions were thrown around.

"I've been to the large cities in the north," Master Thomas said, cutting in on the conversation. Men quieted, and he joined the throng. "Up there, many men are available to join the military, but down here, we are ripe with resources. We're the supplies they need. It may not be war resources specifically, but they still can't afford to keep this going with the strength of our Confederacy."

Feeling satisfied by bolstering their morale, Master Thomas folded the newspaper and tucked it under his arm, heading into the store. William waited outside before picking up the supplies and loading the handcart, following Master Thomas while Henry broke off to run his own errands. They visited the post office next, Master Thomas electing to pick up letters himself that week, remarking on two arriving today: one for him and another for Ms. Mary. He read his aloud to himself, moseying along while William pulled the handcart.

Dear Thomas,

While your letter was on its way to me, General P.T. Beauregard had instructed the Confederate army to fire its first shots at Fort Sumter, South Carolina, a federal fort in Charleston Harbor. The commanding officer, Robert Anderson, awoke to the sound of cannons on April 12. After a few hours, Captain Abner Doubleday returned fire, but it was clear for the next day and a half that we had won the battle! The war has begun …

The handcart hit a snag, and William grunted to pull it over the pothole. Startled out of it, Master Thomas squinted at the boy before tucking the letter into the newspaper. They passed another crowd, similarly gathered outside. William noticed clusters of people all up and down the street. Murmurs passed through them, and louder folks talked as they walked by.

"This will be over in about a week," one man said. "I know the Yankees don't want to fight against us real men."

Another man bellowed out, "I'm not giving up my damn slaves, no matter what they do or say. I paid for them and fed them all their lives, and if the northern government wants them, they will have to kill me first!"

Master Thomas made no remarks about this when Henry joined back up, covered in a cold sweat. He and William loaded up their handcart as Master Thomas watched the crowds moving restlessly between each other. After that, he snapped, and the trio headed out of Fort Smith, returning to Van Buren. The whole way back, Master Thomas pulled into himself, deep in thought.

When they reached the plantation again, he broke from William and Henry, calling out for another "council meeting." It would be all hands on deck: Ms. Mary, John, James, Theo, everybody. Henry looked at William, then nodded at the cart. "Rufus is out now. You gon' have to listen in today. Be quiet and hurry off if you think they'll catch wind of you."

William waited a minute and walked with Henry before grabbing a gardening tool to walk behind the house. Like he was hunting pigeons, the boy crouched and stealthily made his way right under the salon window. Inside, he heard Master Thomas speaking. It was slow and grave. The last time he talked like this was when he gave his speech before they moved from Lacy Springs.

"Most of you know what's been happening. I've kept you updated from Cousin James' letters, the Thirty-Fifth Parallel, and hearsay around the fort. I know y'all are worried, so I'm gathering you here today to say it aloud: the war has begun."

Audible gasps sounded around the room, and William covered his mouth, leaning against the house.

"Now, don't get too nervous. I'm sure it'll be over by summer. There's no way the North can win against the toughest men of our nation. Us Southerners have weathered the most, provide the most, and hell, we came all the way here in three wagons. They're all fat and lazy up north. Comfortable in their houses. As for us, we're people of the land. We grow all these resources that they take from us. Well, they're about to realize what it's like without our support. No farms. No food. They can't survive without us in the Confederacy."

After the speech, William waited till a softer conversation started, the family seemingly more at ease after hearing him talk, before he returned to deliver the news to his own people.

Several weeks later, a neighbor stopped by to invite Master Thomas to Fort Smith. He explained that the mayor, J.K. McKenzie, was gathering the locals for an immediate meeting at the fort's gate. Master Thomas called for William to hitch up his wagon quickly, yelling for John and James to get ready. "You're coming too, boy," Master Thomas snapped at William. "We can't be worrying about the wagon during this emergency meeting, and you're not doing anything important. Get in the back."

Twenty minutes later, the four rushed off the property, heading toward the fort and the emergency meeting, while the messenger rode on to the next homestead. It was the bumpiest ride, and William winced each time the master lashed at Buttermilk's back, driving the horse on mercilessly fast to make it there in record time. When they reached the gates, a sizeable crowd had formed. Mayor McKenzie addressed the crowd from atop an overturned wagon, the hastily crafted stage elevating him high enough to be heard over the murmuring crowd.

"My neighbors in Arkansas have just joined the Confederacy, seceding from the Union in order to be on the right side of this war," his sonorous voice carried over the crowd. Master Thomas hopped off the wagon, joining the throng as his sons did the same. William hopped off, too, steadying the horse and feeding it oats to help ease the bloodied, frothy beast.

"We must have volunteers, as this isn't like other wars. We aren't fighting to defend our country. We're fighting for our homes! Please join us. We'll rely on our boys here to lead the volunteers and train them up to defend themselves. Fight! Fight for your wives, fight for your children, and by God, fight for your slaves! Because without them, we cannot run our houses. We cannot run our farms, and we cannot run our economy."

Master Thomas grimly met the gaze of each of his sons, holding them for a moment before walking over to the growing line of volunteers, signing their names to fight for Arkansas.

CHAPTER 10

The Winds of Change

Van Buren, Arkansas—Spring 1861

The only sounds on the way back to the farmhouse were the wheels' wooden creaks, the evening birdsong, and the occasional sigh. William crouched in the back, making himself as small as possible. None of the Lacy men even glanced in his direction after the rally. Feeling like he did back in the barn, the boy put his head between his legs and balled up.

When they reached the big house, he waited until each man exited, listening for their footsteps to hit the porch, before he hopped out to care for the horse and move the cart to the newly built stables. Meeting him halfway, Henry stopped him.

"What happened?"

"Massa Thomas signed up for war. It's real now. They fightin' all 'cross the country, and Arkansas just joined. They gettin' volunteers up at the fort now."

Henry squeezed his shoulder. "I'm sorry to keep puttin' this on ya, but we need to know what the massa gonna do next. I'll put the wagon up and clean the horses. You go back under the window and listen. 'Liza and I'll wait at home."

William agreed, silently taking his place under the Lacys' salon window. Inside, Master Thomas had gathered the family once more to distribute the dire news. The boys, John and James, stood at the doorway while he broke the news to Ms. Mary and the girls.

"Papa, why are you going? Don't they have enough younger men to fight?" Theo asked. His voice shook with emotion, and William could picture him standing straight, holding himself back from running to his father.

"Son, this is the only way to protect you. Protect you, your mother, your brothers, our whole way of life. This is the only thing that makes us the men that we are, and we must fight when our homes are in danger." He forced a half-hearted chuckle. "Besides, this'll all be over sooner than you think. We will run those Yanks up to Canada before summer!"

A collective sigh ran around the room. More chatter sounded to allay different fears before Master Thomas cleared the room. Then, it was just him and Ms. Mary.

"You're Private Lacy now," she said in a soft whisper. William had to lean in close, almost bracing himself against the window.

"What about us, though? Really. I know you put on a brave face for the boys, especially Theo. He wants to act like our little man, but he's still just a child. How do you know what will happen to us? What will happen to me and the girls while you're gone?"

William heard her start crying. Then, the crying sounded muffled as if she covered her mouth.

Master Thomas spoke, his voice heavy. "Mary, I must do my part in this war, quick or not. I must support the community here in Fort Smith and continue to uphold the values we brought from Alabama—even our family there is counting on me now. I don't love the idea of slavery, but it's the only way we've ever known. We wouldn't have survived the trip, the harsh winters, or the hot summers. Their toil, their work, their value belong to me, Mary. The slaves take care of our family and business. Without them, well, what would the Lacys be? Just another poor family sitting in the gutters. No, I must fight to keep what my forefathers built and preserve our legacy, Mary. We've worked our whole lives to establish the Lacy name.

"As for the slaves, they don't know any better. They're all blissfully unaware of what's happening beyond the bounds of our farm. All they know is how to do the jobs they were trained for. They'll keep on caring for our animals, family, and land. I will return before summer is over, Mary. There is no way in heaven that the Yankees want to push farther into the South."

Ms. Mary stopped crying, and the two stood in silence for a while, only broken by the shuffling of papers. "I brought you some mail from the post. Try to keep the girls' focus on good news. We need it now more than ever. And try to get some sleep, my dear."

Biding his time, William counted to twenty before moving away from the window. As he rounded the corner, he ran into Theo, crying in a bush. The young Lacy boy stopped, startled by William.

"What are you doing here?" he asked, quickly wiping his cheeks.

"I was ... uh, clearin' weeds," William said. The lie sprang to his lips, and he brought his hand up to show the spade—which wasn't there. He had rushed off without it in his hurry.

Theo looked down at his empty hand, suspicion replacing the tears. "What do you mean?"

William shook his head and backed away. "Just pullin' weeds. That's all. I gotta go now. I won't say nothin' 'bout you cryin' in the bushes."

With that, he turned and ran toward the slave quarters, heart pounding all the way. *He saw me. He saw me. Oh, Lord.*

By the time he arrived, Eliza and Henry had gathered most of the community. It was evening, so they'd be eating anyway. William ran up and stopped in front of them, telling the news between pants. "He ... saw ... me."

"Who, Will?" Rufus put a steading hand on his head. "What happened, little man?"

"Theo Lacy. He saw me outside the window!"

Rufus looked at Henry. "We cain't use that again for a while. The Lacys'll be suspicious even more now. Did you learn anything you can tell us, Will?"

"Yes, they startin' a war now. Arkansas is joinin' the war effort on account of President Lincoln tellin' them to free us. They tryin' to free us slaves."

"What are all y'all gathered here for?"

Master Thomas' voice startled them. The man walked up behind the group, and William nearly jumped out of his skin. Eliza started forward, but Henry put a steadying hand on her shoulder, moving to block William from the man.

"We jus' worried over here, sir," Henry began carefully. "William came back sayin' y'all was gonna have a war or somethin'. Everyone at the fort was causin' a commotion, and we jus' wonderin' what's gonna change now."

Master Thomas stood silently appraising them while William tried not to look guilty. *Did Theo tell him I was back at the window? Oh, Lord, I got caught. They gon' do somethin' bad—worse than the barn.* The boy could hide the roiling emotions but not the sweat pouring down the back of his neck.

The white man studied Henry and then turned to address the group, clearing his throat. "Now, I'm guessing the milk's been spilled before I could get here, but that does make the speech a little shorter. Yes, war is upon us. I've joined the 1st Arkansas Regiment, as it's my duty and honor to care for Mary and my children."

He paused, giving them a stern look. "Something you might have heard already is that the Yankees and their president have a lot of contrary thoughts about our livelihoods down here, specifically about you slaves. They're saying quite a lot, and I'm here to set it straight before you get your minds twisted with the wrong information." Pausing, Master Thomas' eyes fixed on William. "The Yankees ain't winning this war. Even if they do, they're not freeing any slaves. Any news about that ain't nothing but lies. Nobody up there is going to treat you any differently than whites down here. I've been up north, and they hate slaves more than anybody down here. Why do you think they're always talking about you? Freedom? No, they're just trying to kill you, so we can't work together on farms like this. I'd think long and hard about any smart ideas you're having in these 'meetings.'

"Lincoln doesn't care for Blacks at all, and he already published in newspapers that keeping slaves in bondage would be a good thing. The man ain't your friend. I'll say it again, so y'all gettin' it crystal clear: if the Yankees win, they will take all the land and leave nothing. Nothing for me and my family. Nothing for you and yours. Eliza, William, Rufus, Joe, and everyone will be cast out into the wilderness, roaming with no home. Everyone understand?"

"Yessuh," Henry nodded. "Think I speak for all of us when I say that." This was met with a chorus of nods as they all muttered, "Yessuh, Massa."

Master Thomas turned to leave with a satisfied expression before stopping and saying as a casual afterthought, "Oh, and by the way, they found Ole Ben between the river and slave shacks on the plantation. He's dead." With that, he continued back to the big house.

The news rocked through the crowd. Ole Ben was Henry's father and William's grandfather, but the man cared for each person in the community. Eliza quietly reached for Henry, who stood stock-still, watching Master Thomas get smaller and smaller. Her rough hands held the man's shoulder as tears rolled silently down his cheeks. One by one, Joe, Rufus, and others came to place a hand on Henry's shoulder or join the cluster of people embracing.

Ole Ben's dead? William received the news with numb shock, juggling a wave of grief through nervous relief. Master Thomas didn't punish him for eavesdropping, but when would Theo break the news?

Joining the others at his father's side, William stared after Master Thomas as he walked back to the big house.

"Now make sure they sound before you trade," Eliza said, handing William a scarf. Inside, some bread, a jar of preserves, and supplies were hidden to trade on William's latest trip. He was about to head back to Coweta with Master Thomas, and Eliza caught wind of Lucinda's budding leatherworking talents. The girl wanted to send her tools to the community in Van Buren, and William would secretly work with Eliza to make it happen.

"I don't believe a damn word of it!" Rufus' voice sounded outside the shack. Soon after, Henry entered with Rufus close behind him. The air grew tense.

"Don't matter if we believe or not. Ain't nothin' changin' around here," Henry said. "Now knock it off. People gon' here if you talkin' so loud."

"What's goin' on?" William asked.

"Was tellin' Henry, ain't no way what Massa said yesterday was true. We gon' be free if we help the Yankees. Ain't ya heard the songs they singin'? O freedom, o freedom …" he started, but Henry gave him a look.

"Don't sing it here," Henry whispered, his voice low and angry.

"… *O freedom over me!*
And before I'd be a slave,
I'll be buried in my grave,
And go home to my Lord and be free."

Behind them, Eliza finished it, her voice resonant and quiet in the small shack. Henry's fists clenched throughout the notes. "Woman, I ain't doin' this again. I'm tryin' to keep us alive. You know what happens to people who sing this? People who get these dangerous ideas?" He pulled William to him, raising his pant leg to expose the old scar—the one Buck gave him when Master Thomas beat him in the barn.

"Y'all want more? More pain? More beatin'? 'Cause that's all these words and songs will getcha. Mo' scars across ya backs."

"Pa, they been talkin' though. It's different this time. Even the Injuns sayin' we gon' be free soon. Not just in Coweta but all over. The war might be more pain and beatin' … but it also could be freedom." Rufus stood his ground while he spoke to Henry. Everyone in the shack did, waiting for his answer.

"You say you hear people talkin'. Well, I hear people talkin' too. Other slave folk down in Fort Smith. They all talk about they massas and how they be treated. Some folks have it real good, and they don't want that to change. What'll happen if they freed and that good life gets snatched away? I get supplies from Shaw's general store, and Frank be tellin' me how they be gettin' favors from they massas, 'specially from folks workin' in the homes. Only God knows if this'll turn out for us."

"God's the one gon' save us," Rufus said. "What else we doin' here? Workin'? They got us buildin', fetchin', growin', all more than over at Lacy Springs. We dyin' here. They ain't enough of us to keep goin' through another winter. If we dyin' anyway, might as well be on our way to freedom.

Eliza stood by her son, holding onto his shoulders and waiting for Henry to say something.

Henry shook his head and hissed out an exasperated sigh. "Y'all gon' get us all killed, but I ain't stoppin' you from livin'. Ole Ben would've said differently, but he dead now. We gotta live somehow."

Listen to ya daddy. Keep ya head down. Live a better life. Some of Ole Ben's last words flitted through William's mind. *Something huge is comin'. I can feel it.*

Near the house, William prepared two horses: one for the carriage to Coweta and the other for Master Thomas. That day, he was to leave his family for the war.

All the Lacys gathered around to wish him good fortune on his way to the 1st Arkansas Regiment. Ms. Mary cried while she held his head, whispering prayers over him. Each of his sons shook his hand except Theo, who got a head pat.

William handed over his reins, which he took before swinging up onto Buttermilk. "Alright, family. Stay strong while I'm gone. We'll win this war before summer is out, and I'll return triumphant. Keep the faith while you're here." And with that, he clicked, trotting out of the farm.

The boy wandered over to the carriage to wait while the family muttered more farewells and gossiped for a minute longer. Sad, James Lacy broke from the others and swung up into the carriage beside William. "Alright, let's get this trip over with."

For the next eighteen months, William made frequent trips to Coweta to trade with the Postoaks and their neighbors. Most times, it was James who would accompany him. Other times, the Lacy man would slink out of that duty, foisting it onto Henry, who was all too glad to make the trip with William. No matter who came along, the boy made sure to break away to talk with Lucinda each time.

The Creek girl would seek him out, ravenous for more news of the outside world. Ever since he brought the whispers of war, she'd press him for each new telling and new song, sometimes several times, just to hear it again. William was all too happy to comply.

James Lacy grew irritated on some trips when they were met with a mirrored frustration from the Creek villagers. Items they requested got harder and harder to come by, and the ones the Lacy community could find for them were of lower quality. While farther away, the war effort seeped into distant communities like these, making it felt all over the nation.

"You know, half of our tribe's gone north now," Lucinda said. Under the shady tree where they would spend time, the girl passed another leather belt to William. He marveled at the intricate pattern while she spoke. "They're heading to Kansas. Some wanted to join the Confederacy, and others wanted to side with the Union."

William looked up from the belt to see her staring off in the distance, her brow creased in worry. "I don't know what's gonna happen to my people. War's comin' whether we like it or not, and nothing we do here is gonna stop it. Life here in Coweta ain't perfect, but it's calm and simple. I know what to do here. If soldiers come in and families move, I don't know what we're gonna do."

"Can just figure it out one day at a time," William said. He ached to put his arm around her and comfort her, but his painful shyness held him in place. "Ain't no use worryin' 'bout stuff we can't control. The war ain't here yet, so we can jus' enjoy today—the sun, each other's company."

Lucinda smiled at those words, and his heart skipped a beat. "Now, William, I didn't know you was a poet. That's very wise words, and I'll take 'em to heart." She stood up and waved her hands as he tried to offer the belt back. "No, you keep it. I made it for ya as a present. Think of it as a way to remember me if ya can't make it up again for another trade with Papa."

Lucinda, I could never forget you. Never. Not since I saw you at the caravan that day years ago ...

"Thanks, Lucinda, but I'd never forget you. There's somethin' you should know," he started. It'd been a long time, and he never confessed that they'd met before he showed up in Coweta. "It's been almost two years now comin' here with Henry, and I've learned a lot. We also been usin' your leather on the farm. Everyone says the quality is better than anythin' at Fort Smith." He rambled, buying time before he brought up the moment they met. What would she think? Would he be labeled a coward for hiding behind the wagon?

"Ugh, I wish I could go to market at the fort," she said, now frustrated. "Papa won't let me sell anythin' I've made. Says I belong to him, so anythin' I make is his. Same with anything Mama grows in her garden. All he does is drink up all our money. Everything we make, and ..." She stopped and caught a sob back. "I just cain't take it. If Mama or me says anythin', he beats us till we stop screamin'."

William put a hand on her shoulder, a brave gesture for him. She cried, and a few tears spilled out before marshaling herself. "I guess that's what I'm afraid of most. It ain't the war, really. It's bein' stuck here with Papa forever. Stuck watchin' him kill Mama slowly and himself with liquor."

"That ain't gon' happen to you," William said. "What do you want to do? To be?"

Lucinda stared back out over the village and off over the woods nearby. "I'm gonna be my own person. I'll live free to make my own decisions as a woman and a free person. Even if my leather ain't the best, or I ain't in Coweta anymore. I wouldn't care as long as I made those choices myself."

"C'mon, boy! Time to head out."

James Lacy called out near the carriage. It looked like the trades were complete. Billy Postoak also stood nearby, but the smile dropped from his face when he spotted the two of them at the tree.

William pulled his hand back and nodded to the Creek girl. "You will be a free person someday, Lucinda. It might not be tomorrow, but it's gon' happen. I know it."

With that, they walked back to join the others at the wagon. William busied himself securing the parcels in the back while Postoak made parting conversation with James. It sounded like they were discussing the same information he and Lucinda talked about: the war. It was at the top of everyone's mind.

"Part of the Creeks joined up with the Confederacy, too," Postoak said, eyeing James. "Hope that means you'll forget about the others sidin' up with the Union. Not all of us is bad, ya know."

"I know. Y'all are the good ones here," James said. "My father went off to war some months ago to join up with the Confederacy as well. We haven't heard anything from him since, though."

"Don't you worry, Mr. Lacy. He'll be back before you know it."

"Oh, I know," James said with a cocky smile, looking down at the man from atop the riding seat. "But mother's worrying herself to death behind all this war."

"Smart woman, war is a business to worry about," Postoak said. "We got half the town missing. All the tribes nearby own Black slaves, and they all traveled here when they got forced away from their ancestral homes out east. 'Removed,' the United States officials say. Exiled, more like it. And just lettin' you know, Lacy, all us Indian nations are separate and sovereign from the U.S. So, we know Indian futures are heavily affected by whatever y'all's war ends on with slavery.

"Each tribe around here discussed slavery already and decided what to do about it. Those councils met frequently this past year to decide for or against. We got five tribes that make up the 'civilized' nations nearby, but they all split now over this issue, just like the white folk. Not too far from now, what is it, September? A few months shy of 1861 ending, the dumbest leader we got, Apothleyahole, decided he didn't like slavery. All that education and he still came up wrong. So, he's to blame for this rift in our people now. He's leadin' a bunch away to the damn Union of all things. That's four thousand men he took away from our lands and families here, movin' 'em north to Kansas." He laughed long and hard, and Lucinda nearby looked away.

"Didn't work out for him, neither, Mr. Lacy. You know what happened?"

"No, Postoak, just spit it out," James said, growing uncomfortable. William noticed the man was drunk again, heaving his sharp, alcoholic breath over the two of them.

"They got decimated is what happened. The southern Creeks, the real Creeks, led by Confederate General Douglass Cooper, attacked them all the way up. Slaughterin' the backstabbin' bastards," he dissolved into cruel laughter again. "Serves 'em right for choosin' the wrong side."

"Thanks for the news, Mr. Postoak. We'll be sure to let the family know," James said. He took the opportunity to flick the reins to get the wagon moving. "We'll be back in a few weeks with more supplies for Coweta. Until then."

Billy Postoak waved them off before turning to Lucinda. William could almost make out his gravelly tone while they rode off. "You about marryin' age now, 'Cinda. Don't let me catch you talkin' to no other slave boys like that one anymore. You're gonna fetch me more than a few dollars to your husband, and they don't like spoiled goods."

A shiver ran down William's spine. Behind them, Lucinda stalked away from her father while he stared after her with a dark, calculating expression. Soon, that same expression turned to William again. He kept eye contact before they disappeared around a bend.

CHAPTER 11

Whispers of Freedom

Fort Smith, Arkansas—Late 1862

The farm was a cold and lonely place once winter struck once more. The Lacy family dwindled as the year came to a close. Both John and James slipped off in the summer to join the Confederate war effort, leaving only twelve-year-old Theo in charge. Ms. Mary and the girls managed as best they could, relying more heavily on the enslaved community to keep the 60-acre farm running. Compared to Lacy Springs, the new homestead lacked the years of foundational work it took to make things comfortable. Insulated walls, well-tilled earth, and even comfortable walking paths were necessary comforts they had taken for granted. Now, with tools in hand, the slaves carved each from the earth or built them from the ground up.

Without the constant, suspicious eyes of Master Thomas or his sons hovering, William and his family could find moments of ease in their work. These moments flew quickly by as autumn's dry winds gave way to the first icy fingers of winter, clawing into their meager shacks. Even in the second year, there was no time to prepare their own quarters for winter, and this one would be more bitter than the first one there in Arkansas. Fewer people to help meant fewer chores done because of the endless amount demanded. Grain silos dwindled to keep everyone fed.

Theo Lacy, a year shy of William's age, was tasked with keeping food on the table for both his family and the slaves alike until his father returned from war. He resumed his father's meetings, guided gently by Ms. Mary at his side, with other slave owners who neighbored their farm in the Van Buren township. Safely protected from war with his age, it nonetheless proved difficult to maintain relations with the others, looking distrustfully at the boy and covetously at the farm—even his mother and sisters.

As careful as they were with their neighbors, also bearing the burden of winter in a war-torn nation, they had to be doubly cautious with the slaves. Since that afternoon, William and the others steered clear of the salon window. No repercussions fell upon them, but information dried up quicker than a creek in high summer. Theo barely passed on any more news from Lacy Springs, and if a meeting was held, it was short. He only delivered news of Confederate victories, assuring the war would end soon, but that tune had been sung for months. The speeches felt hollow to William, cheerless. Even though they should've been delivered happily by the child master, it came with a cruel sneer. Theo made it clear: the slaves were to mind every move and word while the war raged on. The country's slavery issue would be resolved once and for all, and from Theo's words, it would be nigh impossible for William and his community to receive good news, no matter which side won. A man's property belonged to him, no matter what people said in Ohio or Massachusetts. William felt like Theo was preparing to "inherit" his family and himself.

In October, Henry and William arrived again at Fort Smith to gather what provisions they could find. Spirits dimmed by the constant bad news, Henry dragged the handcart from one store to another, receiving the same words from each: barely anything left after the shipments to soldiers. If anything was to be sold, it was sold at a premium.

Passing by the breezy alleyways, the two stumbled across a group of slaves huddled closely together. William shared a puzzled look with Henry, as it was uncommon to see so many slaves together in broad daylight. While not unheard of, word spreads quickly of slave gatherings, and then punishments by their masters swiftly follow that news. Their whispers carried to them, but not their meaning. Fearing repercussions, the two pretended they hadn't noticed the group and ambled over to the next store.

At the back, Henry knocked at the door. It was Johnson's General, one known for its high prices, but they at least kept stock somehow throughout the troubled times. The owner's face appeared in the window, arching an eyebrow until he recognized Henry as a Lacy slave. He waved him inside.

Stooping to drop the handcart, Henry climbed the steps and opened the back door. William grabbed a basket to help shoulder the burden. Henry could negotiate while he carried the provisions. More people angrily conversed in the shop's front area, and loud white patrons gathered in these stores.

"The Emancipation ain't gonna free no niggas here and nowhere else ever."

William suppressed a jump at the man's shout, but both he and Henry ignored the white patrons. A chorus of irritated agreement joined his proclamation. These sentiments steeped Forth Smith with a humming tension that made these trips nigh unbearable for William. He didn't know how Henry navigated the snide looks the storekeeper gave or the raised prices since James left. When the Lacy men came, the store owners dealt with them in the front, cheaper and all friendly. Now, Henry would get another lashing when they got back from Theo for getting a poor deal.

Still, the man accepted the supplies and thanked the store owner, handing over the money while William packed the goods tightly in his basket. The boy itched to be away from there and back in the relative safety of their farm. Henry seemed just as eager, so they secured the handcart and began their return trek.

Their path led again around the alleyway where the group had huddled together. Henry sped up to clear it without looking, but one man called out to them. "Did y'all hear? Lincoln's sayin' we free at the new year! Better get ready fo' it 'cause we already plannin' what we gon' do when the massas let us go."

Henry's fingers tightened on the handcart so hard his knuckles popped. "Y'all shut yo' damn mouths with that talk in the streets. You tryna get us beat?" He whipped his head around, and the men shied back.

"Now, brotha, don't be like that. We sharin' the good news. We gon' be free soon." Another man smiled at them, waving at William. "You and your boy can walk outta here free men."

William's heart lifted. He felt the joy whispered across the few feet between the group and their cart. He'd never seen so many people smiling that widely.

"Stop it! Don't bring him into this," Henry spat and started the cart again. "Y'all keep that talk to yourselves or at night. What's the matta with ya? Don't you know it's—?

"What y'all niggas doin' together?"

The voice from the store shouted from behind them. It came from the same white patron in Johnson's General, but now William could see it belonged to a tall, thickly built white man with a bushy mustache and a face almost purple with rage.

Scattering, the group in the alley took off in different directions as the white patrons came forward, abandoning William and his father, who took up the cart again, moving solidly toward Fort Smith's gates.

"Where do you think y'all goin'?" the man asked as the group surrounded William and Henry, now alone in the street. William looked at his father, who plastered a neutral expression on his face.

"We goin' back to the Lacy farm in Van Buren where our massa is," he said carefully. "Ain't nothin' to do with us. Jus' takin' these supplies back to our folks. No trouble here."

"See, that's the problem with you. Always lyin' to us when we catch you doin' shit ya ain't supposed to. These damn Union battles only makin' ya harder to remember your place." The group clustered closer, and William moved to stand by his father.

"We ain't do nothin' to y'all," the boy said. Henry put a hand over him and moved him back.

The white man with the mustache struck Henry across the face, knocking him to the side. "Smartin' off to your betters? We gonna teach you mouthy niggas a lesson."

Angry fists fell upon both Henry and William. The crowd knocked their cart aside, spilling the supplies into the muddy street. All William and Henry could do was crouch and wait until the rowdy crowd spent their rage on the two.

After a while, the patrons tired out, spitting on them as they walked away with their supplies. "That'll teach y'all a lesson. Don't be talkin' together and spreadin' no damn nonsense—or we won't leave you alive next time."

Bloodied, bruised, and robbed, the two picked themselves up and limped back home to Van Buren. William distantly wondered what Theo would say when they arrived empty-handed, their money and precious foodstuffs stolen.

The boy made it back to the farm with his father, who sent him home so he could deliver the news to the Lacys. William put the empty handcart back in the barn before dragging his sore feet and aching knee home. Eliza rushed over to him. "What happened? It took y'all so long to get back. We already had supper."

"Got beat in the streets for gatherin'," William said. "The white folk caught some slaves talkin' together in an alley when we passed by. They ran, but them white folk caught us and took what we bought." He delivered the news numbly. Eliza quickly grabbed a rag nearby and cleaned up his cuts. She shook her head and hummed a soothing tune.

"Things might be like this fo' a long while. Maybe betta' to take Ms. Mary or Theo with y'all when ya go into town," she whispered between hums. Another slave walked by outside, singing the same melody, low and steady:

> *"Follow the drinkin' gourd,*
> *Follow the drinkin' gourd,*
> *For the old man is comin', just to carry you to freedom,*
> *Follow the drinkin' gourd,*
> *When the sun comes back, and the first quail calls*

Follow the drinkin' gourd,
For the old man is waiting just to carry you to freedom
Follow the drinkin' gourd ... "

It sounded like Little Mary outside or one of her sisters. Eliza finished dressing the biggest cut on William's head before handing him a bowl of cold porridge. "Saved ya some," she said. "Got some cinnamon from Harriet over in the next farm. They's got more than good spices. We share word 'bout what Massa Theo don't be tellin' us, and it's a lot."

Eliza shared more about what Harriet talked about and information from all over the farms between Van Buren and Fort Smith. They'd just started church services for the farms nearby, and Eliza joined with a few others from their farm. The services kept Eliza involved, helping fortify her Christian principles while picking up new songs and signals that only a few could decode. She told William not to repeat any of the songs he heard around their shacks or the church near the big house.

Henry stalked in soon after he finished, watching the people outside warily before closing the door. "'Liza, ain't gon' ask you to stop again. Ain't ya tired of patchin' us up?"

"Henry, it's real this time. Now I hate it y'all got roughed up in town, but that ain't stoppin' the truth from gettin' out. Don't ya see? They madder 'n hornets all stirred up 'cause they know we 'bout to get set free. Ain't nothin' they can do 'bout it 'cept pile on the punishment. The Lord's settin' us free soon. I know it."

"How you know this?"

"Harriet said so, next farm over. The Emancipation document been set now. Us slaves all gon' be free in a few months."

Henry rubbed his forehead, a huge bruise spreading across his temple. "Heard the same thing in town, then got this to show for hearin' it." He pointed at William. "Same for our boy. We ain't gettin' freed, 'Liza. They jus' stirrin' everybody up. Now I know you excited, but we cain't do nothin' right now but work. Don't sing or go to that church for a while now, hear me? We gotta lay low."

Winter crept over the farm, and William did just as Henry warned. Eliza did as well but hated to miss church. They all kept low, only speaking to each other quietly when they passed during the day and sharing muted meals at night. Other folks in the community still carried on and sang the "Drinkin' Gourd" song. William didn't show it in front of Henry, but the song kept his spirits up with the same spark that lit in his chest at Fort Smith. Eliza muttered about making it to the end-of-the-year church service, where more news would filter through.

Trips to Fort Smith were accompanied, which meant they happened fewer times. William caught wind of the small number of free Black people in the town trying to start their own church. These religious meetings rang like a beacon to them all, carrying folks out of the cold into the warm and sharing good news. By the time December 31 hit, William was rushed along to church services with Eliza, like he was caught in a wave. So many members went that it filled up quicker than he'd ever seen it. People whispered about family members in other towns going to their own churches, and he imagined spots like this, filled with people who looked like him across the nation, waiting altogether for something that would change their lives. He wondered if places as far as Chicago, New York, Philadelphia, Boston, and all the other cities he had learned from war news would hold a special watch night service on the last day of 1862.

That Wednesday, his watch night service in the Black church held the community together.

"What do you think people are doin' up north?" he asked Eliza. She'd been talking eagerly to other women. One freed woman had come from Fort Smith, chattering excitedly.

"Oh, William, it's one big celebration up north. I just know it," she beamed. "We cain't be there in person, but we can be there in spirit. Our people all over are listening to spiritual sermons like us, but those states that seceded have all they slaves freed today. Our brothers and sisters up there are free! I bet they all laughin', singin', prayin', and huggin' right now. They like the Hebrews from the Bible, comin' out of bondage."

Around him, people's spirits were lifted by the good news. It seemed that, here, under the night and with everyone together, they could hope again.

"Amazing Grace ... how sweet the sound ... that saved the wretched like me. I once was lost, but now I'm found ... was blind, but now I see."

William stood in a circle with the other Lacy slaves, mixing and talking with slaves from different farms. People sang together before breaking off to talk about plans. No one came up with anything definite, but at least the expectations were tinged with positivity after nothing but bad news from the war. Maybe they'd also be free come morning.

Thursday morning, January 1, 1863, came, sure enough.

William woke to another routine day on the farm. While he still carried the hope from his community last night and the strength they shared during the service, he couldn't help but be a little disappointed that Theo hadn't called a meeting to free them. Henry was silent that morning, carrying over his sourness from the services he missed. That day ended, and another one started.

Then another.

Then another.

Weeks went by, and nothing. No news. Nothing changed in Van Buren for the boy. What happened with Lincoln's Emancipation Proclamation and all the celebrations? Eliza shared that nothing had changed at the other farms either. Other slave masters visited Master Theo and Ms. Mary, but their brief conversations weren't shared with William, and Rufus dared not eavesdrop again.

They must be discussing something about them because every time William passed the big house, the white family and their visitors would stop talking and watch him sullenly pass.

One slave master from the Frederick family Harriet belonged to arrived with a letter. The envelope carried a Confederate military stamp and was addressed to Ms. Mary. The neighboring farmer usually delivered mail on a set day each week, but this one must've been important because he came on a Sunday. William set his cleaning rag down while Ms. Mary opened the letter, tugging the paper from the envelope. Upon reading, she burst into tears, crying for Theo.

The young master ran over from the porch, past William, and supported his mother as she sank to the floor. Inconsolable, the woman keened, crying into the cold dirt. Theo passed the letter to the courier and asked him to read it.

"We regret to inform you that Thomas Lacy, a man of great character and esteem in the community, has been killed in combat, defending Cane Hill, Arkansas. Thomas was seen fighting bravely till his death."

Theo stared at the man dully. "My father's dead …?"

"Awful sorry to deliver this news, son, but yes, it seems that way."

"What would you do?" Theo asked him, placing a hand on his mother's shoulder.

"Well, from a legal standpoint, all his property will now be decided in probate court. That includes your slaves. I'd make whatever peace you can make with your family and prepare to look over some paperwork with a few trips to Fort Smith. We'll be by later with some pie. Least we can do as neighbors."

Later, Master Theo gathered the entire farm, including the slaves, to inform everyone of Master Thomas' passing. The Lacy children and the new widow shed tears over their late father while their slaves maintained a respectful, somber silence.

"Father was killed in war, so that means I'll be taking over the plantation. Nothing's going to change around this farm."

William remembered the times back at Lacy Springs when they wrestled in summer or played marbles in the barn. That boy was gone now, replaced by this harder white man. While still young, Master Theo was no longer a boy and no longer the person William stole treats with, running away from the kitchen together. They had worked together over the past year to keep everything running smoothly on the Van Buren farm and had achieved a tenuous, albeit cold, understanding that they would remain friends. Was that who he was now?

William was a fifteen-year-old slave, and Theo had just become his twelve-year-old slave owner.

Ms. Mary and the girls wouldn't inherit any property from Master Thomas because women weren't allowed to control property in Arkansas. With James and John still fighting, it would be up to Theo to steward the homestead until they returned. *If they come back*, William thought.

Walking back to their home, Henry shook his head slowly. "Ain't no sense cryin' over that man, but I'll cry over what we had. Before we made this journey, we had some type of peace. But now? All that's gone. No matter what he did, Master Thomas took care of us. He decided when to plant and when to harvest. He'd negotiate our supplies in Fort Smith. He built relationships with the neighorbin' farms. Theo—Massa Theo—ain't his daddy. Don't know what we gon' do now that he's dead.

"Without a grown white man in charge. Things gon' get even harder. They only held back at Fort Smith on account of the Lacy name and Master Thomas' friendliness. All gone now."

Figure 11 – 1: A newspaper clipping of Theo Lacy Sr. in the *Santa Ana Register*

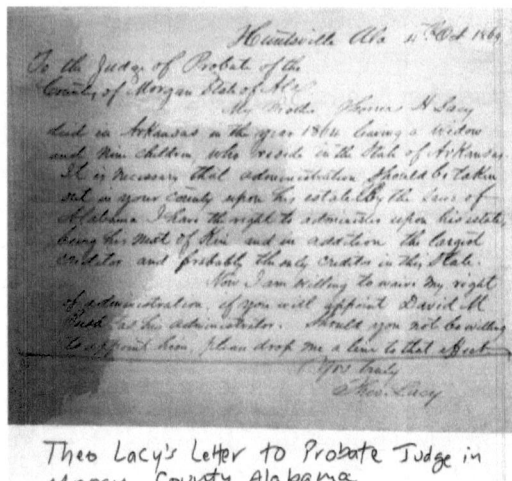

Figure 11 – 2: Great Uncle Theopolis Lacy's letter to a probate judge, asking for Thomas Lacy's will to be probated in Morgan County, Alabama

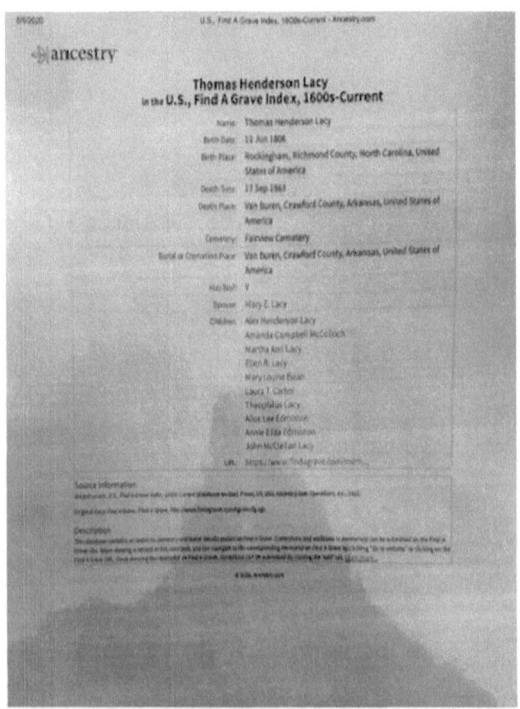

Figure 11 – 3: Thomas Lacy's census record

CHAPTER 12

A Promise Made

Van Buren, Arkansas—March 1863

Before long, the death of Thomas Lacy faded into the new rule of his boy, Theo. The young master worked the enslaved community much harder, running them ragged like in their first year there to keep them busy. However, the work before, while tiring, had meaning behind it, and this work rang false. Cruel. Even Ms. Mary intervened some days, asking the young master to give them a day of rest on the Sabbath.

"These niggas ain't in God's eyes," he responded. "But they can have one day. Can't have more dyin' before the harvest's finished."

The emancipation that the slaves hoped for so deeply died along with half of the population. Only Henry, William, and Joe lingered on. Rufus didn't make it to the following spring. They found him dead in the cold, frozen from hunger, on a secret walk back from Harriet's place. Now mostly alone, the family stuck together, William keeping an eye on Joe, who had a wild look after the news of his brother.

They continued trading at Fort Smith and into Indian Territory despite the level of interest and supplies drying up. Trips to Johnson's General in Fort Smith took on a different tone when folks saw Master Theo walking ahead of the handcart. The store patrons whispered when Theo went to talk with the store owner, ignoring William, who waited nearby to carry the provisions back. Even with a good year behind him, Theo Lacy wasn't his father, and the resources his farm created were a far cry from the shrewd harvests Thomas wrought.

Everywhere he looked, his own weathered, hungry face stared back at him from other people. Both Black and white folk, Indians, and everyone felt the bitter struggle of wartime. A full stomach and a happy smile were rare sights.

Winter of 1863 crawled by, and William kept up Eliza's news sources within the church meetings, keeping up the grapevine where he could. From hearing the news, cities all across the South struggled with food supplies, like Fort Smith. The Confederate army was large and consumed all the farming resources to maintain its fighting strength throughout the states. The opposing forces, both Union and Confederacy, snatched up all livestock, grain, and even winter preserves when they passed through Fort Smith. The military sometimes purchased the supplies, but sometimes, they just left without paying, remarking that they were fortunate to supply the war effort.

In some places, William heard the army even torched entire farms solely to keep the leftover food from being stolen by Union forces. This sent shockwaves through the Southerners, worsening the already terrible food shortage they suffered. They couldn't last much longer, and with the war that should've only taken a summer moving into its third year, William knew something had to give.

The men in Fort Smith echoed these thoughts, in varying degrees, across the town. From general stores to plazas to alleyways, the shared sentiments were of how the war had no end in sight.

Many tools from the Van Buren homestead were breaking, and Henry, with all his craftsmanship, could only stretch them so far with repairs. Can't repair without resources. Wagon wheels and tills needed iron, which was snatched up as fast as food for the soldiers. Iron grew so scarce that even their horses had to go without shoes, and not just horses went without. Ms. Mary and her children had difficulty securing shoes since the cobblers were off to war.

Seamstresses sewed military uniforms, hoping to be paid for their efforts. Hatmakers, ironworkers, carpenters, and anyone with a skill or medical talents were forced to work for the Confederate soldiers. The general message was that it took priority over any civilian affairs.

Even schools shut down with nobody to teach. The Lacy children quit their lessons when their teacher was impressed into service as a nurse at the nearby Confederate hospital.

Now, around the house more, the girls and Ms. Mary planted a garden to grow food for their family. William and Henry went fishing to help supply food to their own community. What the Lacys didn't eat first left very little for them to survive on. In secret, they carried the fish back after dark to roast them over a fire, handing out pieces to neighbors who came hungry. The entire farm was backed into a corner without money, grain, seed, or tools.

Theo sent Henry and William out again into Indian Territory, assigning them a mission to find a place with food. They didn't have much to trade, but with the good faith Thomas put in places like Coweta, maybe they'd help them through this rough period. A few industrial tools existed on the farm, but they wouldn't do anyone good if they all died of hunger.

William inspected the worn and partially working ones before placing them in the wagon. Henry added a fishing pole to gather more food on the trip. The almost empty wagon was a sore sight compared to what they used to bring to Coweta. William hoped Postoak would understand that no rum was to be found anywhere near Fort Smith.

Giving the fort a wide berth, the two nevertheless had to pull the wagon aside on the road when a rumbling shook the dirt. They hid in a copse of trees nearby as columns of uniformed officers marched through: the Confederates, all dressed in gray now. The Arkansas Confederate cavalry returned from battle. There were so many that it took about an hour for them to pass by. Unnoticed, the two waited till they completely disappeared, and the last soldiers entered the fort before hurrying along their way again.

When they arrived in the tiny Creek village, its quiet, empty houses surprised William. It hadn't been long since his last visit, but the place looked dead. They stopped at Billy Postoak's house first but found no one inside. Abandoned, covered in dust, it looked like the occupants had cleared out quite some time ago. Panicked, William broke from his father and ran to the next house. "Lucinda?" he called out. "Lucinda!"

A deep pit opened in his chest, deeper than he'd ever felt before. *Lucinda's gotta be okay. If she's gone ... I ... Who am I without these trips to see her?*

Henry called after him, but lingered near the wagon with their precious few supplies for trade. William's mind was far away from the trade now. He no longer cared about the items, the wagon, or what Master Theo would do back in Van Buren if he lost them. Without Lucinda, those long, empty months between seeing her would become unbearable.

Henry moved the wagon to the next house while he ran, calling for the Creek girl and the Postoaks. No animals, not even dogs, lazily grazed outside the houses anymore. Just like their owners, the livestock disappeared. Henry stopped to talk with two boys, younger than William by four or five years, who were alone in a house. There were no adults nearby.

One house sat at the end of the street, the chief's old house. Its gardens were moved back, clustered around the house, and everything outside used for decoration was torn down. It also looked abandoned, but William saw clothes drying outside on a line. Maybe they knew where the Postoaks had gone.

William approached the house, quiet now. If he ran over yelling, it might spook whoever stayed inside. Whatever happened to his village, the last remnants wouldn't take kindly to a stranger shouting.

From the log cabin door, Billy Postoak emerged, followed by Luvinia and Lucinda, staying farther behind him in the shadows.

"Weeeeell, if it ain't the Lacys," he said with a snide glance at the cart. "Comin' by here again to trade, but I don't see nothin' back there we'd want. No gift either to apologize for comin' last time mostly empty-handed either." He stared around. "Where's Thomas? That fool barks like a dog, but at least he brings the best rum to be had 'round here."

"Dead," Henry said. The word dropped like a stone between them.

"Ah, my ... condolences," Postoak muttered, off-balance now with the news.

"Lucinda," William said and moved onto the Postoak's yard. He ignored Billy as he walked forward, trying to see the girl better. She retreated farther into the shadows. "I thought y'all had left, and I'd never see you again."

Before he could climb the steps on the porch, Billy Postoak had his rifle up and aimed at William's forehead. "Stop right there. What d'you think you're doin' comin' up on a man's property without anythin'? No gifts? Nothin' to trade?"

"Now, hold on there, Postoak," Henry said and moved forward to stand next to William. He put his hands up. "We don't mean no harm. The boy's jus' excited is all. They friends ever since we started tradin' up here a few years ago, see?"

"Oh, I saw," Billy lowered the gun and spat. "You keep your distance from my property, nigga. People already came up here and took everything from us. Now I ain't lettin' nothin' else go. Confederate soldiers popped up here not three months ago raidin' and took all the squash from my garden. Took our horses. Our pigs. 'Bout took my wife and daughter if I hadn't come out with this rifle." The man shook the firearm at Henry. "They made off with half the village and what was left. Took what they could and ran. I stayed here. This is our land, and I ain't runnin'. Also ain't lettin' anyone take anymore from me neither. Everything here is mine."

Billy Postoak had the same wild look in his eyes that Rufus did. He saw some things, and those things broke him.

"Honey, they ain't here to do nothin' but share drink and trade. Just like the good ol' days," Luvinia said and stepped onto the porch. William about gasped. The beautiful woman was covered in bruises. Her arm was snapped, and she cradled it against her chest. She tried to place a hand on Postoak's arm, but the man jerked back. She winced.

"We did come here to trade. And I saved one last thing for you, Postoak," Henry said. Returning to the wagon, he opened a small drawer, revealing a half-empty bottle of rum. Postoak's face lit up like a firefly.

"Well, Henry, I always liked you best. You know that? How about we talk about these trades?" He shouldered the rifle and walked over to him, all smiles and friendliness. William stood on the porch as he walked past, staring at Luvinia.

"Ma'am ... you look like you need some bandages ..."

"Oh, I'm fine. These things is jus' takin' a while to heal," she smiled at him cheerily. "You go on now. I know Lucinda been wantin' to talk to you since you visited last."

With that, Luvinia ambled off, and he turned to Lucinda's silhouette in the doorway.

"Lucinda?" he asked. "I ... I thought I'd never see you again, back when I first got here."

Sunlight glinted sharply off the metal. The girl moved forward, equally covered in bruises, but not as bad as her mama's. She held a knife close behind her. "Jus' William, huh?" She stared after her dad, who was now bantering cheerfully with Henry after a long swig from the rum bottle.

"What did y'all bring this time? Cain't be much considerin' the state of everything."

"Let's go to the oak tree," William said. "We'll let Henry and Billy deal with that."

They walked quietly under the shady tree where they had made so many good memories. Memories of happier times. Lucinda was just as lovely, and William's heart about burst seeing her look so sad.

"William, I cain't stay here anymore," she said. Taking a deep breath, the girl turned, looking him dead in the eye. "Last time we talked, I said I'd be free, and I meant it. You're the only person I can trust in this whole wide world. So I'm tellin' you this so you'll know I ain't dead. I'm gonna be free. Soon.

"I'm tired of watchin' my daddy take his anger out on Mama. Tired of watchin' her die every day. I know she doin' it for me. So he won't hit me when he's mad. When the Confederates came and stole everythin', they ... they hurt Mama. Tried to hurt me but Daddy stopped 'em before takin' us inside." Hot tears streamed down her face while she spoke, the words all tumbling out like the damn broke.

William pulled her to his shoulder and squeezed her as tight as he could, trying to hold together whatever was broken in her. Like a storm, the girl gritted her teeth, only letting out the occasional sob so nobody could overhear. Even desperate, defeated, and on the brink of hopelessness, the Creek girl carried a strength, a defiance against the world that tore at her. In that moment, love took root in William's chest, a love that grew so deep and strong in his heart that its strength would break rocks.

He would do anything for Lucinda Postoak.

After her tears dried, he brushed a hair behind her ear. "I wanna be free, too. Things is just as bad back in Van Buren. It's why we only got tools to trade here. Master Thomas died in the war, and his sons is gone, too. It's just Theo now as massa, and he ain't keepin' things up. They ain't no food back home. Black, white, Creek—don't matter. Everybody's hurtin' everywhere."

Now that she'd gathered herself more, Lucinda absorbed the information, tapping her chin while she thought.

"Where would you go? How you gonna get free?"

"To Kansas, where the rest of my people went."

"What if you get caught?"

"What if … we don't?"

She looked around before looping her little finger around his. "Jus' gotta promise me you'll watch my back."

"You mean … me goin' with you? You don't even have to ask. I promise to watch your back, always," he whispered, heart pounding.

"Good, but we gotta run …" She met his eyes fiercely.

"Tonight."

CHAPTER 13

A Midnight Flight

Indian Territory—April 1863

The moon rose high, lighting up the night-drenched countryside. William lay awake near the cart, staring up at it. Not a cloud in the sky and the spring weather brought a gentle warmth. *Lucinda couldn't've picked a better night*, William thought.

As the hours dragged by, his anxiety warred within him. While he would stick by his promise, the repercussions roiled in his gut. Deep down, he knew he couldn't return to the Van Buren farm. Barely anything waited for him there besides pain and his remaining family.

Henry had stumbled back to the cart to sleep hours earlier, finding William already tucked in. He roused the boy, letting him know the trade wasn't successful. Postoak had nothing left to give, so they'd have to make the long, bitter trek back to Van Buren in the morning. William said nothing, merely nodding and turning over in his blanket. Wearily, his father made a sleeping pallet on the other wagon's other side, taking advantage of the pleasant night.

The empty Creek village grew quieter at night, and William could believe it was totally abandoned. Postoak didn't keep a cookfire going, he guessed, to deter any more looters from discovering their home. He closed his eyes but knew sleep wouldn't come. It was too late now to catch any. Instead, he prayed.

God, if you listenin', I know I ain't the best, and this is the first time I'm comin' to you for favors, but I ain't askin' anythin' for me tonight. Please watch over Lucinda. Give her the freedom she so deserves, and give me the strength to help her find it.

His lips moved as he prayed with no sound. A subtle creak sounded from the Postoak's house, and William almost missed it if his ears weren't extra sensitive to the sound. Silent, he rolled out of his blanket, rolling it up behind him as he caught sight of Lucinda's form slinking away from the old chief's house. She seemed unprepared. Now puzzled, William lost focus and snapped a twig as he walked to meet her. Cursing in his mind, he darted a glance back to check, but Henry stayed asleep, his chest rising and falling under his blanket.

Lucinda stood near their shady oak, and he arrived shortly after. Together, they walked around it between the deep roots, then out into the field. During all their talks, they never wandered too far, and a thrill took William as their feet hit unfamiliar ground. Mushy footprints sounded in the air, but he was less worried now that they were farther away from Coweta.

Stooping down, the two kept as low as possible in the wide-open field. They soon broke through a tree and brush line, passed an empty log cabin, and wove in and out of game trails. They'd only been traveling for about twenty minutes, but the giddiness overcame William, and he took her hand, pulling her gently into a run. Laughing now, the couple raced forward under the moonlight, sprinting toward a stream.

Still giggling, Lucinda pulled him to a stop before they hit the water. "Hold on a minute. I gotta get somethin'." Turning, the girl moved to a large tree near the water's edge. William followed, watching her curiously. Lucinda moved a large branch, grunting as she heaved it aside, revealing a basket filled with hard-tack bread and several jars of jam.

"You prepared a stash?"

"I knew this was comin' weeks ago," she said, smiling at William. "Stroke of fine luck you came when ya did. I would've been gone tonight. For good."

"You two up to no good tonight?" Henry's voice came from behind them. William whipped around, fear tingeing their good night. Lucinda went still behind him.

"Pa, we headin' for Kansas," William said, choosing his words carefully. "I know it ain't right, runnin' off in the night like this, but what else do we have? Massa Theo gonna tear into us when we get back. Way I see it, one less mouth means one less thing to worry about."

"Please," Lucinda added. "Please don't tell Billy. I cain't live here no more. That man's gonna kill me and my mama both."

Henry studied the two of them and sighed. "I know, girl. I ain't stupid. Jus' pain and sufferin' is all that's between Coweta and Van Buren. But Kansas? What's in Kansas?"

"More Creeks," Lucinda said.

"You got supplies? Awful long way to Kansas," Henry said, and William started forward.

"You ain't bringin' us back?" *We gotta s'vive best we can.* The words echoed in William's mind. With Henry there, he thought their escape was short-lived.

"No, they ain't no s'vivin' here. Not anymore. Best chance you kids got to live a life is somewhere far away from here." He reached toward his belt and pulled out his good fishing line. "Here, take this with you."

"What're you gonna use to fish?"

"I got more line, boy. Don't worry 'bout me."

William joined his father above the creek and accepted the line. Attached was a fine iron hook, and he slipped a pouch filled with cheese and dried fruit he must've got as a trading gift from Postoak. Henry pulled his son into a fierce hug. "You get outta here and live the life we never could. You hear me, boy?" He kissed his temple, making a sharp, quick move before pushing him toward Lucinda. "You get outta here, and y'all make it to Kansas."

William nodded and joined Lucinda, barely catching a whispered "thank you" before she took his hand. They ran off into the night. William didn't know tears could come when you were happy.

North. Ever north.

The two ran through the night, North and east of Coweta, up toward the Arkansas River, and straight through Indian Territory. Lucinda pointed out where to wade across the Arkansas River, which was now drier before the rainy season fully hit. To be free, even in Kansas, the girl explained they'd need to pass through the Creek Nation and into Cherokee.

William knew a few rumors about an "Underground Railroad." He prayed fervently that they weren't all just hearsay because their lives would depend on at least one being right. As they caught their breaths, Lucinda confirmed that at least one thing was true that William overheard from Harriet's farm: a Cherokee school nearby would harbor them. The tiny schoolhouse served as a mission alongside a lake. From there, they would get their start, grabbing information that would lead to the next safe spot. This reminded William of the Hebrew slaves being led out of bondage to freedom by Moses. He could remember sitting around the fire back at Lacy Springs while he recounted the ancient story—only when the Lacys were far away in the big house.

He and Lucinda wouldn't come across a red sea, but he hoped any obstacle would part for them.

Two days of hard running along Texas Road at night and following water during the day finally led them to the lake and the Cherokee mission. Hiding in the trees to watch, the two studied the place to make sure it matched the description they had both heard from people. The tiny schoolhouse did look similar to the details: a log cabin built in the same style as those in Coweta. Lucinda monitored the door, waiting for something. They needed to see who lived at the mission to ensure it was the right one.

She whispered to William, "Stay behind this tree until we see the priest. Then we'll know it's the right place."

William nodded. He knew they couldn't afford to make even one tiny mistake on this journey. It would mean being turned in to the authorities and returned to their previous masters—or worse.

Finally, as the sun set, a man walked from the nearby trail back to the building. He was dressed in long robes, covering his Cherokee frame. Lucinda sighed in relief and walked with William a few paces behind, all along the treeline to the mission. Catching the priest's attention from the bushes, the girl called out, "We're a friend with friends."

The priest stopped carving wood and peered around, finding the two in the bushes nearby.

"Friend with friends," she hissed again. *Was it right?* William thought. *Did Harriet give us the correct phrase?*

"Follow the drinkin' gourd?" the man's shaky voice replied.

With the response, Lucinda motioned to William, and the two emerged from the trees and hurried to the mission. The priest watched back toward a road nearby, waving them quickly to the doors.

"Wait, I know you," he said to them when they were safely inside. "You're Postoak's girl from Coweta over yonder. Haven't talked to your family since we delivered goods and baptisms this past summer. Is all well with your father and mother? Will they be joining you?"

Lucinda shook her head. The priest seemed to understand without her saying anything. He opened his mouth to speak, but she cut in and said, "You told me if I ever wanted to follow my people to Kansas, I should come here first. Make sure no one followed me, and you'd help. Well, here I am."

"Here you are," he replied, nodding before turning to William. "Looks like you were followed, though, but I bet this young man is someone you trust?"

"With my life."

"What is your name, son?" the priest said amicably before catching himself. He let out a soft sigh. "On second thought, don't tell me. This isn't a friendly visit from my Coweta friends. You two are running for your lives. The less anyone knows, the better, and this is a lesson you both should take to every stop along the way. Remember: talk little, always listen."

William repeated the words, which made the priest happy. "Good, now come. Let me show you the hiding place. You'll need to get there quickly if I give a warning shout."

The two followed him as he moved to the western corner. There were only so many places to hide in the tiny cabin, so William wondered how they'd find anywhere a cursory look wouldn't reveal them. The priest shoved a table over, which creaked with age, before kicking over a thick, dusty rug. Underneath, a single hole in the wooden floor stared up at them. He placed his finger in the floor and pulled.

Hinges swung open, quieter than the creaky table, revealing stairs that flowed downward into the hiding hole. Lucinda and William explored the place to make sure they knew where to crouch should they have to do so quickly. Above them, the Cherokee priest passed them food and then arranged comfy floor mats for them to rest.

In the still night, they heard the priest gently snoring in his cot near the fireplace. William felt a hand on his back, and he flipped over to see Lucinda awake.

"You think Henry said anythin' when he got back?"

"I dunno, probably not. He ain't a man to go back on his word. I'd guess he left back to Van Buren just as fast not to be awake when Postoak—your father—woke up. He'd be hoppin' mad."

Lucinda curled in on herself, looking like a lost little girl instead of the young woman she was blossoming into. "You think my mama's alright?"

"I hope so, 'Cin, but you cain't be worryin' too much. What's done is done. You know she'd want the best for you."

Lucinda sniffled but nodded. "You worryin' at all? Seems like I'm the one all caught up in this."

"Yeah," he whispered. "Honestly, been so worried 'bout us makin' it, didn't have time to think of my folks at home." Thinking about Rufus hurt. Without his stepbrother and now him, Henry lost another person, but he couldn't let that distract him.

"We got time to worry when we safe in Kansas," he said. "For now, we gotta focus on that. One step at a time."

He reassured her, stroking her forehead until she fell asleep. However, regardless of what he said, his thoughts turned to what Theo Lacy and the others would do without him. One less mouth to feed for sure, but also one less pair of hands to work the fields and care for horses.

Watching Lucinda sleep calmed all his worries. He was exactly where he was meant to be.

The priest was so concerned about being overheard that he only whispered instructions for the next stop in their hiding hole, in Cherokee, and only to Lucinda. William waited next to them while the priest did so, counting their trail rations.

Later, on the road again, Lucinda shared that the next place would be an Ottawa Nation school. The headmaster there was someone trustworthy who understood why people used the railroad to get to Kansas. He would help them one step further. They needed to repeat the priest's name, which Lucinda swore not to reveal even to William, and only tell it to the headmaster once they arrived.

Another day of walking at night and resting during the day brought them to another wooden building, and this one differed from the Cherokee mission they'd left. Further, in Indian Territory, the Ottawa school was built with logs that ran vertically instead of across, similar but different in style from the schools the Creeks and Cherokees built. Puffs of thin smoke rose from the chimney, promising a way to keep the night chilliness at bay.

A little braver now, the two crept toward the Ottawa school, hitting the location in the early evening. With no one in sight, no carriages or animals, the light approach seemed like the practical thing to do. William went up the steps to knock, telling Lucinda to wait and run if he gave the signal. Everything seemed to be the way the priest described to her. Once he knocked, they both turned and ran to hide behind a tree outside, waiting to see if the person who answered also matched the priest's words.

No one came out.

The two waited until the sound of horse hooves clopping on the road reached them. From the opposite side, a man halted his horse near the entrance and dismounted. While shorter than the Cherokee priest, the man fit the headmaster's description as a broad-faced Ottawan man, missing an ear. The two made sure he was alone, waiting while he put up his horse before they approached.

"Friend with friends," she said.

To that, the headmaster narrowed his eyes and looked past them where they sprang up, possibly noting the direction they came from. Lucinda stepped forward further and said, "Degataga."

The man's eyes widened. "You're from the Cherokee mission? That old man's still findin' people to send? Come in, come in, make haste now."

Finding a similar situation waiting for them, the two gratefully accepted food and a place to rest for the night. A similar hiding place was revealed to them should something happen: a secret handle hidden in a log bed's frame. Once opened, the bottom log slid forward, allowing the runaways a place to hide. The schoolhouse boasted a much larger room, with attached bedrooms and beds built with logs. The headmaster offered them rooms to sleep in. William couldn't believe it. An actual bed to sleep in? He thanked the headmaster for his kindness.

Before they could fully bed down for the night, a knock tapped at the front door—all three fell silent. Lucinda took all of one second to rush to the secret hiding hole, waving William to move inside. The two crouched under it while the headmaster slid it back into place. "I'll see who it is and tell them to come back in the morning." He said in a low voice to them. "Hello?" he called out louder toward the front. "Who's there in the middle of the night?"

His footsteps receded while the two huddled close together.

"Think it's my papa?" Lucinda asked. Her voice was even, but that close, William could feel her body shiver.

"We ain't goin' back. Even if we have to fight for it," he replied.

Agonizing minutes ticked by before the log bed rolled back, showing the headmaster's relieved face. "All is well. You can come out now." He set the rifle he carried down by their beds. "Was just a student's father. In all the commotion, I forgot he came to drop off some firewood for the children before heading out of town. I let him know to leave it outside so he can be on his way."

William and Lucinda let out the breath they were both holding. "Thank God it was just that man. We'd be dragged back if my daddy caught up with us," Lucinda said. "We'd have to go back to our old lives."

"I'm relieved as well," the headmaster said. "No old life for me to return to. If any of us are caught helping slaves escape to Kansas, it's a severe punishment. The usual is six months to a year in jail and expensive penalties. I'd lose this schoolhouse, and the children wouldn't have any place to learn. With no resources or reputation, I'd lose my standing as a teacher, never finding work again.

"It's worth it, though," the man caught himself rambling at their scared faces. "Each life saved is worth the risk, no matter who comes to my door. Seeing two lovely young people, barely out of school yourselves, I couldn't live with myself knowing you'd be out there with no advice or people to guide you. Kansas will be much different, trust me. The Creeks left Indian Territory, where you might've grown up, to escape the war, but they'll welcome you in as free people."

The man left them to bed down, promising to give them more instructions in the morning before they left.

CHAPTER 14

The State of Freedom

Indian Territory—April 1863

Explaining the next step of the journey, the headmaster doled out their breakfast: fresh eggs and onions fried up in butter. William savored the rich breakfast slowly. After a diet of dry bread or barely anything for weeks, the first bites sent his stomach roiling. He swallowed some water and paced himself.

Thanking the headmaster for his kindness and sharing knowledge about the next safe place and such generous food, William and Lucinda struck out north once more. Determined, the unexpected support from these complete strangers brought color back into the world. Living under Theo's rule, with the ever-sinking numbers in his community, William adapted to a deep sadness. Now, though, in stark contrast, these strangers breathed new shades of relief within him, slowly, like a paintbrush dripping watercolors on a page. Hope returned.

Lucinda led him through Miami, Peoria, and Quapaw Nations, passing by Indian schools and missions, much the same as the first two. These strangers provided cover, protection, and supplies. Some gave careful instructions to uncover hidden canoes near the lakes and rivers, which were usually impassable. But under the cover of night, the two would push the canoe into the water, sending silent ripples across the surface, and travel through the water. The other side meant one more obstacle between them and anyone who might've given chase.

However, as weeks passed, both William and Lucinda relaxed more. Instead of constantly looking back in fear, they turned their faces north toward a new future.

Finally, they reached a location that marked a milestone. Another tiny mission, the Quapaw Nation, was their last stop in Indian Territory. A young woman, bright and friendly, carried a water bucket on each shoulder. By now, the duo traded off the first contact duty, ensuring the information given was correct. The young Quapaw woman twirled around, looking for the source of the "friend with friends," said gently from the tree line.

Beckoning them closer, the woman knelt to place the buckets down. They conversed briefly, Lucinda first in the Indian tongue before William joined. When they headed toward the mission, William carried the buckets back himself.

In another log cabin, called a longhouse, as William found out, the Quapaw woman set down three bowls filled with steaming porridge. While he wistfully thought back to the eggs earlier, the young man dug in gratefully. The woman told them how close they were to making it out, delivering instructions while Lucinda helped her tidy up. William went outside to chop wood. The two picked up general chores to reciprocate the generosity of these brave people on the railroad, simple gestures though they were.

Before they left, the woman handed William a tiny cross. "To remember that God watches over you."

Lucinda rolled her eyes whenever the woman went back to the longhouse. "These missionaries be helpin', so I s'pose I better be grateful, but that white god they keep ain't brought nothin' but broken treaties and sickness to my people. The Breath Maker gave us our ways long before we were forced to abandon our lands. You keep whatever you need, William. I won't never trust these churches. They divided my people so many times, ain't about nothin' left of us. My grandmother's grandmother's stories of our ancient ceremonies and rituals are all I took with me."

William thought back to his own violent baptism. Since then, he'd seen a fervent community built on churches, and Lucinda was right; the strangers that guided them all came wrapped in the light of Jesus. He pocketed the small cross. "I'll keep it safe here. Better take all the help we can."

He thought about mentioning their first meeting again, but a noise startled them from the road. Talking masked the hoofbeats of riders approaching the mission.

They had only seconds to dash to the treeline, throwing themselves under the bushes before the three riders dismounted at the mission. So close. William clutched the cross in his pocket while the lead rider kicked in the door, entering the longhouse with the other two. They were unarmed, except for the knife Lucinda kept strapped to her leg under the medicine bag.

"Where are the runaway slaves?" the man shouted. Dressed in old military uniforms, now blackened with age and dirt, the law officer pushed the Quapaw woman out of her house. She fell into the dirt. Behind them, the other two ransacked the mission, dumping over tables. Beside him, Lucinda had the knife out. He took her wrist gently and whispered, "Ain't nothin' we can do."

"She's gonna sell us out," Lucinda said. "We gotta run now."

"We cain't. They might see us. We betta wait a moment."

The Quapaw woman looked over to where they were hiding. "Ain't no slaves here," she said. "'He has sent me to proclaim liberty to the captives'—so says the Lord in Luke 4:18. I minister to all souls in need, as Christ commanded. But if you're asking whether I hold any man in bondage, well, I serve a higher Law."

Another officer appeared from the house, holding the bowls. "Sir, there's three bowls inside, still wet from being cleaned. Ain't nobody else here except her."

Savagely, the lead man kicked the Quapaw woman before removing a rope from his saddle. "Tie her lyin' ass up. We know you helpin' slaves across the border here, and you just got caught. 'Servants, obey your earthly masters with fear and trembling,' as Paul writes in Ephesians 6:5. The law of this land is clear, and so is God's order. Romans 13:1 commands submission to governing authorities. You're not preaching Christ, ma'am. You stirrin' rebellion, and we ain't lettin' you keep at it anymore."

Screaming, the officers tied her up and threw her over the side of one horse before riding off. Her panicked prayers faded into the distance. Once everything fell silent again, Lucinda stood up, sliding the knife back into its sheath. "Maybe her god'll protect her. Maybe not. I sho hope she'll make it out alright."

William removed his hand from his pocket. He'd been squeezing the pocket cross so tight it cut into his palm, a bloody cross now embedded in his hand.

After another half-moon of travel along roads at night, hiding at any sound of hoofbeats, the two passed into the high prairie grass of southeast Kansas. The star Lucinda pointed out led them true—into the newly born state.

Created in 1854 by the Kansas-Nebraska Act of Congress, the Kansas Territory was fought over by pro-slavers folks from Missouri and free-state folks back east. Both flooded into the state, hoping to muscle their way onto the folks in the area.

Congress decided to allow the people of the state to determine whether it would be a free or slave state. With their muskets in hand, Missourians established towns along the border in places like Fort Leavenworth, while free-staters established smaller cities such as Lawrence and Topeka. These direct challenges to the people of the Kansas territory made Kansas bleed daily over the issue of slavery. In the end, the free-staters won out. It made more sense for the young duo to flee in that direction.

Road-weary and weather-beaten, the couple started a new string of stops. No longer relying on Indian missions and schools, the Kansas leg of their journey changed to depending on white abolitionists. These white preachers supported their journey to a place called Mound City. The sleepy town grew into a legend for escaped slaves and a thorn in the sides of slave catchers. Figures like John Brown and James Montgomery fortified its reputation.

William repeated these names, learning them by heart in case he ran into them.

Amid the complicated instructions, the preacher told them more about John Brown. The man was an abolitionist preacher who reviled slavery. He used his spiritual teachings across Kansas to rail against its evils. Using his movement, he attacked bushwhackers from Missouri and slave owners to free slaves nearby. Shepherding these slaves to Mound City, he found new places for them in Lawrence and then on to Nebraska to be free.

William and Lucinda listened quietly to the tales, filling in blank spots from rumors that dripped into Coweta and Van Buren. Now, they had the complete picture.

In 1858, not but a handful of years earlier, John Brown launched an attack on a military arsenal in Harper's Ferry in Virginia. He intended to ignite a race war there between the enslaved and their masters—attempting to start the war much earlier. Eventually, as William heard in the song, he was captured and hanged. Thankfully, some of his followers fled, even though most were killed in that battle. The preacher shared the name Augustus Waddles as a comrade they could speak with in Mound City. John Brown had used his house to help his cause, stacking as many as one hundred former slaves there until he could get them to a safe location.

As for James Montgomery, he led the Second South Carolina Colored Troops, being named Colonel. Due to tuberculosis, the man was relieved of his command and sent back to Mound City.

Such towering men and their efforts reassured them that walking freely in Mound City would be safe. The preacher corroborated their last instructions received from the Quapaw woman: keep off any road leading to Fort Scott. Soldiers used it often, and so would slave catchers, bandits, and any other ne'er-do-well in the area. Money was scarce now, and travelers were easy prey.

Heeding the cautionary advice, William and Lucinda waited by a thin trickle called Little Sugar Creek. So close, the stakes rose considerably for the abolitionists. Slave catchers patrolled the areas, lurking to catch people when they made their last desperate run. So, the railroad stops here had to coordinate more carefully. They set up a system to alert the next stop with descriptions of the people to be ferried. The last preacher delivered this news to the next, saying he'd whistle when ready.

So, the two waited for the signal in the night.

Just as a cloud passed over the new moon, a sharp whistle sounded from across the creek. With Lucinda close behind him, William crept out, and the two scurried toward the birdcall. A white man sat in the bushes. He brushed his beard and pointed northwest, saying, "Go up the river a ways and into a cave. Move through it till it ends. Then you'll be in Mound City."

Thanking him, the two rushed off, carried through by a surge of optimism.

They reached the cave, and its mouth yawned open. Nothing but darkness showed beyond where the moonlight stopped. William halted Lucinda before she went in.

"We shoulda brought a light. What if there's a bear in there?"

"I'll take a bear over a slavecatcher any day," Lucinda said. "C'mon, we almost there."

Holding hands, the two entered the cave, and the darkness swallowed them. William latched onto Lucinda's sleeve tightly as water came up over their knees. The creek ran through the cave, but it got deeper the farther they went in. The water grew icy, sapping strength from their already exhausted bodies.

In the pitch black, the cave's walls drew in tight around them, so tight in places that they had to crawl and squeeze to move through, holding their breath underwater. Shivering now, the two stopped frequently, trying to warm up, the cold chewing them faster than anything before.

"Why didn't that man say we should bring a fire?" William said through chattering teeth. "It's like winter in Van Buren again but wet."

"We couldn't keep a fire anyway," Lucinda replied. "Too wet, like ya said. We jus' gotta keep goin'. We almost there, Will."

Staggering now, the couple sloshed through more water. Hours passed before they stopped to check a cave wall. Were they walking in circles? Lost? William almost sobbed in panic. All this time on the road, only to die shivering in a cave right before the end.

"Was this all a hoax? That man coulda lied to us, sendin' us in here to our deaths," Lucinda said, her worries echoing softly off the cave walls.

"We could turn 'round," William said but knew it was an empty thought. They had already doubled back. If they tried to retrace their steps, it would make them even more hopelessly lost.

Lucinda hugged him tightly and whispered a prayer to the Breath Maker. William's fingers found the cross scar in his palm.

After taking a few deep breaths, the two worked out a plan. They'd follow the cave wall, stretching their arms to feel the texture and call out any variance as they went. It took another hour, but William finally caught another hole they'd missed earlier. "Here!" he called out. "Oh, thank the Lord, we found it."

Lucinda followed his hand to the opening and slipped through, with William close behind. A warm breeze stirred in the new cave passage, and the two walked free of the icy water from earlier. When they dried up more, William's knee seized up, and they had to rest again. Lucinda pulled some herbs from her pouch, sprinkling them on a scoop of jam for William to eat. They rested once more while the herbs took hold.

"We gotta go, 'Cin. I don't know if I'll get up if we stop," William said. Climbing to his feet, he gritted his teeth and pressed forward through the pain. Lucinda caught him under his armpit, and the two hobbled through the darkness.

They came to a dead end. Dry, but dead all the same. Exhausted, the two fell against the wall and held each other. William whispered to her that he'd get them out, one way or another. The girl nodded but quietly stroked his back.

A rock moved above them. Startled, the two looked up to see a face smiling down at them from the roof—a white face.

"Y'all made it," the man said, lowering a rope to them. "Welcome to freedom."

William looked at Lucinda before cautiously taking the rope.

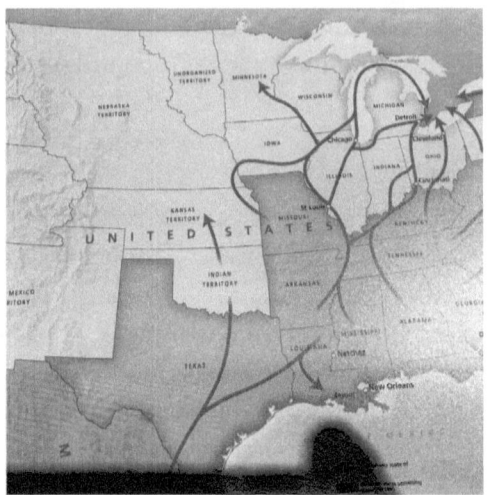

Figure 14 – 1: Map of underground railroad path through Indian Territory

Figure 14 – 2: Sign for Little Sugar Creek, a notable spot in the escape path

CHAPTER 15

Welcome to Mound City

Mound City, Kansas—April 1863

Sliding free from the cave, covered in mud, William and Lucinda came up into a trap floor in a small cabin. They must've been lost all night and into the morning because the sun hung high overhead. Frank, as the man introduced himself, offered them sips from his canteen. The clean water and sunlight restored them fast.

He helped William hop, alternating with Lucinda. The town lay close by: Mound City. Continuing from what the preacher said, Frank explained how the free city worked. Since Kansas was a free state, they would be considered free people now.

"But be cautious," he quickly added. "Just because this here's a free state don't mean slavecatchers ain't stalkin' the place. People get stolen back if they recognize ya. So I'd be careful who you talk to in the first few months. Once ya got a nice reputation established, they cain't do nothin'. People'll vouch for ya in about half a year. Till then, though, I'd lay low and make friends. Don't tell nobody about where you from except bare bones information—never mention bein' enslaved."

"'Sides that, welcome to Mound City. I'll introduce ya to some good folks. They'll get ya settled in a new place."

Frank was a man of his word. The couple followed him to a cozy log cabin on the city's outskirts. There, the man ensured they bathed in cold water to scrub their muddy trek off. The next day, after ensuring they had enough breakfast, he produced new clothes from a trunk. He explained the garments matched the current fashion in the city, passing them off as native Kansans at first glance.

The first week or so, he helped them slowly acclimate. Frank brought the young couple to church with him as they knew no one. The United Brethren Church, filled with a mixed community, was stark with about six pews on each side, complete with a humble altar displaying a picture of Jesus, showing a white man with a beard and long hair. Mid-construction, William ducked under boards holding up the church's doorway to enter. Everyone they talked to welcomed them with soft smiles and their names.

Another couple, a few years older than them, took a shine to the newcomers. Benjamin and Caroline Smith talked to them about living in Mound City, careful to ask them gentle questions that wouldn't reveal too much. Friends with Frank, the abolitionist couple also shared information with them altogether, pointing out store owners and farmers they could trust in the area, as well as the schedules of the more prolific slave catchers. The Smiths opened their lives to the young couple, offering their own home. While they had to alternate between their place and Frank's, for the first time in their lives, both William and Lucinda felt like they were in a place where they could be themselves.

More freed Black men and women floated through their lives as they settled in Mound City. The church changed hands with a ladies' organization Caroline was a part of, and she invited Lucinda to attend meetings alongside her. While there, the group covered topics around the abolitionist movement and how they might turn the church building into a school. While Lucinda was attending meetings, Frank, William, and Benjamin met with another important figure in the city: James Snoddy.

Meetings with Snoddy often fell into talks of his newspaper, The Border Sentinel. While discussing his past with many people wasn't wise, Frank and Benjamin encouraged William to share his stories with Snoddy. The man wouldn't publish them, but verifying hearsay from as far south as Fort Smith would really help his paper, building a bigger knowledge base.

Snoddy's influence opened doors for William. Sharing his tales, the young man received odd jobs around town. People knew Snoddy vouched for people of good character, so while William was new and likely a runaway, people invited him in under Snoddy's good name. Finding work otherwise was difficult. Between the slave catchers and the general poor conditions from the war, William carried the lion's share of work, throwing himself into making a name for himself as a good worker. Lucinda spent her time helping care for Snoddy's household, selling old medicine remedies to folks who came by.

At first, William didn't know what to do with money. His first week's wages sat in his hand after Snoddy handed them over with a smile. He stood there, staring at the currency and feeling its weight in his hand. *What do I do with it?* he wondered. Was this what the Lacys had to deal with?

Frank, thankfully, dropped by to visit with the newspaper owner, and seeing William standing there, he quickly explained what each bill and coin meant. His head spun by the time he met up with Lucinda after work. The young woman beamed, comparing her earned coins to William's and talking excitedly about how much corn it would buy. William gave her the wages, happy that she had a better head for money. The barter system was all William knew, and his exposure to trade was only through the Coweta visits. Henry or a Lacy man would make purchases in Fort Smith, and he just carried the goods. Now, the couple had a semi-consistent income.

Just as surely as the welcoming arms did, the income changed their lives. Through the ladies' group, Lucinda met a woman named Elizabeth, who expanded on Lucinda's savvy money skills. The two went to market together every Sunday, conversing and giggling to buy grain and eggs if they had any. Elizabeth's warm candor eased Lucinda into the market's merchant group, who quickly grew to love the fiery girl with her negotiations. William swelled with pride when she returned home, boasting of a good deal made at that week's market. He wondered if Master Thomas, when he was alive, would've enjoyed supply runs with the Creek girl.

Nearby landowners now paid them directly, and they collected the fees with gratitude. It wasn't long before they carved a cozy place for themselves in Mound City, earning respect from the community with their cheerful attitudes and hard work. Odd jobs flowed to them from surrounding farms, and when those were completed, Snoddy and Frank supplied them with chores around their houses.

A lucky break occurred a few months after their entry in the form of a small home near James Montgomery's farm. The earlier tenant, a war widow, had vacated the premises to move somewhere without bad memories. She sold it to them for a minor fraction of its actual worth.

Lucinda danced through the threshold, her finger tracing outlines around the room, where she could start building a life. Together, they mapped out a garden near the house to plant crops and medicinal herbs. William brought all his knowledge to bear from his farm work. However, when the harvest grew this time, it'd feed him and Lucinda, not go off to fill the Lacys' pockets.

Frank and the Smiths came over with tools to celebrate the couple moving out of his place and held a housewarming gathering. William eagerly started plowing with the middle buster tool Frank offered. Earlier, at thirteen, he could barely handle the one in Van Buren. Now, though, the young man built up enough strength to till his own field, preparing it with the turning plow the Smiths let him borrow. The work was hard, but the thought of growing his own food kept him pushing through the sweaty days. Lucinda cooked dinner for him, and the two would eat freshly cooked veggies at night, using spices she carried with her from the Creek village.

Frank popped by William and Lucinda's place a month into their stay. His visit was brief, bringing some good news that they could soon own the land under the house as well—for only $27. Excited at the prospect, the couple scraped and saved, pulling extra odd jobs well into the evening. Work became scarce again at the farms nearby, so they had to source more work farther from Mound City.

Steadily, more former slaves entered Mound City, making the work harder to come by. Freshly out of dire straits, the couple bowed gracefully aside from the easier jobs in the city so other folks could get a foothold. Since they were more established and people knew them, it was safer for William and Lucinda to seek work farther outside the city.

The one good thing the nearby Fort Scott brought was an answer to their work issues. One morning, William visited to find more for his land savings fund and saw several Black men walking toward town. Feeling friendly, he joined the group, ambling alongside them.

"Where y'all headed to?"

"We goin' down to the courthouse lookin' for work," one said. The other two stared at William, half-suspicious of him. "You sound like you from Alabama. Are ya? Welcome to join us either way. My name's Edward."

"Nice to meet ya, Edward. I'm William." The young man offered his hand, and they shook. "You recognized it from how I talk? Yeah, I'm from Alabama, but uh … moved here a few months back."

While walking to the courthouse, he discovered the three were runaways like he was. After sharing their stories, they found an easy camaraderie, joking about various tales from Alabama and Arkansas. Frank told Edward that the courthouse had many errands to be done. If you waited outside, someone would offer you a job.

They shared more accounts from Alabama when a soldier approached the four of them. The man swaggered up to them, hiking a boot up onto the lower steps. "You boys want to make somethin' outta your lives?"

William had never seen colored soldiers before, and now he could talk to one. His nerves kicked in again, freezing him to the steps between Edward and the others. Edward spoke up first and said, "Lemme guess. You want us to join the war effort?"

"Bet your buttons, I do," the soldier replied. "I know y'all gather 'round the courthouse for work. The Union army got mo' money to pay and work forever. Jus' come by to talk with 'em. You'll see."

Curious, William followed, motioning for Edward to do the same. The four walked with the colored soldier to Fort Scott, tagging along for the eight-mile trek. Typically, William wouldn't leave so far, but Edward's fast friendship and the soldier's confidence carried him way past the boundaries of Mound City.

He barely got in a word between the soldier's bragging and Edward's digs. The two bantered back and forth, and Edward's easygoing nature infected the group. Soon, they shared stories between the digs. The soldier's name was Ralph. He was a recruiter from Fort Scott, sent to drum up more bodies for the war. Fort Scott was his station, and he showed it off proudly when they arrived.

Ralph talked about how it was named after General Winfield Scott and was established in 1842 as a United States Army military station that protected settlers while they put down roots. This reminded William of how Fort Smith started. William thought it was dingier than the Arkansas fort, but what it lacked in color, it made up for in people. The whole place bustled with folks running to and fro. When he'd left Fort Smith, it seemed like a dried-up husk. Fort Scott was growing.

Ralph continued to talk about the 1st Kansas Colored Volunteers—his troop—and how they were using it as a quartermaster supply depot and training center for the war. When they entered the walls, the sheer size stunned William, and all comparisons to Fort Smith disappeared.

Hustling between soldiers, washerwomen, couriers, farmers, tradesmen, and crying children, the buzzing base swallowed up the five. William struggled to keep up with them as Ralph led them through the crowd. Nobody looked down at him here; people barely noticed him at all—too busy. Former slave or no, William felt a tightness loosen in his chest. Mound City gave him hard work and earned coin, but Fort Scott gave him a sense of security amongst the milling people.

"Ralph! Bringin' more trash in?" a yell cut through the crowd from another soldier. When Ralph spied the man, his face broke into a huge grin. "You know it, Paul. Find these lazin' about at the courthouse jus' like you said."

Introductions went all around as the blue-uniformed soldier joined them. They moved to the side, talking loudly to drown out the crowd's noise.

"Colored men to arms for your fellow man and your country!"

Another soldier, like Ralph and Paul, standing on a concrete block across the way, yelled out his message. "Join the 1st Kansas Colored Volunteers and fight to eradicate slavery. Get paid when you do it!" His voice carried to the small group, but he shouted this to a cluster of men dressed like William standing around near the fort. *They must be lookin' for work too,* William thought. One by one, then in twos and threes, the crowd broke apart to talk with the shouting soldier. He gestured to a booth down the road where a line of men started.

"You look interested," Paul said, following William's gaze. "Let's go sign y'all up. Better to strike when the iron's hot."

Paul led them through a few alleys to cut around the main thoroughfare. They approached a row of tents outside the fort. They needed to go to a different place to sign up. A flag flew over the tents, and colored men with blue uniforms trained a few yards away. William looked for a white officer, but after a minute of searching, he realized there were none. Everyone at that camp was colored, just like him. Not only that, but these men carried 1858 Enfield rifles, marching in time like a real army. *Can people like me really fight?*

Struggling not to freeze up again, William took in everything, inching around the camp while Ralph and Paul explained the training efforts to Edward and his friends. According to Ralph, the colored troops drilled in front of the fort all day to prepare for the inevitable battles. Each man carried a rifle, and they drilled with them. A waist full of equipment also adorned each soldier, filled with things William was sure were meant to take another man's life.

The 1st Kansas Colored Volunteers was a regiment of Black soldiers, making a name for themselves across the eastern edges of the state. Paul continued to explain that this stemmed from their battle at Island Mound in Missouri. At the battleground, the regiment was organized in August 1862 by Kansas Senator James Lane. The senator had moved from Indiana to Kansas to join the free state movement and rose to prominence and notoriety through his leadership. Lane served in the Mexican-American War about fifteen years earlier, so his tactic came from seasoned knowledge. Senator Lane brought all his faculties to bear on the forefront to stop the spread of slavery, and Kansas looked like the place to make a stand. Paul couldn't keep the admiration from his voice, talking about their regiment's founder.

Evidently, Senator Lane had written to President Lincoln to request permission to raise the colored regiment in Kansas. However, he was still waiting for a reply. He'd formed it anyway, telling the officers it was a moral and spiritual obligation. William nodded as he heard the news, seeing how everyone was caught up in it. The senator was right. William knew in his heart that God supported their cause.

They'd need one commanding white officer for the entire regiment. So, Senator Lane turned to Captain James Williams, who already had experience like his in the Mexican-American War. Captain Williams had served with the 5th Kansas Cavalry when the current war began but ultimately resigned from his role to join Senator Lane. He agreed to lead the 1st Kansas Colored Volunteers. By January, just a few months earlier, he formally acquired the role.

Ralph took the story over from there, explaining the long fight to create it. Senator Lane reached out to prominent colored men as recruiters to fill their ranks. He offered William D. Matthews, a colored man like themselves, the rank of Captain if he could raise one hundred men from Leavenworth, Kansas. Another colored man, William Seamon, received a similar offer of captaincy if he would help recruit men from the southern parts of Kansas, specifically around Fort Scott. Not just ranks, but money came with the offers: $13 a month, minus three for uniforms, of course.

Ralph finished it by pointing at the bigger tent in the middle. "He's in there right now. We gotta help him get his captaincy. If he can be our officer, we can show the white folk us coloreds fight just as hard as any of 'em."

William wanted to make that a reality. He'd earn the respect he never gained as a hunter or a farmer. He would find it as a soldier and make something out of his life, exactly like Ralph said. Edward and the others were just as fired up, promising to return with William to sign up to help with the effort. The group headed back to Mound City.

William returned to his home to find Lucinda working in the garden. Riding the high of good stories and newfound friends, he launched into retelling his day. Lucinda was excited at first. However, when William's tale turned toward the story of the 1st Kansas Colored Volunteers and the legends behind their creation, her face lost its smile, and she slowly set her trowel down, dusting off her hands.

"Will, I hope you ain't thinkin' of bein' a volunteer," she said.

His smile died down. "O' course, I am. They makin' somethin' of their lives. Makin' money too, and fightin' to protect they lives: thirteen whole dollars a month, Lucinda. You ain't gotta sell no more medicine. Can jus' stay home with ya garden."

"I didn't run all this way jus' to stay home," she spat. "And I didn't take you with me jus' so you could run off on some fool's dream in the army. People die at war, Will. Are ya stupid?"

Anger rose before he could catch it. "I know that! Lost Master Thomas to it and the others 'fore we left. You weren't there. They all workin' together—coloreds, like us. You can walk free and in the open."

"Don't want to hear any more about no 'war effort.' We stayin' out of it. Look at what we got, Will. Nice home, a growin' garden. Ain't it enough?"

William didn't want their first fight to end badly, but he didn't know what to say. He knew Lucinda only saw people die at war, but it'd be different for him. He felt it. No matter what she said, he'd prove he would be the soldier she needed to defend their home.

Figure 15 – 1: Frank's cabin outside of Mound City

CHAPTER 16

The Meaning of War

Mound City, Kansas—April 1863

The next day, William returned to Fort Scott. He approached the tent where a group of men waited to sign up. When it was his turn, he marched up under the tent's overhang.

"Sir? How much does it pay to be in the army?" *Lucinda will be happier with the whole thing if I get a good amount.* "And what d'you do as a soldier?"

"How old are you, boy?" A white man appeared behind the signup desk. He had a commanding air. His spotless uniform and white beard added to his presence.

"I'll be sixteen in a few months, sir."

"We need men, not boys your age. Too young to fight. Carry a rifle. Definitely too young to earn the thirteen a month."

"Well, who takes care of your horses?" William shot back.

The captain shot him a weary look, studying him up and down while grinding his teeth. Finally, he gestured sharply to a stout fellow tacking a war horse a few yards off. "Go see that man," he said, leaving it at that.

William nodded and sped off, barely catching muttered words behind him. "Half these contraband are too young to be useful. Need more folks helping out anyhow."

Contraband? He talkin' about me?

Introducing himself to the horsemaster, William fell into step with him, helping complete the cleaning of the horse. It'd been a while since the young man had worked with horses, not since the Lacy farm back in Van Buren, but the work came fast from muscle memory. The horsemaster was impressed, hiring him on the spot.

"Haven't seen this kinda talent in a while. You're welcome on my staff, boy," he said.

"Thank you, sir," William said. "And uh … what's 'contraband'?"

The man sighed but set down his work to explain. "It's what we callin' runaway slaves here. Y'all greenhorns gatherin' here to find work or join the cause. Before the war, the Fugitive Slave Act would force us to return slaves to their owners. But during the earliest part in Virginia, three slaves made it to Fort Monroe, and General Butler, who was stationed there, refused to hand 'em back to the rebels when they knocked to retrieve 'em. General Butler explained that since they seceded from the Union and formed their own country, he had no obligation to return them, especially since they was buildin' they own fort across the river to attack Fort Monroe! He was a lawyer, so he used that law speak to get 'em to leave. Ever since then, word spread it's legal to keep y'all fugitives. Besides, it weakens them damn rebels. They can't use you to work and strengthen their armies since y'all can fight for us. We hopin' the rest of the Union will join in soon."

Lucinda gave him a sidelong look that William had been getting used to seeing since he brought up the army encampment and possibly joining at Fort Scott. She wasn't thrilled to be accompanying him to the fort, but work was work, and they needed the money to buy land before it got bought up by someone else.

"You know I hate these places," she said. "Army's always trouble. You promise me you ain't joinin'?"

"I cain't, 'Cin. They don't take boys my age," William said quickly. "Captain said that yesterday, but they do got work. More since men got recruited. That many people always need somethin'. They's gotta be meals to cook, laundry to wash, and I'll put my old horse work to good use. We'll be landowners soon 'nough."

The two entered Fort Scott, and Lucinda used a reference from a soldier's wife from Mound City, endearing herself to the military Quartermaster Sergeant there. While she had to lie about her past, saying she was Spanish, the man offered her forty cents a week to peel potatoes and help with the laundresses.

For the next few weeks, William and Lucinda hiked the eight miles each day to Fort Scott to keep their newfound income, making it back in time at night to care for their growing garden. Lucinda grew more sour by the day, stating how she hated lying about her family. The few Cherokee people she saw there were treated poorly, barely paid, and worked just about to death under suspicion of being spies. Other "contraband" came as well. About forty other people mixed with the two, mostly colored and fresh out of slavery.

The work was as tough for William. It reminded him of their first year at Van Buren, setting up the farm. At Fort Scott, six hundred men needed clean uniforms, food, and well-prepped horses. It took all their energy to keep up their hopes of saving the money. Days passed, and they had less and less time to tend their small garden. Weeds crept in.

William fell into old habits of blending into the background, so it was easier for him to overhear conversations around the fort. William found Edward, now a soldier, along with Ralph and Paul, and they would share brief breaks to talk about the regiment.

A week later, William found more Creek soldiers when he moved to a new stable on the fort's eastern side. He eagerly made their acquaintance before asking if they had heard of Coweta. Unfortunately, they were from farther north. The group he found had been with Opothleyahola when they traveled north from the Creek lands in Indian Territory. The Union army had recruited them from an Indian reservation west of Mound City. Confederate Indians attacked Opothleyahola's group, and this solidified their decision to join the regiment—for revenge.

This news did little to cheer up Lucinda, as the people she knew back in Coweta were most likely dead. Though she ached to talk with them, Lucinda had to keep her distance. If they saw her talking with other Creeks, it might reveal her as one of them, and she could lose the meager pay promised.

Lucinda carefully peeled potatoes, dropping them into a large pot while William rested nearby. He'd come to the kitchen between jobs to spend more time with her before heading off for the day. Nearby, some soldiers ate the cooked potatoes and chatted about the recent victory at Island Mound near the Missouri border. Not much older than William, he roused himself and joined them.

"What's shootin' like? I've been hunting before but never handled a gun myself. And what happened at the battle?" William asked. Behind him, he heard Lucinda toss a potato a little harder than necessary into the pot.

"Some of us 1st Kansas men were foragin' for food at a nearby farm when we was attacked by Missouri bushwhackers. We had our hands full of chickens, pigs, grain, and anythin' edible when they jumped out of the bushes at us. Captain Armstrong and Crew ordered the others—about sixty strong at the time—out of Fort Africa to engage the guerrillas in their hideout."

"Fort Africa?" William asked.

"Yeah, it's a farm that was taken over by us 1st Kansas boys to use as security, where we can gather more military. A rebel sympathizer named John Toothman owned the farm, but he and his family fled as we approached. The rebel guerrillas shouted at us, callin' us all kinds of names, but we sent all that right back at 'em. Needed to keep them distracted while reinforcements was comin'. See, that whole thing at first was a distraction from us takin' they pigs and such. We all gotta eat, right? Better us than them.

"Anyway, they opened fire on us, and we fired back. There's nothin' like it, and I can't explain it till you do it for yourself. They say we made history as the first coloreds to enter the war. Definitely terrifying at first, but boy, it felt good to give it to 'em after hearin' all the things they was callin' us. We struck a blow for freedom for us and all those still enslaved across the South."

Lucinda had stopped peeling and was listening from the kitchen. William asked if they had more to tell, spellbound by the story.

Another soldier continued, "The rebels set the prairie grass on fire to get us all worked up. It raged on into the afternoon. Captain Seaman ordered us to get clear of the smoke and get eyes on the rebels. Our Cherokee officer, Captain Sixkiller, rode into it himself, leading the charge. He spotted a large group of rebel soldiers trying to use the smoke as cover, and they were shocked that it didn't work. They got tore into with Captain Sixkiller's rifles, and the rest of us sprang into action, driving them out of the area. Sixkiller is amazing! Killed two men with his rifle, then another with his bayonet, and the last with the butt of his rifle. It took six bullets before he fell dead, and that's why the Cherokees all mad as hell. Them Missouri guerrillas left the field, and we tracked them at least ten miles away from where we fought.

"During the battle, Lieutenant Minor and his company joined us. That'd make Minor the first colored officer to lead Black and Indian men! Can you believe it? We made history for sure over in Island Mound. Now that we won, they gotta let us keep growing and fighting. Don't know why they won't let Black officers lead anymore. The government stripped them of their officer rank and said no Black soldiers could be officers. It'd conflict with white soldiers. The First Confiscation Act, passed by Congress, allowed federal forces to take and seize property owned by rebel soldiers and use it for our needs. The Second Confiscation Act, signed last year in July, gives us permission to take their whole property—it's why we snatched up all those pigs in the first place. We also can protect slaves who come to join us.

"As long as he was near the federal army, places like Fort Scott, you're safe from slave catchers. The Confiscation Act allows us to recruit more colored soldiers."

William felt something settle in his chest. *That's why I feel safe here. Not only am I 'round lots of people like me, they all protectin' each other.* "Thanks for lettin' me know. Seems like y'all don' great things out there. I'm proud to meet the first colored soldiers who won in the war. What's your name?"

"William Matthews," the talkative soldier said, proudly shaking William's hand. "I recruited most of these men you see myself. Hope we can count on you to help when you're older."

The days swam into one another in a rush of soldier stories, dirty horses, and peeled potatoes. Walking to the fort each day, the two developed even harder calluses on their feet. Soon, Lucinda reminded William that they were supposed to be paid for all this work—in all the flurry, William forgot.

"The ladies reminded me on Sunday that we gotta ask, so don't feel too bad," Lucinda admitted.

"Alright, well, now we just need to figure out who gives out the money," William said.

Agreeing to find out together, the two went their separate ways until lunch. Lucinda slipped back into cleaning up cooking pots. The other girls left her the duty since she was late that day, meaning she'd need to walk out of the kitchen past the soldiers' tents to get the pots washed up in a fountain nearby.

She took two with her, huffing as she trudged along with them. Already exhausted from the long walks and hard work, Lucinda struggled to get them down to the washing fountain. She decided to set them down for a moment to stretch.

A hand tangled in her hair and snatched her backward.

Jolting with dizziness, the girl had the wind knocked out of her, and stars swirled in her vision. It took precious seconds to get her faculties back, and by then, she was dragged into a tent by one of the soldiers. The man put a sweaty hand over her mouth as she opened it to scream. He was too late, and she shrieked before he covered it.

Lucinda's legs and arms shook, and she bit deeply into his hand, tasting coppery blood.

"You damn bitch," the soldier shouted, slapping her across the face with his wounded hand. The blow stunned her, and she rolled backward, flailing wildly and knocking over his supply rack, causing a vicious clang.

His hands clamped onto her left arm, squeezing so hard she knew there'd be bruises. The man forced her down, using his knees to kick her legs open. Sobbing, she summoned more strength—to either grab her knife or scream. She chose the knife.

But it wasn't in her sheath.

Spying it in the tent's corner, the man must've removed it while she was stunned. He had wild eyes, distant like an animal, as he flipped her skirt up, exposing her underclothes. With a sharp rip, he tore them free, and Lucinda knew she had seconds before the violence, and her strength was failing against the large man.

Breath Maker, please ... help your lost daughter, she prayed. *Don't let another girl's blood soak into the earth.*

Careful words tumbled from her, and she balled her hand into a fist as her eyes closed. She'd wait. Wait until he thought she'd given up, and then, when he least expected it, she'd gouge out his eyes. Lucinda pretended to faint, shivering as unfamiliar hands pressed into her throat.

A click sounded.

"Get your hands off her, and stand up slowly," a low growl sounded from the darkness.

The soldier stopped, pulling to look behind him, and Lucinda leaped into action. She dug into the man's eyes with a sharp nail, scratching as hard as she could. Nothing popped, but a satisfying amount of blood sprayed out into the tent.

Screaming, the soldier fell backward, writhing in pain. William's surprised face was revealed at the tent opening, holding a long rifle that must've been hanging outside. He reached in to quickly pull her free, and she needed it. The fight took out almost all her energy; she leaned heavily into William to keep on her feet.

Stumbling away, William dropped the rifle near the man while he shook. Thankfully, most people were away, so the man cried in his tent alone, and nobody saw the two sneaking off back to the more populous areas.

Behind a store, William removed his jacket to cover Lucinda's torn dress. She shivered violently, gulping in air like a fish, eyes distant, and black hair falling about her face.

"Hey, 'Cin. Lucinda?" William gently cupped her shoulders and put his face in front of hers. "You safe now. You safe. Ain't nobody hurtin' you."

It took a few minutes to calm her down. In the meantime, he spoke gently to her about the rifle and his first time holding one. Master Thomas never allowed him close to one because the general sense was that slaves holding guns was a good way to get themselves killed. The fact that he could pick one up meant he could protect her better from events like this.

"Take me home, William Lacy," she said. Each word about broke him, hearing her so shaken up. "Now."

Leaving work without saying a thing and without pay, the two walked back to Mound City with William holding Lucinda up. After clearing the fort a good mile or so, some strength returned, and she could walk home, albeit slowly, without leaning on William.

Their tiny farm waited for them, and William started a fire when they got back. It was quite a while before sunset, and he'd forgotten what the place looked like in daylight. They usually left before the sun rose in the sky and returned long after it set. *What's the point in havin' a home you ain't never in*, he thought dully.

Their meal was simple. He warmed up some bread and used a smear of butter, passing it to Lucinda, who'd taken up a spot by the fire. She ate a little and kept silent the whole time. William thought back to the fort and all the soldiers there. They came back from battles, making history. Nobody would dare mess with them or anyone they knew.

"I'll get a rifle for us. May cost us a little more, put off our land buyin' plans, but it's time we got somethin' to keep us safe here," he said. Holding that rifle and stopping another man in his tracks made William feel powerful—an unfamiliar, heady feeling that carried him through the horrors of the day. He'd seen Master Thomas and Theo practice with one back in Van Buren. Was that why they always acted so superior? Access to the power of rifles?

"I ain't never felt so powerless, Will. If you hadn't showed up …" She couldn't finish the thought. All cried out from the road, Lucinda sat, staring at the fire hollowly.

"Don't think about what might've happened. Focus on what did happen. I saw you scratch that man. You didn't need me there, 'cept to help pull you up," he said, sitting beside her. He put an arm around her, but she stiffened.

"I ain't never goin' back there again. That's what war does to people, Will. Turns 'em into animals that attack each other. It chews up everyone and spits 'em out like some beast. It happened to my people. Happened to whites, Blacks, Indians, men, women, kids—don't matter who you are."

"It's different, 'Cin. I seen some things and heard people talkin'. Yeah, of course war does that to people. It ain't all happy and pretty, but we gotta fight to protect what's ours. Can't just lay down and die when tough times come in. The way I see it, these men makin' history, makin' the world a better place."

"You think you different, William Lacy?" Lucinda jerked away from him. "You ain't. It'll chew you up and spit you out just the same as that man in the tent. I won't be here to see it happen to you. And how dare you ask me to watch, knowin' what it did to Coweta. What it did to my mama."

Stalking outside into the garden, Lucinda left William to his thoughts in their house.

CHAPTER 17

Sunlight in Quindaro

Fort Scott, Kansas—June 1863

Regardless of what happened, William had to return, not just to get answers and justice, but to retrieve Lucinda's hard-earned pay. He completely understood why she wouldn't return to the fort and tried to further solidify why he needed to be there just as powerfully.

He kept himself in check, entering the training grounds again and not seeking out the man who tried to hurt Lucinda. He'd know him by the scars across his face now.

Pulling the Quartermaster Sergeant aside, the officer was about to give him a dressing down till he saw the look on his face. "What happened, boy?"

"'Nother soldier tried to hurt my girl, sir," William said, clenching his fists. "She clawed him good before she got away, but if nothin' happened, he'd've hurt her real good. She's my age and worked here for the last few weeks. Remember Lucinda?"

The officer looked sick and rubbed his forehead. "Ugh, yeah, I know her. Good girl, hard worker. Did she come in with you?"

"No, she don't wanna come back here now."

"Smart girl, good head on her shoulders," he said. "We'll send her wages with you when they come in. It's fine that she can't make it." He turned away, returning to his work.

"That's it?" William almost shouted. "I heard stories of honor and people makin' history. That all the regiment has when a rape almost happened?"

The sergeant whipped back around and prodded a finger into William's chest. "Rapes happen every day. We living in war times, boy. I'd man up and get over it fast. I'm sorry about what happened, but if we strung up every man here that ever did anything, we'd have no soldiers left." He shook his head. "You're contraband. Don't forget. Kids like you disappear all the time. If that bothers you, march right on outta here and back home."

Stunned, William watched him walk away. Lucinda was right about one thing: war changed people. He couldn't help but compare the officer to the rowdy soldiers he talked with in the kitchen. They were so excited, riding the high of a battle. What was a soldier if not that? Would something like this happen to him if he joined up?

The Union army wasn't proud of its soldiers who won battles for them, and it'd let Lucinda get chewed up and spat out along with them. No protections for "contraband" like them.

He thought back to leaving Lucinda at home. She'd already started the washing, got breakfast ready, and was tending the garden in time for him to leave, promising to talk to Snoddy again for more work in Mound City. She'd bounced back after a good cry and a few hours in her garden. It didn't matter what the Union soldiers or their officers believed. He was mighty proud of her and proud to be alongside her. She survived more horrible things than the soldiers and kept her love and kindness.

War meant protecting her and the tiny home they started. She didn't see it that way, but he had to join up and be the soldier she needed. He fought for scraps of peace between what the Lacys demanded all his life. With Lucinda, he'd found happiness, belonging, pride. The army almost took that away and was unapologetic, but he knew the tides shifted with them, whether they would care for small people—contraband or not.

She was beautiful, of course. Everyone who saw her would agree, but it was more than that for him. He finished his work for the day and headed back as fast as he could to a place that sprang up like prairie grass overnight: home.

Lucinda was on the front porch, waiting for him with a steaming bowl of soup. It smelled heavenly after the long day. The firelight framed her silhouette like before, the day he arrived on their escape from Coweta. Now, the girl shone as mistress of her own home, instead of a slave in someone else's.

"William, come on in. I've got somethin' to say," Lucinda said, sliding his bowl down the table. She'd waited to eat with him in the late evening.

William kicked off his dusty boots, bought used from the army supply, and gratefully accepted the bowl. "I do too, 'Cin." Her tone made him nervous, but it did nothing to diminish the swelling of his heart. The feelings carried him through every hour at work and followed him back home.

"I need to say my piece first," she said. "I never thanked you properly for savin' me. Sorry about that. The whole thing happened so fast. I never tol' you, but ... somethin' similar happened back in Coweta. The Confederate soldiers who came through did that to my mama and tried to get me, too, but Daddy came by and rushed them off. Never was the same after that. It made it real hard for anythin' to get done, and ever since, well, I just hate seein' anyone in uniform now. Damn military men ruined my life and my people's lives.

"But you came in after me, Will. Daddy shouted to scare 'em other soldiers off, but you came into the tent after me. Nobody ever done that before." She placed a hand on his. "So, from the bottom of my heart, thank you."

William teared up. Here was this beautiful, fierce, brave, smart girl—someone everybody loved once they met her—and he was the first to stand up for her. She'd been fighting for a scrap of peace her whole life, and everyone tried to take it from her. He got up from where he sat and crawled over, pulling her into a fierce hug.

"I love you, Lucinda," he said. "I love you so much." A little stiff at first, the girl's shoulders fell, and she melted into the hug, bringing her hands up behind his back to pull him in closer.

"I love you, too, William."

"I got somethin' to tell you, too."

She sat back, watching him by the fire, letting him take his time to find the words.

"We didn't meet first in Coweta. I first saw you near Lacy Springs. You and your daddy came by as traveling merchants. Shoot, this must've been near seven years back now. This group of boys caught you then, too. They was draggin' you to the river till I threw a rock."

Lucinda sat upright. "That was you?"

William nodded. "Ashamed to say that was all I did. You took care of the rest. I sat back, frozen. Couldn't even move. Just like when you talked to me unloading all them boxes when Master Thomas first met your daddy.

"All my life, I got shocked still, like a rock in a river. Couldn't do nothin' when Buck got free and kicked me or when Henry and I got beaten in Fort Smith. But earlier, when I heard you scream, I moved. My whole body reacted, and I was in that tent with the gun before I knew what was happenin'. You melt me, Lucinda. Make me a better person. And I wanna do the same for you every day of my life. Till I die."

Lucinda grabbed his shoulder and pressed her lips against his, crushing into him like a wave breaking on the shore. "Be my man, William Lacy," she whispered, slipping out of her dress.

For the next few weeks, William and Lucinda fell into a routine. William walked to the fort, working all day with his horse duties, and deepened his friendship with Ralph, Paul, and Edward. Lucinda continued with her odd jobs around Mound City, mostly working at Snoddy's house but getting the occasional extra work from ladies she met at the church. The two returned each evening, exhausted but satisfied. While their savings for the land grew, it came at the cost of neglecting their garden. With Lucinda's best efforts at the end of each day, it still wasn't enough to tame the weeds.

Between laboring, survival, and socializing, the two explored each other, rejoicing in the safe home they'd created with each other. It took a few awkward nights to figure out what even to do; the teenagers' only knowledge of intimacy came from Bible readings or watching animals. They let their love for each other and eagerness to please lead the way. The more they lay together, the closer they felt, gratefully drinking in the deliciousness of someone else caring about who they were and feeling happy, peaceful, and loved.

In late May, William arrived at the fort to start his regular work. The place barely contained all the recruits, now boasting over six hundred soldiers, and the support staff needed to keep the place running. That morning, the 1st Kansas had been bivouacked outside the fort, filling up the large flat area between the fort and the nearest city. The regiment stayed outside for months since the colored soldiers weren't allowed in the fort alongside their white counterparts.

To adapt, the colored regiment created their own organization, grouping into company streets between tents and training in the public areas where they could find room. Many townspeople took exception to the colored soldiers drilling with actual weaponry in broad daylight, despite their legal right to be there. William saw them receiving the same postal mail for their officers, the same uniforms, and dealing with the same enemy. When he heard the whispers from townsfolk, it irritated him. Since Lucinda's near-miss, William could see how people acted more clearly.

When a group of men jeered at the training of 1st Kansas soldiers outside, something came over William, and he grabbed a piss-spot from the nearest windowsill, dumping its disgusting contents onto the hecklers before speeding off. A wave of giddiness overtook him as he raced up the steps two at a time to flee the scene, and that rush soured to guilt when he rounded the corner. *I'm not a kid*, he thought. *If I wanna be a soldier, I gotta start actin' like one. Not dumpin' piss on people.*

The sun dipped farther in the sky, and William tiredly shut the stable door in the military section. Some contraband workers trailed off, setting their work down to join the crowd. Lieutenant Minor, one of the men who delivered news, stood on a concrete block to make an announcement. Curious, William joined the growing crowd around him.

"Attention, everyone, the 1st Kansas has received marching orders from the Army of the Border and General Blount today. We're to move south to Indian Territory toward Fort Gibson to protect the road between that fort and ours here. We're leaving at first daylight."

Hot and sweaty from the afternoon work, William wiped at his brow, sharing looks with strangers. The news was needed, but nobody knew what to make of it. Others in the crowd yelled questions, but the lieutenant couldn't answer all of them.

William finished his work and traipsed homeward, wrestling with his thoughts on what tomorrow would bring. He was too young to join the war effort and couldn't follow the regiment back toward Indian Territory. Regardless of his involvement or how many pieces of military uniform he wore, his contraband status made him a target anywhere else.

Lucinda rolled over in the hay bed they shared, pulling herself closer to him on the chilly night. "Oh, did you get our wages? Been a long time since we added more to our savin's jar."

Sleepy until she asked, the young man's eyes flew open. He cupped a hand over his forehead and winced. "Sho' didn't. Sorry, it's been a hornet's nest over there. The 1st Kansas is movin' out on marchin' orders. I'll get 'em tomorrow, though. Promise." He thought back to the last conversation when he brought them up. The Quartermaster sergeant mentioned it, but he was so angry about what happened to Lucinda that it didn't seem important. He had to keep reminding himself that all the back-breaking work came with pay now. His whole life told him otherwise.

"I deserve to get paid," he whispered, hitting his fist gently against the bed. "I deserve to get paid. I deserve to get paid …" The mantra followed him into sleep.

Lucinda leaned out on their porch to see a strange sight: William walking home midmorning. She hadn't left for Snoddy's place that day to start work, so she was bringing water to their failing garden. Limp, lifeless sprouts grew in the soil.

"What's the matta'?" She fanned herself with a rag, Kansas summer in full swing as soon as the sun came up.

"They all gone. Left in the mornin'," William shouted back. He kicked a stone clear across their yard, sailing off into the space behind their cabin. "No wages since the Quartermaster went too. Must've forgotten in the scramble."

Lucinda's hands tightened on the porch railing. "Weeks. Weeks, William. I almost got …" she trailed off, legs shaking with anger. "We put ourselves through hell to save for this house. Now they just up and disappear? The army ain't nothin' but sickness and heartache, Will. Do you see it now?"

William shook his head. "I'm goin' into town to the courthouse again. Maybe they got somethin' else for me." He felt heavy and didn't want to fight with her about the soldiers. The news that they'd left and had taken all their income with them was already devastating enough. He saw how much she poured into their garden, and they'd sacrificed time to make it better with the promises of wages. Now?

He hung his head and ambled to the Linn County Courthouse in Mound City. Like always, a group of men lingered around the steps, contraband like him, trying to find a way to scrape by. As he approached, most of them wore discarded military uniforms like he did. They were also discussing the same issue he had: wage theft, courtesy of the Union Army.

The men were about to head to another fort called Leavenworth in the north, about a two- to three-day walk. Since they already had the routine down for military maintenance, it seemed only fitting that they continued it with another group. The second reason was that William Matthews, the sergeant of the 1st Kansas, had some disagreement with the Army down in Fort Scott, and they chose to go to Fort Leavenworth instead. He'd overheard it in the early morning before they left.

"Matthews is honest. We always had a kind word, and he made sure to pay me before they left. Said he felt bad that he couldn't get everyone what they were owed, but the marching orders had to be followed. I trust him to find us more work up in Leavenworth," the man said.

William sensed truth in their words but dreaded bringing home the news to Lucinda. He knew she'd fight tooth and nail if he tried to go to another fort to find work. What choice did he have now? All the other work was taken in Mound City, and he knew exactly how to keep a fort going. Like the other contraband, his choices were limited. It was either try Leavenworth or get desperate.

Re-entering his house, he waited for Lucinda to return. She was baking some potatoes for dinner that night. He knew there was a little thyme saved, so he placed that on the potatoes with a pat of butter each, keeping them nice and hot for when she got back.

She set her travel sack down by the door and took her place, sighing gratefully. "Ahh, that smells good. Thank ya." She blew on the fluffy, buttery potato piece before taking a bite and chewing happily.

William tried to keep the talk light but couldn't hide his nervousness around the topic. Finally, Lucinda tapped the table. "What's wrong, Will? Looks like you got somethin' on your mind."

"We gotta find work, 'Cin. The garden ain't comin' up fast, and we gotta eat."

"Somethin' tells me I'm not gonna like this."

"They got more work in Leavenworth. It's ... another fort."

Lucinda sighed and left the table. "Another fort? We jus' spoke this mornin' about the army stiffin' you. And now you wanna go off and join again? How many times they gotta prove they no good before you catch it?"

"Cain't squeeze the plants to make 'em grow faster," he said. "And cain't pull these potatoes out of nothin'. I ain't happy with it neither, but we gotta do somethin'. I don't expect you to come too, but it's what I know now. I have to try. They sayin' William Matthews is up there, and he paid some other folks this mornin' 'fore he left. So, I'm thinkin' maybe there's at least one trustworthy soldier up there."

Lucinda shook her head. "You gon' do it anyway, so I won't waste my words. But mark it, Will. Nothin' good's comin' from Leavenworth."

"Things will be better if you there."

Lucinda grabbed her knife from the kitchen and strapped it back to her leg. "Next time someone grabs me, I'm cuttin' they hand off. I'll follow you, Will, but I'm watchin' everything on the road."

Four hard days of walking brought the small group to a town at the bend in the Missouri River: Quindaro, Kansas. The little village belonged to the free state but was so close to Missouri that its borders bled into slave territory. With no army and no community like in Mound City, the two kept a close watch for any strangers approaching the group. It wouldn't be like before. Now they had to watch for slave catchers again.

Wooden buildings comprised most of the city, complete with a busy river port. As they entered the town and looked around, it seemed like it was mostly populated with free coloreds like them, way more than Mound City. It had several parlors and hotels filled with businesses. William was flabbergasted, taking in the sights.

Once solidly in Quindaro, they discovered connections to Mound City in the form of abolitionists. A healthy group of them lived there, and they were vocal enough to find without looking too hard. The group explained that the town was founded by abolitionists, originating from a need for an established community to stand up to the Missouri slave catchers. Feeling a little better, Lucinda exchanged names with a few key members, promising to deliver letters back to Mound City on their return journey. Meeting so many like-minded people sent an excited thrill through the couple. Could this be an even better spot than Mound City? Lucinda admitted shyly that it was a good idea to come.

William was distracted by a wondrous new sight: steamboats. He'd seen them in Memphis, but that was a long time ago, and he was only a child. Now, with the freedom to explore, he would visit the ports where Quindaro made a big name for itself as a place to land steamboats.

Free state lovers needed a place to dock their boats on the Kansas side of the river. William found out Quindaro offered a safe place to dock since pro-slave forces had taken to blocking passage upriver.

"Y'all new to Quindaro?" a white man said, approaching the two. William nodded, shaking hands with the man. He introduced himself to the two of them as Mr. Freedom."

The alias seemed a little odd, but William had met several people who had to lie about their names, so he took it in stride. Lucinda followed behind them as Mr. Freedom pointed out spots in Quindaro, keeping a suspicious eye on him. His amiable charm and helpful information eventually won the two of them over, and they ended up staying up late in the back of his haberdashery, sharing stories of Mound City and Fort Scott to catch him up on the goings-on down south. In gratitude, he asked them to stay the night there.

A few more people greeted Mr. Freedom, contrabands like them. He asked William and Lucinda to help cook and prepare dinner, talking with the frightened runaways from Missouri. Under Lucinda's calm hand and William's inspiring stories, the newcomers fell into an easy camaraderie, explaining that they were about to keep heading north to Nebraska.

They found out that Mr. Freedom was another stop on the Underground Railroad. Many runaways never stopped in Kansas but kept going straight into Nebraska. The thought gave the couple pause, and they conversed with each other into the early morning, sleeping fitfully in the new place. Even among friends, they had a hard time letting their guard down completely.

The place reminded them of the missions they stayed in on their way through Indian Territory, which didn't help the anxiety. After a few days of this, Mr. Freedom asked if they were traveling to Nebraska, too. He didn't want to make any broad assumptions, but neither William nor Lucinda mentioned travel plans, and it was strange for people to lurk around Quindaro dressed like they were.

"Honestly, sir, with what we're seein' here in Quindaro, we're not wantin' to go up to Nebraska," William replied. "We was headin' to Fort Leavenworth, but with all the good work to be done and friendly people, Quindaro seems like a better option."

Using his connections, Mr. Freedom helped them get a room in a small boarding house near the river, which suited William perfectly. He could wake up to mornings with cozy riverboats trailing into the port at dawn.

Lucinda also found a good spot, running into a schoolteacher who knew the Smiths from Mound City. She quickly got a job at Quindaro Freedman's school as a caretaker, preparing meals and cleaning the two-room schoolhouse. Folks around the town warmed up fast to the newcomers. They started saying "good morning" to many people before leaving the street in front of the boarding house.

With the stark change in energy, after a week, the couple talked extensively about whether it was worth it to seek their lost wages in Leavenworth. With the steady work in Quindaro and the community, it didn't seem worth it to continue saving for land outside Mound City. William was all too happy to give up on something that settled Lucinda's mind more, even if the passion he felt didn't leave. He felt like a soldier was who he was, and somehow, he would need to confirm it.

Finding a poster outside the parlors, William noticed the writing surrounding a picture of a stagecoach and a horse train. He took it inside to ask if anyone could read and explain its meaning. Most of the posters were for jobs.

The bartender read it aloud for him, explaining it was a job offer. The advertisement was for new stagecoaches that ran daily between Quindaro and Lawrence, Kansas. They needed people to drive the wagons and keep the horses healthy.

Well, this is a sign if I ever seen one, William thought and asked for directions to their business. Not two hours later, William donned the stagecoach business's livery and began work in their stables, the newest hiree of the Robinson stagecoach line. Learning from earlier, he respectfully verified where and how his wages would be paid. He was happy to find out it would be cash paid daily after work.

With the work set, Lucinda found a second job in a kitchen near Mr. Freedom's haberdashery. This matched well with William's schedule, as he ran the Robinson stagecoach most of the day and tidied up their stables in the evening. Occasionally, Lucinda would come by and catch a ride with him, lending a helping hand and a warm smile. These days made William deliriously happy. A good job, a happy girl, and well-earned pay. *Heaven on Earth,* he thought.

Mr. Robinson took an interest in his newest employee, wanting to reward him for his hard work. One day, when he overheard him and Lucinda discussing their old home, failed garden, and problems with the boarding room, he offered to sell them a small house in Lawrence for a portion of his pay. It would commit him to the company, but he was happy to do it for someone with an extraordinary hand with the horses. William and Lucinda agreed, thrilled to have a stroke of luck.

With the deed done, William became a homeowner overnight. The weeks in Quindaro slid over him like a warm summer breeze, and he couldn't help but keep moving at such a fast pace.

The house he now owned was larger than their place back in Mound City, still with one room and a chimney. It came with a deep, fresh well, and a cornfield surrounded it, planted and kept by a coworker from Robinson's company. Complete with a small porch, barely the width of the door, and propped up by bricks, the couple settled into their new home.

CHAPTER 18

Growing a Family

Lawrence, Kansas—Summer 1864

As the center for the free state's movement, Lawrence, Kansas's popularity boomed, especially once the armed conflicts started. The efforts to ensure Kansas remained a free state continued to fuel the city's passionate populace and, equally, its hatred of pro-slave forces. Arriving there as the days grew long and hot, William and Lucinda discovered another buzzing town like Quindaro. It was home to about seventeen hundred people, including James Lane, a U.S. senator, and William's employer, Charles Robinson.

The two strolled down Massachusetts Street, where most of the town's business district lay, lined with saddle shops, machine shops, lawyers' offices, hotels, and bakeries. They had to cross the Kansas River by ferry to continue their journey.

Robinson's stagecoach business supported the business in both Lawrence and Quindaro. Its name came from "pile of sticks" in the Wyandotte Indians' language. It became important enough to connect both the Santa Fe Trail and the Lane Trail for settlers moving westward. This drew Robinson's business sense to operate a stagecoach line between the two growing hotspots and increase his staff by hiring folks like William.

His work stretched on every day, so Lucinda would go to the coaches on Sundays. She'd ride with him, continuing the earlier tradition and spending the whole day with him. The rides eastward meandered over smooth, mildly sloped hills, and the Kansas River Valley area grew lush and green as spring blushed stronger into summer.

One such Sunday in August, Lucinda leaned over, wind blowing her hair back. She wore a large hat tucked under her arm for the windier parts. She confided in William that she might stop the Sunday rides since she fought through so much nausea. Once in Lawrence, and the stagecoach passengers filed off, the two trekked across the city to find a doctor who'd see them.

Sixteen-year-old William discovered he was going to be a father.

Lucinda, at seventeen, reeled at the news of impending motherhood. The two would have much more to consider now, but a radiant joy washed their worries away. That evening, hugging each other outside the doctor's office, they found peace in their world and new hope for the future.

Lucinda's mood dropped on the way home. She knew nothing about birthing babies and let William know all about it, walking from Robinson's stagecoaches to their house. William floated through fatherly daydreams at work, but Lucinda's worries brought him back to reality. He'd have to provide for them when Lucinda had to stay home to care for their baby. It'd be a joyful time, but dread crept in as well. How could you provide for three when the salary he had now barely made it for his half?

William went to work as usual the following Friday, but Lucinda's day took a different turn.

The morning's sun rose fresh over the town's roofs, and she'd started her day's work, attending the schoolhouse to keep it clean and tidy. On her way, trails of black smoke whirled into the sky. More joined them, making progress to where she walked.

A newspaper sat outside the general store. August 21, 1863, was the date that burned into her memory as people ran around her. She tried to stop someone, anyone, but the panicked crowd kept pushing past her, almost knocking her over as people joined in. She finally caught a thin man as he stumbled, crashing into the newspapers and knocking them over.

"Hey," she shouted, shaking the man. "What's goin' on? Why's everybody runnin'?"

"They killin' everybody!" His shrill voice, squeaking with fear, forced out word by word through gasping for air. He exhaled more before his breathing came back under control. He pushed her aside in his flight, tearing off to join the others running. "They killin' the men! It's William Quantrill's bunch, the raiders, and they burnin' everything!"

A chill ran down Lucinda's neck, and she grasped her knife, safe in its leg holster, before her hand traveled up to her stomach. Grimly, she set her shoulders and rushed back homeward, thankful she hadn't made it the whole distance to the schoolhouse before hearing the news. It still took too long to get there.

Hoofbeats sounded behind her as she rounded the cornfield. Adrenaline surged as the young woman ducked into the corn, cursing when she had to pull her colorful dress in behind her. A tickle in her mind said the men on horseback knew where she was headed.

So far, their home sat undisturbed in the raid, even with most of Lawrence now up in flames. The towering smoke billowed over the trade district: saddle shops, machine shops, lawyers' offices, hotels, and bakeries—everything she walked past in the morning. If she were lucky enough, her tiny home would seem deserted, and the raiders would pass her hiding place undisturbed. She prayed for a watchful eye from the land spirits. Panting, she crossed the threshold and tumbled inside.

From the yard, cornstalks parted for racing horses just a few seconds before she shut the door. *They know I'm here*, she thought, moving to a spot behind the door and drawing her knife. She fought to calm her breathing. This wouldn't be like Coweta when her mother was taken; she was grown now.

As heavy boot steps hit the porch, she drew her knife. She had the element of surprise but would have to make it count. No matter what, she wasn't going down without a fight. Visions of a destroyed Coweta and her daddy swam up, blurring her eyes with tears.

The door opened, and a tall, broadly built man strode in carefully. He flipped the table over violently, tumbling everything to the floor in a large heap, ripping open their storage bags and upending boxes. Lucinda waited patiently in her hiding spot for the right time.

One step, two, and as the door swung shut behind him, she leaped like a mountain lion, tackling him to the ground. The man's hat flew off, revealing raven-black hair and reddish-tanned skin. Her knife flashed toward his throat—then she froze. Just above his collarbone was the coiled serpent of the Wind Clan. Her breath caught before she forced out, "You're Mvskoke?"

His eyes widened, then darkened with shame. Men called from outside. "Hey, you messin' around in there?"

Turning his head to the door, the man shared a look with Lucinda, who shook her head grimly with the knife still poised near his throat.

"All clear," he shouted back. "Nothing but dead abolitionists. I'm looking for rum."

A chorus of laughs, followed by "drunk," sounded from outside.

"That'll give us a minute," he whispered, "and I ain't no Creek. I'm white, no matter who my papa is. Now, I won't kill you, but you can't say nothin' 'bout recognizin' my tattoo. The raiders will kill us both if they think I ain't white. You need to hide."

Lucinda withdrew her knife, crawling off the man as fatigue set in. "I won't say nothin'," she whispered. "But why? Why y'all doin' this?"

"Quantrill's men hate the abolitionists here. They know if any men, young or old, are left here to fight, they'll join the Union. So, they came to cut that off at the root. We're here to make sure the homes don't house men that'll come for Confederates later."

"Ain't no men here," Lucinda's icy cold words trailed out.

"I can see that," he replied. "You can come with me. I'll protect you in the group."

As he stood up, Lucinda flashed her knife again, her hand instinctively flying to her belly. The half-Creek man stared for a moment before smiling sadly. "I won't disturb you no more, but I can only buy you the day. Once the raid is over, flee far from here. Don't let your roots grow in bloody soil."

He swiped a dark bottle from the table and went to the door. When he opened it, he slouched and sloppily closed it, calling, "This place is lousy with tonic—just needed a taste to be sure. Leave it alone, and I'll come back later to find y'all some real medicine."

"Damn drunks," a raider laughed. "C'mon, we got more work to do, and leave some for us."

The raiders continued jeering, and Lucinda listened for them riding off, curling up on the floor and pressing her forehead into the wood. She rocked back and forth, praying in gratitude as the hoofbeats diminished into the distance. Only the wind through the corn sounded outside.

William saw the smoke before the stagecoach made it to Lawrence. Coming to a stop near the border, the passengers got out, giving William an aghast look before sprinting off into the burned city. It took him a second to wrap his mind around the devastation—Lucinda!

Wheeling the coach around, he drove the horses hard to reach his house. Once he neared the cornfield, he pulled them to a stop. Leaving them in the middle of the road, he jumped from the driving box and hurtled through the field toward his home. "Lucinda!"

Night covered his house. With no fire lit, it stood cold and dead. His heart pounded as panic took hold, and he practically jumped up the steps. Tearing the door open, William scrambled around the room, stopping when he spotted Lucinda's form curled up in the corner. He roused her, and she looked around in a daze.

"You alright? You hurt?" he said, squeezing her to his chest. "I thought you was dead, 'Cin. What happened?"

"They came to kill all the men," she said, exhausted, "and they did. Two hundred people dead in the city. All the shops burned down."

William couldn't understand how she escaped, even as a woman. God must've had a hand in shielding their farm. Bowing his head, he prayed in gratitude over Lucinda and held her close. He didn't know she was crying until he felt a spreading warmth on his shirt. Her gentle sobs felt like sighs. She hid these parts, even from him, even now. He stroked her hair.

"I thought you was dead, too," she said in broken words between jagged breaths. "If you was home, they'd've killed you like everyone else. Black or white. Didn't matter. The war's reachin' over here, too. It's like some disease you cain't fight. A sickness takin' people over. It feels like a matter of time befo' it takes us."

"You're safe here, 'Cin," he whispered to her. "That was mighty scary for both of us, but you safe now. I'm here."

She let out a strangled cry and buried herself closer, and in return, he squeezed her tightly. "Don't matter what happens. Diseases, war, raiders, I'm always gonna love you, 'Cin. I'm gonna fight so you never gotta feel this way again."

William cleaned up the house while Lucinda rested. He put everything back where it needed to go and swept out the debris. He noted a missing rum bottle he was saving for a celebration but counted himself lucky it was the only thing gone. He went back to find the stagecoach in the same place. He cleaned up the horses and placed them in the cornfield, leaving the coach where it was.

With the place settled as well as he could, they bedded down for the night. William slept fitfully, waking up every hour or so to pace and listen for any signs of a return. Lucinda mentioned they had a day, at least, but he trusted his senses.

Come dawn, the two used the stagecoach and went to check on their neighbors, finding the same story from the survivors' mouths or written in bloody script on the burned ground. Men lay dead or dying in their homes or businesses destroyed by the raiders. With no soldiers to protect Lawrence, the place was an easy mark. They must've received word that the 1st Kansas was off fighting in Arkansas.

William met with other church members in the town to begin cleanup, led by the surviving clergy. It took days to rescue all the survivors. He checked on the local Black church to ensure the pastor was alive. Johnnie Little, William's pastor, stood before the ashes of his church, praying earnestly. Together, they worked to build a list of the congregation members so they could verify who was still alive.

It took another month to revive the congregation, at least for everyone left. They conducted church outside, like in William's youth. He arranged logs like the wooden pews Ole Ben preached near, carrying the way forward. Through the despair, William reminded the members that a church wasn't a building; it was the people inside.

Lucinda helped with the recovery efforts, but a thought nagged at her throughout: don't let your roots grow in bloody soil.

"Well, where in this world ain't the soil bloody?" she said softly to herself, rubbing her swelling stomach.

After rebuilding the church and convening the Lawrence survivors, Pastor Johnnie Little suggested that the couple be married. It didn't sit right with the holy man to watch the couple's family grow without a blessing from the church. As August's raid faded into memory, William latched onto the support this would bring. "Y'all can come with me to Leavenworth as a wedding gift," Pastor Little said. "I'll marry you in my house since it still stands, and after, we can go gather supplies and food. The trip with all that fresh air will do you some good, and I know everyone here will appreciate the stock."

William thanked him and shared the news with Lucinda that night. She stirred their soup pot, almost bursting with the baby as her belly sat low in the dress.

"How awful kind," she said flatly. "You mean to tell me the good pastor will allow us to run a big ol' chore to the next town for the low trade of marryin' us? Why you even wanna get married, William? What's gon' change?"

"We could die tomorrow," William said. He'd paid attention to Lucinda's souring mood through the rebuilding efforts. She had never really approved of the church, but he thought the recovery efforts would change that. "I want to make sure everyone knows we belong together. The church members, the community, God, everybody."

"Why does it matter besides what's between you and me?"

"It just does."

"No, you didn't even think about no marriage until this pastor brought it up. Is you Christian?"

"I don't know. I think so. Got baptized."

"Mmm," she hummed out. William knew what that sound meant. *"Sounds stupid, but I'm not gonna say anything."*

"Why you gotta fight this? It'll help us belong to this place. We all gotta lean on each other if we gonna make it."

"What if I don't wanna lean on these folks? Everyone I knew died in that raid. I don't even know if I wanna be here in Lawrence anymore. Now you come in spoutin' marriage talk? 'Specially from that man. I see how he took this 'shepherd' role real quick. Everybody joined his church now, and everybody listenin' to him like he God himself. I don't trust him."

William understood where she was coming from, but he knew the dangers of going outside the community. Lucinda and her family fended for themselves for a while, more so after Coweta was destroyed, but William saw what happened to people if they ran across the folks in charge.

"The church here is helpin' folks. If we get married, it'll give those people hope that somethin' good's comin' in the future. And I wanna celebrate you, 'Cinda. Give me a happy day to carry forward."

She stopped stirring and moved closer, taking his hand and kissing his cheek. "I'll do it for you, Will. You a good man and deserve to have that happy day."

The lead-up to their wedding was a flurry of happy activity. The church members flocked around the couple, alternating between cooing at Lucinda's belly and patting William on the back for making the right decision. The young man felt buoyed by the flood of support, which carried him through their trip to Leavenworth to retrieve emergency supplies. They discussed the wedding along the way, the folks buzzing with good-natured humor.

When the day came, Pastor Little introduced William to another colored minister named Jesse Simpson, who'd be presiding over the ceremony. He shook William's hand and presented him with fine clothes to wear for the day. In the flurry, the young man found himself at the altar in a house decorated with flowers. Pastor Simpson set up an altar and everything, so much so that William felt like he was in a church and not someone's home.

Lucinda walked in, holding a fresh-cut bouquet of wildflowers. The church women must've fussed over her something fierce because she looked like one of the beauties from Memphis he had seen long ago. She wore a fashionable bell skirt and a tighter corset that stretched over her belly. The sight took his breath away.

She walked slowly, joining him at the altar. As the pastor started the ceremony, he leaned in and whispered, "Ain't never seen you look more beautiful." Smiling, Lucinda took his hand, and the couple stood against a large blue wall.

"It is especially sweet to marry this young couple today. We so sorely needed somethin' after the events of earlier this year. Joining marriage and motherhood is holy in the eyes of God. Surely, the good Lord will smile on you both for all the days of your lives."

After the wedding script, Pastor Simpson handed them rings. When he gave one to Lucinda, she hesitated, then reached into her sleeve. With steady hands, she tied a beaded bracelet around her husband's wrist, the blue and white threads of the Wind Clan stark against his skin. The preacher stiffened. "What's this now?"

Her voice was sweet, edged with steel. "A family tradition. Surely God won't mind."

William nodded, and the preacher continued. They jumped the broom. Once married, the newlyweds dined at a grand feast, stuffing themselves with the good food cooked that evening.

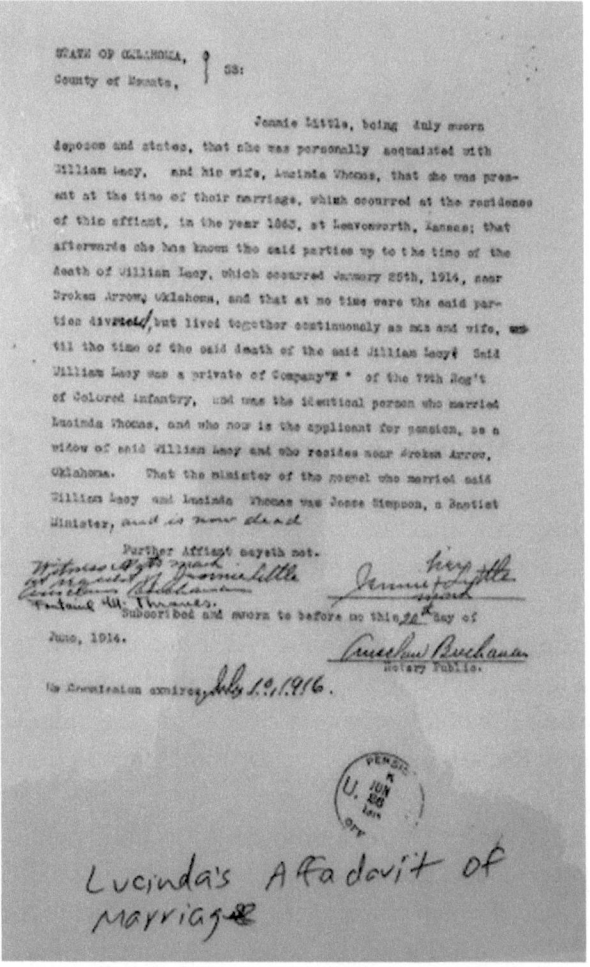

Figure 18 – 1: Lucinda and William Lacy's affidavit of marriage (used later as evidence)

CHAPTER 19

The Kansas Militia

Mound City, Kansas—Fall 1864

November marched back around in 1863, and the young newlyweds reached their first month of marriage. Married bliss sat well with William, who allowed the good-natured congratulations to boost his mood. As a good Christian husband, the young man tethered to the support of the Lawrence community, even knowing it would come to a close soon. Lucinda, who'd been just as happy declaring public love for him, felt much more distant in her joy.

Outwardly, the contentment showed, especially in public. However, when they were alone, she withdrew more, sharing less of her thoughts with him, even through her growing pregnancy. Facing the struggles together, William considered this union a blessing that Lucinda would adjust to once the ever-present emergencies were dealt with.

As fears circled their household, he clung to those fleeting bubbles of support with the Lawrence church-goers. He couldn't read or write, and neither could Lucinda. Even though the reprieve of rebuilding and sharing floated the couple, it would soon stop, and they would resume the search for work, but now, William had to shoulder the brunt of it as Lucinda would be caring for their child.

His bad knee ached again, worn out from moving all day. He was afforded some sitting time with the stagecoach, but restoring a razed city took legwork. As Lawrence grew again from the sweat on his back, the young man became increasingly more aware of the dwindling access to emergency supplies. Soon, the town would be back on its feet and returning to how things used to be—possibly with fewer jobs.

The city and state politicians continued to drag their feet on resource distribution, and what trickled down to Lawrence was still a pittance compared to the war effort. As it raged across the states, events like the raid on Lawrence were addressed, but not fast enough. It crippled the area, with Quindaro reeling at the sudden loss of its major sister city. The growing reality was that even though the people had survived, two hundred men were killed in the raid, and now, there was no more money in Lawrence.

Rubbing his knee, William stood up from the last grave. It took months to properly bury and give ceremonial rites to the discovered bodies, and he'd made sure they were all honored. These were men he saw daily, talked with on the street, bought their bread, and shared their fight for a good life. He owed this much to them.

With this done, no more church members could give him extra supplies. Pastor Little had his congregation set up, and they also ran dry with their newlywed gifts to him and Lucinda. Everyone in Lawrence moved toward "business as usual," which he found out, walking through the streets, meant he was back to contraband status. In their eyes, the young man was friendly but, ultimately, not useful anymore.

Mr. Robinson had fled Lawrence at the first sign of smoke and returned to find half of his business burned to the ground. When William appeared again, showing that he survived the raid, Robinson had to break the news that he was closing up shop. Keeping the business going wasn't worth it, which meant fewer workers to run the coaches. William fought not to explode at this conversation—this man, who'd sold him land and given him a shot, now offhandedly reduced him to beggar status. All these people in Lawrence turned their backs on William when he desperately needed the work.

It was the same story in Quindaro.

Without a steady flow between the two cities, even his friendly relationships there were strained. Businesses dried up, closing ranks to protect their interests, leaving William and Lucinda, close to bursting with the baby, in the cold.

He approached her, practically shaking after another business in Quindaro turned him down. The travel between the cities had taken its toll, and he sank into a chair at home. Waddling when she walked, Lucinda, now so swollen, brought a plate with freshly baked bread and cheese and set it down.

"This is too much, 'Cinda. You eat this. I had a few apples on the way back from Quindaro," he said, pushing the plate toward her.

She sat down, tearing half the bread off his plate before pushing it back. "You the one walkin' so eat up. I'm just here in the house all day."

William chewed on the bread, anger diffusing into despondency. He covered his face with a hand, fingernails still gritty with grave dirt, and stifled a frustrated sob.

"Will, ain't ya done with this yet? We don't belong here. I knew it the moment you returned after the raid. This place ain't for us. But ..." she said, reaching over and putting a hand on his, "... was important for you. I saw how happy it made ya to get that church weddin' and rebuild with all them people. Some parts were nice, I'll admit. But they ain't like us, Will. We ain't got kin ties to this land. They was happy enough to partner when we all had to come together, but now they on their feet again."

William shook his head. "Robinson's line got me the first job where we got paid regular for hard work. You had your schoolhouse. We got Sundays together and even a house here off o' Mr. Robinson's kindness. It don't make no sense that it all dried up now."

"Makes perfect sense," Lucinda said. "Ain't everybody around to help out when times get tough. They all pull back to they families and think about themselves first. Just how things is. Sorry you had to find out about it now."

He shook his head. "They'll come 'round. I'll ask again tomorrow."

"Will, ain't ya tired? Stop pretendin' you a Lawrence man. Maybe it would've been real if we had come here first and had more time to build up family. But we didn't. We outsiders. They gon' clan up just as fast. So we'd better do the same."

"Clan up?

"Yep, go to where people know us."

"We cain't head back to Arkansas."

"No, but we can get back to Mound City. We got close folks there, steadier places to earn work, and that fine house we left."

William scratched his chin while he thought. "I guess if we goin', we goin' now. No sense waitin' with the baby almost here."

Thankfully, Mr. Robinson did a final kindness and let the couple borrow a horse to carry Lucinda. She rode on the animal while William walked, traveling down through the state back to their old home. They left without a single goodbye to the people of Lawrence. Lucinda rode a little straighter once they lost sight of the city, but William couldn't help but feel a sharp pang of regret. For all the frustration of the last few days, those sunlit rides with Lucinda between Lawrence and Quindaro were his happiest memories.

The ride was quiet, with William keeping a close watch on the road and Lucinda holding herself still on horseback, riding sidesaddle to find some comfort on the journey.

Mound City was still there, as was their home. The emptiness was still there, too, without the 1st Kansas Colored Volunteers nearby at Fort Scott. They were still in Arkansas, fighting for the Union, so it continued to be a dead end. The one lucky stroke was finding their old place still intact, even with the garden—overgrown but lively. The six months away felt like a bittersweet dream.

With William's help, Lucinda hopped from the horse and waddled over to their house, checking on the plants outside. She made a mental list of things to do while William checked the house, ensuring there were no unpleasant surprises. The couple settled back in, thankful to be someplace else, with people they knew nearby. William also made a list of things to do, one being to return the horse. The other was a way to make sure they wouldn't have to go through this again. Lawrence left an impression on him about what it means to find a community.

New Year's was a quiet affair. The couple marked a safe few weeks of concentration with their garden, cleaning up their house, and reestablishing friendly connections. Elizabeth, an old friend, brought along more people to visit them and welcome them back to the town. Through the unseasonably warm weather, Lucinda found comfort in bringing their garden back to life, a sure source of food and security for them both. With January being so mild, they leaped at the chance to start planting.

The couple donned charitable clothing from the church members nearby. Lucinda wore a new floral print dress with two-toned shoes. She was grateful for the garments but continued to carry her old tools from Coweta and wrapped her head to keep the sun off. She saw the folks coming by from outside and touched William's arm to let him know.

"Welcome back, you two," Elizabeth said warmly, leaning against the low fence around the house. "Came by to say hi and introduce y'all to someone."

"Hi there, Lucinda, my name's Carolyn. I'm the midwife here at Mound City," said a plump, tidy woman who stepped forward and placed a hand on the gate. "Mind if I step in? I'd like to take a look at ya."

William helped Lucinda to her feet, the wind stirring her floral dress. He went to open the gate and welcomed the church ladies in. "I'm William Lacy," he said, shaking Carolyn's hand. "This is my wife, Lucinda Lacy."

Lucinda beamed and walked a little closer, hand on the top of her heavy belly. "Pleased to have y'all here. Now, what's a midwife?"

Carolyn smiled. "I suppose you might've heard of midwives before, but they'd be called *pucase* where you're from. Or for you, William, you can just call me Granny."

"You're a root worker," he said, recognizing the terms.

"That too," Carolyn nodded. "But in any case, let's go inside and sit down. Lots to say and no sense standin' in the sun to say it."

William instantly had a warm affection for Carolyn and prepared the way for them all to take seats around their small table inside. Since the birthing time was close, Carolyn explained what they needed to know about it.

Any woman, even one as healthy and strong as Lucinda, would be at risk when birthing a child. The pain involved, plus the lack of proper medicine nearby, required the people to come together for the event. She, Elizabeth, a few more ladies from the church, and a doctor would be present to help. William needed to take the chief role of keeping Lucinda clean while in labor. Besides hemorrhaging and infections, a load of complications could happen before the baby was safely caught and brought into the world. Carolyn kept the information light so the couple could absorb the sudden vast amount of information at their doorstep.

As the hours passed, getting answers to questions they hadn't known they had to ask, the couple grew more nervous about the imminent birth. How could anyone endure such a terrible thing and survive with so much that could go wrong? Carolyn sensed their fears and put a hand on Lucinda's knee, shaking it gently.

"If I thought you couldn't do this, I'd have let you know by now. But both of you are young and strong. This shouldn't be more than a walk in the park for you, my dear. Keep a good head on, and you'll make it through with a happy baby soon enough. May I?" she indicated to her stomach. Lucinda nodded.

Placing her hands on her belly, Carolyn screwed up her face and squeezed gently. "Hmm, seems like you returned to Mound City just in time. I'd give you another week, maybe less, before it happens," she nodded. "I need to prepare, but I'll return soon. Don't you worry."

A week later, William stood outside his house, folding up the latest newspaper. Edward had come by, another welcome sight after leaving the Mound City area for so long, and delivered some news about the 1st Kansas. Neither of them gave up on supporting their fighting brethren.

"Just makes me proud to be a colored Jayhawker," Edward said, leaning against William's fence. "Them 1st Kansas boys already won a battle over at Island Mound in Missouri. Know it don't say it in the newspaper, but that makes 'em the first Black folks to fight in this war."

"Wish I was there," William said. He looked off to the east. "Them natives got the same treatment. Paper sayin' they even had white folk fightin' with 'em. Callin' it 'integrated' with Black officers. Captain Seaman and the others received a new name for the force: the 79th United States Colored Troops."

Edward laughed. "That's a mouthful. I'll still callin' 'em the 1st Kansas like everyone else in Mound City."

"They'll always be the 1st Kansas Colored Volunteers."

From behind the two, the midwife, Carolyn, hefted a large bag, sweat beading on her brow. William quickly set the newspaper down and hurried to help her. "Sorry 'bout that, ma'am. We just got to jawin' and didn't see you comin' up the road."

"Aw, don't you worry none," Carolyn said. She gratefully allowed William to take the bag. "My husband says he gotta put a bell on me since I'm so quiet around the house."

Edward laughed and waved. "I'll come back with the next edition, Will. Best of luck with everything."

William and Carolyn walked up into the Lacys' home, and he helped her get a cot set up in the corner. For the next few days, Carolyn stayed with the couple to be nearby when Lucinda went into labor. She brewed some medicinal teas, conversed with Lucinda, and used additions from her garden to provide some ease. They debated back and forth on proper herb usage. Lucinda struggled to sit up in the bed under her full moon-sized belly.

"You about ready to burst," Carolyn said as she brought her a steaming cup and helped her drink. "Should be any day now."

And in two more sunrises, that day came.

Carolyn instructed William to keep hot water nearby. As the midwife hovered nearby to assist the birth, Lucinda asked her to explain what she could do to help. They argued for the first bit before the pain gave way to shrieks. Scared, William sat nearby, alternating between following orders and standing over Lucinda helplessly. He saw her walk away with her head held high after being carried off and remembered her fearlessness as they fled Coweta. Now, above the determined, pain-stricken face of his wife, William didn't know he could love her even more deeply.

After hours of screaming and cursing, and with William's good hand now sore from her bone-crushing grip, the couple welcomed a healthy baby girl into the world.

"What a head of hair," Carolyn said as she cleaned and swaddled the baby. "Six pounds and you can take this bet. She's out right on time. What's her name?"

"Didn't think of one yet. We've been so busy gettin' the house set up," William admitted, a little shy. Lucinda nearly passed out from the strain, so he cleaned her up before getting water ready close by. "I have an idea, but I'd like Lucinda's okay."

Lucinda stirred after a long nap. Carolyn had already packed up and made her goodbyes, promising to check on them later. The baby girl was healthy, and with no complications, she was confident they could recover on their own. "Especially after all the fight she had in her over medicine," she had said. "That girl's sharp. She'll make an excellent mama, and you too, Papa."

Papa.

The word sank into William. He was a papa now.

"Will?" Lucinda said. She coughed and reached for the water.

"I'm here." He brought the infant over and helped her sit up. Together, they cradled the girl as she babbled softly. "'Cinda, I was thinkin' about back before we got to Arkansas when we was with the Lacys. There was an accident in the river, and it always stuck with me. Ms. Mary, Mas—Thomas Lacy's wife—well, they lost a child that day to the river. Ain't never found her again. When that happened, was like all the light got pulled out of 'em. We got settled in Van Buren, but everything was different.

"Feels like everything's different here now, too, but there's so much more light. So much more to live for now. I didn't think I could get any happier with you, 'Cinda. But this … You made me a papa. Rebecca was the name of that baby girl they lost. I want to name her Rebecca in honor of that."

Lucinda stared up at him before kissing their baby girl's face. "Rebecca it is, then. She bringin' so much light into our lives."

Throughout the spring of 1864, William, Lucinda, and Rebecca mixed well into the Mound City community. From friendly visits with Edward to talk over the newspaper to doting walks with Carolyn and other ladies to see the new baby, the young family conversed with both Black and white neighbors near the Montgomery farm.

With another mouth to feed, William worked extra hard, rising a little earlier and finishing way later, to bring their field back up to date. In between this, he'd go to town occasionally to do odd jobs and scrape more money for essentials. Sometimes, he'd finish morning work on his farm before heading to a neighbor's to work on theirs. People left to travel to Topeka or Kansas City and needed extra help to ensure their plants were well cared for. On other days, he'd help with harvests, moving loads of wheat, corn, or hay around, and making friends with the other farmers. No matter how much work he had, he'd always make it back home to join Lucinda and Rebecca for dinner.

Doing all this traveling and talking got him further acquainted with Mound City. After working in Lawrence for so long, slight peculiarities stood out when he stopped to think about them. While Mound City suffered its own problems during the war, it was no stranger to recession from lack of trade, and the townspeople showed fierce dedication to each other. After Quantrill's raid, Lawrence maintained that fevered community for a while, but here in Mound City, it thrived.

The place was full of abolitionists, and he saw a steady stream—still, to that day—of escaped slaves passing through toward freedom. It remained a persistent stop on the Underground Railroad, and two years earlier, the area had already supplied the 1st Kansas boys, even before they got complete legality in the eyes of the U.S. government.

Now, William and Edward read news of tens of thousands of Black soldiers organizing around the country. A special article discussed the foundation of a new bureau: the Freedman's Bureau, created specifically to manage the influx of colored men as soldiers in the United States Army. While the Confederacy, they reported, had won most of the major battles, the Battle of Gettysburg came as a critical loss.

The people of Mound City caught wind of the return of a home-grown hero. General James Montgomery, born in Ohio, had moved to Kansas in 1854 and purchased a large tract of land. William had taken a job there earlier and walked the land himself. He was just as excited as the townfolk, all buzzing for his return. He matched their enthusiasm to drive pro-slavery people out of Kansas and bring their state into the Union as a free state.

One neighbor, a man who hired William for odd jobs, gossiped about the general's return with other men. Most proudly stated their affiliation with the Self-Protective Company.

The name rang a bell for William, and he recalled that John Brown, the man hanged at Harper's Ferry, worked with the group and General Montgomery on occasion, frustrating those that would spread slavery west.

As his neighbor handed William his pay for the day, the man shook his head when talk turned to the failed rescue attempt for John Brown. "No reason to talk about that," he murmured. "It's been many years, and people still bring up that travesty. We should've been there for him."

William studied General Montgomery's farm on his way back home. He passed the prominent place, slipping between the cluster of small homes like his. The towering legend accomplished so much in his time. He'd most likely meet the man since he lived nearby.

The time finally came, but both William and Lucinda were told that the general was recovering from a respiratory illness, one reason for his return. A small contingent of soldiers escorted him to his house, and his staff leaped into action, but in all the excitement, there was no time for visitors. Instead, people gathered outside his home to show respect and discuss his accomplishments. Through this gathering, the couple learned more about how he led a battle against the U.S. Army in retaliation for executing five free men at Marais des Cygnes in Kansas.

The people mentioned his religious fervor. As an evangelical minister, his ideology hardened regarding slavery in his home state. This happened five years prior, and the men declared soon afterward that he had turned his sights on leading the 10th Kansas Regiment. Even as a minister, he was intimately involved in the sacking of Osceola, Missouri, during a cold September of 1863. The entire town was burned, killing over two thousand people and destroying businesses and homes. They stole horses, cattle, and flour, freeing over two hundred slaves in the process. Nine local men were tried and executed. Besides these memories, he'd led men in the Battle of Combahee Ferry and Olustee, Florida.

Lucinda shivered. "See, Will, war saves no one. Just like in Lawrence, our side is doin' it to theirs."

"There's a difference, 'Cinda," William replied. "They freein' people after all that."

"Still sounds like a zealot to me. Some of the other ladies agree at church."

"They say the U.S. Army authorized him to lead the Second South Carolina earlier this year," William said. "Edward mentioned seeing it in the paper. It was also a regiment of colored men like the 1st Kansas."

"I don't think we oughta talk about this now, Will," Lucinda said, giving him a look.

After the excitement, William threw himself into the small church of Mound City's regular routines. Sunday services had him, Lucinda, and Rebecca showing up. They all agreed it was a calm place in the storm of their lives.

Through these services, Lucinda reconnected with her old friends, explaining what happened after they left for Quindaro and the harrowing experiences in Lawrence. They each took turns holding baby Rebecca while she spoke.

William made fast friends again, and they were happy to see him with a healthy, growing family. Snoddy and the others fell back into an easy routine with the couple coming by their places for work or company.

The young man found himself seeking shelter in the church with these abolitionists. Despite all the hell breaking loose and the strangeness of the church members in Lawrence, the good people of Mound City shone with the light of God in them. William took to more Sunday services, staying after to talk about Bible stories he had never had the chance to learn more fully.

Ole Ben used to preach back in Lacy Springs, and the story of Moses always stood out to William. Moses led the Hebrews out of Egypt. The story of Daniel also made him want to know more about how he survived being thrown into the lion's den. Then, how David beat Goliath—all those years ago, when Ms. Mary read that story before the awful accident.

In all these stories, slaves were taught to obey their masters. It was how Ole Ben raised Henry and then William. But how could God look down on all this war, pain, and suffering and still infuse the holy word with teachings like those? Did he and Lucinda defy God by running away together?

These heavy thoughts spilled out amongst the safety of his friends in Mound City's small church. The pastor and other members encouraged his curiosity and were happy to satisfy it. Slavery was indeed a sin, and it was their right to emancipate themselves from the torment. No self-respecting Christian would enslave another person for their own gain, rob them of the fruit of their labor, and doom them to a life of ignorance and poverty.

William brought these encouraging words back home to Lucinda, who didn't attend church with him. She still carried her feelings from Coweta and her intense distrust of the folks worshipping the "white" savior. However, seeing William so uplifted by the community, she came with him once a month to break bread with their friends. Black, white, freed, and fugitive, the small group was special to have so many different people coming together to worship.

As the daughter of a Black slave woman and a Creek man in Indian Territory, Lucinda's family kept to the old ways. Her mother passed on her medicine bag and stories of the Breath Maker. She learned all the rituals to bring the rains back. Through this, Lucinda could recognize good people and knew the spirits wouldn't bring bad luck to her for supporting the church members.

One night, Lucinda shared with William the stories her mother passed on.

"The spirits exist in and around us, Will. If you holy enough, you can even speak to the dead," she said, cradling Rebecca as the baby softly slept.

"The dead? What you wanna talk to them for?"

"All kinds of things," Lucinda said. "But our other rituals didn't focus on them. I used to love the Busk Festival. We'd have a ceremony for four days, signaling the start of a new year and when the corn gets nice and ripe. This was a time for healing, gettin' right with the spirits, and forgivin' each other. Daddy never went, even though my momma told him he should. She was the one who gave me all these stories, even though she wasn't Creek like Daddy."

"These all important to you?"

"Of course they are. They make me who I am. All my best memories were from these festivals, too. Was the only time I got to see everyone all together."

William lay back in bed, thoughts swirling. *'Cinda found so much of herself in those stories. But what do I got? Pictures of the churchgoers, the people outside Montgomery's house, and his own family next to him flooded his mind. I got somethin' alright.*

Figure 19 – 1: General James Montgomery's tombstone, found in Mound City, Kansas

CHAPTER 20

Troubling the Waters

Mound City, Kansas—October 1864

An icy chill sliced through the fall air, brushing down through the men's collars outside the courthouse. The job seekers huddled together on the steps, grumbling about the same things, and this gave William a sense of comfort, something stable in the world. He smiled and joined the group, saying hello to familiar faces and shaking hands.

Edward brought the local newspaper, the Border Sentinel, by to discuss here instead of at the house, gathering more men to him as he read. One by one, smiles dropped from the men's faces. Edward's voice moved from incredulous to somber to angry.

"A pro-slaver named 'Blood Bill Anderson' and his guerrilla followers had overtaken a train in Centralia, Missouri. This train carried a load of Union soldiers on leave to see their families. Guerrilla troops, led by Anderson, including two men aged 16 and 17."

They're the same age I am, William thought.

"Frank and Jesse James," Edward continued reading, "aided Anderson in seizing the train by force before rounding up and executing the soldiers on board, even though they were all unarmed."

Aghast, William and the others shared their sad looks with Edward. When he finished, people muttered angrily, asking to see the article or having him reread certain parts for names. Some folks recognized their kin aboard that train or were worried others were in the area and might've gotten caught up in the attack. Edward all but had to shout to get them to quiet down again.

In all the hubbub, a politician exited the courthouse steps. The suited man produced a telegram sent over from Fort Scott. "Got some news may be of interest," he started, his sonorous voice carrying out and stilling the crowd. "Don't start a panic, but do take some precautions. A man named Sterling Price, who used to be the governor of Missouri, is now a general in the Confederate Army, and he's stormin' his way across Missouri. Looking at the way he's moving, folks in the town over thought they'd better warn us. He might be headin' westward, toward places in Kansas. Even us here in Mound City. He's probably aimin' at Kansas City, but we're in the way.

"He's burnin' homes and killin' folks who ain't pro-slavery on his path. Now, we all pride ourselves on our abolitionist roots here. So General Price will catch wind of this place quickly if he comes near. We'll stay near the telegram for more news, but I'd prepare yourselves and your families for somethin' to happen soon."

William's head spun, and someone—Edward, when his face swam into view—placed a steadying hand on his shoulder. "Will? Will, ya alright?"

His vision swam as a fierce anger rode up through the young man. What started as fear quickly burned into rage. Visions of soldiers riding out of Fort Smith years ago, shouldering rifles and ready to kill, popped into his head. Fresh in his memory was also the raid on Lawrence. Lucinda had barely survived, thank God. Those men on the train, Quindaro, and now Mound City?

Ever since he'd left Coweta with Lucinda, his life had been on the run. Someone was after him. He was looking over his shoulder constantly, in fear of getting beaten senseless like in Fort Smith. All he and Lucinda wanted was a safe place to raise their child.

The cruelty pressed into his head like a hot knife. Before, he hadn't known any better. But now … now, William tasted sunshine on a stagecoach. He held his baby girl in his arms. No, he wasn't a slave anymore. It didn't matter what people said. He was born free and would fight like hell to keep it. These Confederates were doing the same to keep them in chains. The war spilled out through the states, reaching even into sleepy places like these farms in Kansas.

It's never gonna end, he thought, staring back at Edward. "It's never gonna end. They gon' keep killin' and burnin' until we all dead."

Edward's mouth pulled back grimly. "They certainly gon' try."

Mound City sprawled out around them, and William looked at the men there. Each one was either an escaped slave or an abolitionist, but all had come there because there was enough to build a life. Even when times got hard, the people came together to help each other out because they—to the most recent newcomer—understood what it was like outside their community's safety.

"Well, they findin' themselves a fight if they come anywhere near Mound City," William said. Another man near him nodded. The thrill of camaraderie emboldened him.

"We not lettin' anyone take our lives and families away. 'Specially not these damn pro-slavers and they evil lies!" William shouted. The politician stepped back, turning toward the courthouse as the men outside riled up. They clustered around William and Edward.

"We gon' fight for everythin' we love here in Mound City. If we fight together, we win."

Edward and William rounded up the other able-bodied men to start training to defend their homes. Everyone knew the Kansas regiments were too far away to help, and the towns were left unprotected by the federal government's forces. General Price knew this, too.

Every Saturday and Sunday, the men met at the courthouse to train in warfare. Now seventeen, William was old enough to carry a rifle alongside his friends. When Edward first passed him one on the dirt training ground, he almost dropped it, surprised at how heavy it was. Even before defending Lucinda, the weapon carried weight beyond simple metal. Edward showed him how to load, fire, and care for it to be reliable in battle. The shots empowered him. Looking around at so many other men training, he felt a part of something, like what he did could make a real difference.

A few weeks later, Mr. Snoddy offered William his own hunting rifle for training and, eventually, in the battle to defend Mound City. He could carry it home with him and care for it himself. He tripped over his thanks, shaking his hand enthusiastically.

As another Saturday rolled around in October, the familiar training was interrupted by two men trotting up on horseback. One man was Mr. Snoddy, but William didn't recognize the other.

"Gentlemen," Mr. Snoddy said, his voice carrying over the group. "If we get called to defend our town, this man will be our commanding officer." He waved a hand at his companion. William's eyes widened when he realized who it was—General Montgomery, the legend in the flesh, had left his homestead.

"I'm General James Montgomery," the man said. His voice rang out in a sharp command, and everyone stopped what they were doing. "I was sent here by Governor Carney to help you organize and fight for Mound City, the state of Kansas, the U.S. Army, and your families. Now, let's train hard and hope we don't have to use any of this knowledge if the danger passes us by. Any questions?"

Shocked and speechless, all the rookie militiamen, William included, stayed silent. Most had heard of the man moving back into his farm nearby, but his recovery kept him behind the walls. Setting his illness aside, the man stepped forward again to help his hometown.

Throughout more training, William couldn't help but think more about his time at Fort Smith. Lines of soldiers passed by on horseback near the fort just a few years earlier before the U.S. Army split in two. The colored soldiers from Fort Scott, later on, also marched and practiced as they prepared for war. Now, here he was doing the same. Any time soon, it wouldn't merely be practice anymore. He'd be going into battle alongside these men if those vicious raiders came by. Now, he could stand directly in the path so that Mound City wouldn't look like Lawrence.

What would it be like to kill a man, though?

The question fell like a wrench into his brain. All the fire from earlier spurted out. Of course, keeping Lucinda and Rebecca safe and free was paramount, but bringing death to another person? Could he actually do it?

When he went home that evening, he dragged himself into the cabin and set the rifle down. As usual, Lucinda ignored the shiny metal, setting down dinner. The smell of corn stew hit him. Fresh herbs from the garden were now a regular occurrence, filling his home with spicy scents and making his mouth water.

As usual, Lucinda kept an icy distance from discussing his training. She'd accepted the news when he told her but seemed to pull farther away from him every day. That night, as he entered their home, she cast a sidelong glance at his rifle when he put it up. William kept it on the wall, hanging off hooks he installed himself. After he finished and had taken off the uniform coat, he sat down to dinner.

Lucinda had Rebecca in one hand as she served, and William quickly jumped back to his feet to help. "Lemme get that, 'Cin."

"I got it."

"No, you got dinner." William kept his voice low and gentle, and not just for Rebecca. "Let me serve it. Sit down and take it easy."

His wife turned a sidelong look at him before doing as he said. She stepped lightly to the table and set Rebecca down on a specially made spot.

"Thanks," he whispered, pouring their beans from the stew pot. A fierce anger rolled up his body when he set the bowls down, looking at his family. It wasn't fair that they had to make do with these dregs when some officers probably ate well, growing fat off the misery they stole from the poor citizens in their bloody wake. "I gotta confess somethin'. Feels like no matter what I do, war's gonna come and eat us all up. Me trainin' like I do to make sure I can defend us … It's got to you, too. We ain't talkin' no more."

Lucinda looked up at him. "You fightin' the white man's war, and it's never gonna stop. Sure, this time it's comin' up the line where we live, but the best thing to do is to move. That's what my people did until they got caught up in the nonsense. Now look what happened.

They all chewed up or dead. I know you gotta do somethin', Will, but you can't ask me just to watch it happen or be happy about it."

"What else we s'posed to do? Let 'em come kill us all in our homes?"

She sighed and rubbed her forehead. "I don't got the answers tonight. Let's just eat."

The next day, William took Rebecca to church. Maybe they'd have the answers if he met with older folks who had survived much longer. God had to give someone the answers to how to live in troubled times.

After confessing, William sought guidance from the pastor, asking God to bring him strength and pledging his life to Jesus Christ. The pastor led the service, welcoming him to the fold as a disciple of Christ. Through it all, William poured out all his fears. He didn't want to kill someone, even if they were attacking Mound City, without protecting his soul first.

The baptism in Lacy Springs held on like a cobweb in his memory, but he was mostly ashamed of his behavior. As a child, he had no idea what the presence of Christ, the Redeemer, would symbolize amongst the people here. He wanted to make it right. It had to mean something to God if he chose on his own accord.

Lucinda was almost forced to do the same thing he did that day in the Tennessee River. Much more than a forced washing, William recognized now that something much worse might've happened to her back then if he hadn't intervened. Now, as runaway slaves, they had grown up and could make better decisions. William needed to feel like he was part of something, and with how good the people of Mound City were, the church seemed like the best place to join more fully. Even Lucinda had made friends with the kind folks attending church, working for them, and becoming a staple in the ladies' group. At this point, they'd all need to stick together. Surely, she could see that it would be something else to talk about instead of just the training.

On a cool October morning in 1864, a knock came at the Lacys' cabin. William opened the door to a blast of morning air, along with his immediate neighbors and Edward, standing on his porch.

Sleepily, he wiped at his eyes. "Morning," he said, a thrill catching up to his groggy brain. "Wait, why are y'all here?"

"We need you to get to the courthouse," stated one man.

"First, get your next neighbor. We're splittin' up now to find more men," Edward added.

The group stirred on his porch, some armed already. The hairs on William's neck stood on end. This wasn't the first knock to ask for a courthouse meeting over the last few weeks they'd all been training. The way everyone behaved now, though, got adrenaline shooting through William. He said his goodbyes before the men left his property, walking quickly to the next one. He passed his rifle, but before grabbing it, he swung by the bed where Lucinda and Rebecca slept peacefully. He kissed his wife on the cheek, stirring her.

"Will? What's goin' on? You up early," she said. Her hand came up to stifle a yawn.

"Neighbors came up to get me. We meetin' at the courthouse."

"Now?" Lucinda sat up in bed, her arm cradling the sleeping Rebecca to her chest. "Why?"

"Cain't say. I'll be back later." *I hope.* He kept the last part to himself.

"Will? Will?!"

Ignoring her, William grabbed the rifle from its resting spot and checked for ammunition in his carrying bag. In the doorway, he turned back to catch a glimpse of Lucinda, now rocking Rebecca, crying and awake. The moment slowed as he took a mental picture of his wife and child, promising himself to do whatever was needed to protect them.

In the cold morning air, William trudged directly to his neighbor's place to check on them. Gathering speed like a storm, the growing group of folks in the farm community, led by William, made it to the courthouse. Hours passed as more gathered there, more men he'd trained with, now recognizable faces, as a sizzling charge entered the air. Everyone was on edge.

By midday, all the young men in town, Black and white, from Mound City and the surrounding communities from Linn County, Kansas, milled about the courthouse steps, awaiting instruction.

As the sun started to sink, General James Montgomery and Captain Snoddy rode up on horseback, complete in military uniform, stopping their horses in front of the crowd. From their training, everyone grew silent, giving their attention to the leaders. Snoddy raised his hands to direct attention, and even William held his breath.

"Good people of Mound City, the Confederate General 'Pap' Price has turned west from St. Louis. From what we can see, he's now heading toward Kansas to burn down Kansas City and Leavenworth. Pap won't spare any person—woman or child, colored or white—when he comes through the state. He's already burned most of the eastern part of Missouri, targeting any town even rumored to have abolitionist sympathies. He's out for blood.

"This man's already racked up ten million dollars in property damages in his own state, attacking Fort Davidson in Iron County and fighting several battles with General William Rosecrans across Missouri. We know Pap's goal is to disrupt the election coming soon in November. He wants us frightened. He wants us staying home instead of voting. If he can prevent us—by killing us or through terror—he'll do it."

William remembered Edward explaining the election and government news from the newspaper a few days earlier. Edward remarked on similar tidings, saying that the incumbent President Lincoln was prosecuting the war and trying to keep the nation together. This cemented other info, too, like how Southerners wanted General George McClellan to run against him. He'd been fired for lacking aggressiveness as a soldier. With all this going on, the election was in a crisis, with little confidence from any side. Edward shook his head, ending their meeting with more rumors that other countries might be coming in, like France or England, to join forces with the Confederacy.

However, Lincoln was popular, and despite all this mounting evidence, the current president held the people's hearts, spanning across soldiers, abolitionists, and most Northerners. He'd need every available and eligible man to vote to keep the nation together. Pap Price knew this, and so did Snoddy.

"We're having our first national election for the presidency in Kansas. Pap knows this, and he's trying to scare as many men as he can from Missouri and Kansas out, away from their homes and courthouses to benefit the Confederacy."

Pulling a crumpled piece of paper from his pocket, Snoddy cleared his throat and read it out loud to the crowd. William was thankful to Edward and Snoddy for interpreting these things for men like him who couldn't read. His voice rang out, delivering Governor Carney's directive. The order was General Order #1, calling all eligible men in Kansas to report for militia service. It further detailed the massacre in Lawrence as support for his decision.

William settled back, letting the orders wash over him. The governor himself realized the importance of involving *all* men, not just whites. He was part of the call. This was it—the call to war.

A militia was formed immediately to protect their homes. The men around him were organized into six companies, preparing for the next battle.

That October passed in a rush. William had never been around so many people and was reminded of his time at both forts. However, living in a swiftly forming militia was a far cry from the more organized movements of the military establishments.

Getting more news from Edward, he learned that all around them, over twelve thousand men had rallied to the meeting places with their arms and ammunition, following the call to arms by Governor Carney. Major General Dietzler stepped up to lead the Kansas Militia. William became swiftly embroiled in the politics, thanking God he'd made peace before doing so. Even with the threat of violence, dizzying political struggles took place around the colored forces.

Original militia law did not include colored men like him. The writing called for "able-bodied white men between 18 and 45 years old." This critical line spat in the face of all the abolitionists in the free state of Kansas. They made it clear, with all that was happening, how could colored men be considered equal in a free state while simultaneously being prevented from fighting for it?

Edward brought a copy of the Leavenworth Evening Bulletin, which called the law an "unwise act." It further stated, "Here is a class of men—good, tried, and true—who we could use to a great advantage, but we are deprived of their aid and assistance in the defense of our state." Nearby, the town's mayor, close to Fort Scott, openly called upon his citizenry, "without regard to color," to organize units to defend their homes against guerrilla attacks. Not three weeks later, when Leavenworth was placed under military guard, its colored men were brought in and organized into fighting companies, asking them to report for duty. Men poured in from Quindaro as well.

William watched all of this, a storm gathering above his head. Just like the other colored and white men, he'd trained hard to defend his home. However, the hovering age of eighteen disqualified him from joining the militia, regardless of skin color. He'd already had a hard time joining because he wasn't white, but his age was another matter entirely. Despite this, he showed up to sign up anyway, a fire burning in his chest. It was lit that day on the courthouse, and it'd burn him up alive if he didn't follow it.

It didn't matter if they'd placed some official garbage on his name. William Lacy would become the protector of his family. He knew that was what he was born for.

This fire burned up any fear of death or nervousness around lying. He'd strike a blow for freedom throughout the nation, even back in Fort Smith, where Henry, Eliza, and the others were still enslaved. He'd do something to help them, too.

Thinking about them brought him back to Lacy Springs. They didn't even experience the travels through Memphis and Little Rock like he and Henry did. They were still stuck in that old world where only the masters mattered, and nothing changed. What possible future would they have if no one stood up? If no one remembered they were there ...

William would.

He'd fight for Lucinda and Rebecca. Fight for Henry and Eliza and all the people he remembered back at Lacy Springs—all the people forgotten, buried by bloody history and cruel masters.

If he had to be eighteen, that's what the officers would know. The years of surviving, hard work, and fatherhood put muscle and confidence in William, so when he marched up to the courthouse, nobody questioned him in the lines forming. The men at the courthouse put him with the other colored men who were enlisting in the fight. William joined the others he trained with, glancing at Edward and his neighbors.

When it was finally his turn, there was little pushback. He simply signed an "X" on the official documents. William Lacy was now in the Kansas Militia.

As the intensity of his deception settled down, more anxieties came on. He was a soldier now, and the identity was ill-fitting with the freedom fighter and man of God. In such a short period, he overheard other soldiers talking about how they'd be separated from the white soldiers, often to be used in direct battles as prime targets. The Confederates were even more aggressive with colored soldiers, seeing them as a direct threat.

Thinking back to Quantrill's raid on Lawrence, he remembered their violent assault as they burned down people's livelihoods, scattering the broken bodies of men to the wind. They targeted colored men and white men, anybody who'd stand up in a fight. He knew from the rumors that those raiders had joined up with Pap Price. It was a battle primed for revenge, but it only made William sick.

Sorting through all this news was troubling, even with folks like Edward reading to him so they could share the burden. Often, he'd take the farming information and other good news to the ladies' group at church to spread some cheer, having them read these to him before they prayed for guidance. This was also to double-check if some information was real, as some men at the courthouse could spread nasty rumors to get people riled up.

One day, a lady came across some troubling news, even in the gentler newspapers. She read to William about a massacre in the Leavenworth Evening Bulletin. William quickly thanked her and took the paper away, leaving to find Edward in town. After the two got together, Edward dispensed the information more fully.

Pap Price's twelve thousand cavalrymen had turned away from burning and sacking St. Louis, now moving westward toward Kansas City. At a rapid pace, the raiders moved across Missouri. In smaller towns, the Confederate general would notify the townspeople of his army's presence and ask for conscripts and volunteers to grow his force, threatening anyone who would disobey.

William's blood boiled when Edward confirmed the following lines:

> *Bloody Bill Anderson and Frank and Jesse James had joined forces with Pap Price. The group reached Lexington on October 14th, and one of his men, Captain George Rathburn, had already issued a General Order showing Lexington's mayor had surrendered the town to the Confederate government. The rights of non-combatants and private property must be respected. All white males between seventeen and fifty were ordered to report themselves to the headquarters at the courthouse, and the Confederate soldiers would repossess any public property belonging to federal government officials.*
>
> *If anyone attempted to resist, and if any shots were fired from the houses at Confederate soldiers, those homes would be burned down. Proper vouchers would be issued for all property taken for public use in the Quartermaster's department. Pap Price gave this same treatment to most towns between St. Louis and Kansas City.*

Meanwhile, General Curtis, in charge of the Kansas Militia Cavalry, was camped at Charlot in Kansas City. Seizing the opportunity, he sent General Blunt and his volunteer cavalry east toward Warrensburg and Lexington. A spy in Pap's camp reported that Price now had a force of over 20,000 men, augmented daily by his forced conscriptions along his route. The spy also shared that Pap Price intended to move to Kansas City after Lexington by following the river. After he conquered Kansas City, the man was hellbent on pushing far into Kansas, Indian Territory, and Arkansas.

Lexington's citizens had already seen combat in the Battle of Hemp Bales years earlier. In 1861, the rebels, with Pap Price at the helm, grabbed victory by drawing federal troops out of the courthouse and tightening bales in a circle. They'd previously soaked them in water to avoid fire. Ultimately, the federal troops surrendered. After that, Frank James had been captured and forced to swear an oath to the Union by federal troops. This time, however, the outcome was different.

In response to this news, Kansas City was placed under martial law, rigidly enforced by the military. All available men were put to work, constructing long entrenchment lines across the east and south borders, creating a formidable obstacle for the rebel army. Officers also ordered men to get to the front.

William leaned in closer as Edward put the paper down. "Ralph was there, William. He sent me a letter after the battle."

"What did it say?"

"He said Captain R.J. Hinton, his commanding officer, was placed in charge of his group of colored men. This meant everybody from the Leavenworth Battalion, thirty parrot guns under colored Lieutenant Minor, two companies from Wyandotte, and another from Shawnee. Some troops were attached to other brigades, but all were ordered to the front.

"Ralph said he could see Pap and his boys comin' up near Lexington before the first shot got fired. But General Curtis was surprised when Ralph's folks, the 1st Regiment Kansas State Militia, refused to cross the state line. They said they all needed to defend Kansas and not move into Missouri. The military men got mad at that, sayin' that's the problem with militias. They called them 'unorganized' and 'they didn't know who to report to' and didn't have good equipment.

"The Leavenworth battery deserted, and others moved back to Wyandotte. While General Blunt prepared to engage at Lexington, he had his 2nd brigade withdraw. By the time this happened, Pap Price's folks across the way also set in. They engaged lightly with parrot guns and howitzers. Price's men advanced slowly, leaning on their strength in numbers and relative advantages.

"But then the trap sprang shut.

"General Blunt's slow retreat was purposeful. He fell back to test his enemy's strength. The command was given to withdraw. At the same time, Colonel Moonlight's 11th Cavalry covered the withdrawal, and the retreating fight was maintained for over six miles. Blunt planned to test the enemy's forces the whole time, and that'd been done. Now armed with more information and safely away, they counted their minimal losses and set up again. General Curtis could now disseminate reliable information to the militias, reuniting them in harmony and the spirit of action. They just needed to wait for the enemy to reappear."

CHAPTER 21

The Battle of Westport

On the Missouri Roads—October 1864

At seventeen, William Lacy rode out with the militiamen, a group filled with Black and white, angry Kansas residents prepared to defend their homes. Mr. Robinson loaned him a horse to ease his travels, and Snoddy's rifle bounced gently against the saddle. Surrounding him, the others in the militia were the colored members, and the white volunteers rode a short distance behind them. Even though they rode in two groups, they each wore determined looks—all ready to deliver swift justice to Pap Price.

Four days passed before they reached Hickman's Mill, where the 6th Kansas State Militia reported for duty. No board was ready when they arrived, so the groups had to break camp. It reminded William of traveling with the Lacys to Arkansas. This time, trained men, led by officers, organized their encampment, setting up better resting conditions near sheds and fences around the mill.

General Samuel Curtis, General George Deitzler, and General Blunt joined forces to outline plans for this ragtag army arriving from Kansas. William tracked their movements, trying to maintain some semblance of order when the camp inevitably devolved into chaos. The command structure wobbled when colored troops were involved.

He was thankful for Edward and Ralph's forewarning. Integrating a militia with a regular army took finesse.

Ultimately, Colonel Charles Blair, a tough but respected officer, was assigned to lead the newly arrived militia units, including William's brigade. William and the other men from Mound City leaped to attention when he came by to introduce himself and give them orders.

Unfortunately, the tenuous calm broke when another officer got into a screaming match with the Colonel. Brigadier General William Fishback, another member of the Kansas Militia, grew frustrated with the arrangements, feeling like the militiamen were deliberately kept out of the regular army for a reason. If they weren't treated like regulars, why did they have to follow their commands like regulars? He made this known to the Colonel, saying they should only follow militia officers.

William overheard these shouts, discussing them with Edward, but the growing consensus in the camp was to stay put for more orders. So, on October 15th, those orders came by. William and the others packed up and broke camp, heading back to protect their state. Fishback and Snoddy led the militiamen, and Snoddy muttered about how the men from Mound City needed to return to prepare for Pap's men to arrive. He continued when the men asked why they were leaving, simply stating that they were unprepared for the rigors of army life. William noticed neither Snoddy nor Fishback sent word to General Blunt or Colonel Blair that they were pulling out.

As they headed home, William grew more confused about the long ride to Missouri, only to turn around and hike back. If they had to expend all this energy and fight against so many fears, what was it all for? Why were the leaders acting like this? He'd been ready, for whatever it cost him, to kill another man. Kill a white man. He could still picture himself in the barn, freshly bleeding from Buck's kick, when Henry explained his place. If he couldn't even talk back to a white man, killing one was surely a grave sin.

On the way, he shared these thoughts with Edward and the others. How were they supposed to be ready to kill white men? What would the others say? Sure, the men from Mound City were abolitionists, but still whites. How would they react, and how could they trust them not to turn on them when the war was over? Would they become afraid of their colored neighbors once violence took place? The people of Mound City took in runaway slaves and stood their ground against pro-slavery aggressors, but this militia would put that to the test. Some others shared his fears, but Edward put them to rest, leaning on their years of friendship and goodwill and pointing out they were willing to die alongside them for the cause.

Chasing after them, General Blunt caught up to the traveling militia, along with the 15th Cavalry. He galloped up, passing the troops with a set, angry face and immediately laying into Snoddy and Fishback. William couldn't hear every word, but it sounded like he was ordering them back to Hickman Mills. As General Blunt yelled it back over the men, he heard clearly: "Thousands of rebel soldiers are on their way toward them, and I need all you men from Mound City and Linn County to stay and fight for Missouri. I know every man in Linn County will want to do his duty when the time comes … and men, it's here."

Shaken, the men of the 6th Kansas State Militia milled about until, again, they were ordered to head back to Hickman Mills. William rode toward the front, so he turned back around. He had to yell what was happening as they passed people out of earshot toward the back. He shook his head. There was more organization in the devastation of Lawrence from beleaguered survivors.

A man called out, "What's goin' on? Why we turning' back?" Another added that they'd whip them right there in Missouri. Everyone roared in approval, including William, feeling the thrill of belonging to this group of fighting men. Everyone was itching to put their training to the test and tired of the endless walking to nowhere. Tired of the confusion. Still, the disorganization itched at William.

As they arrived at Hickman Mills, William was stunned to see a group of soldiers place Colonel Snoddy under arrest. Resisting a little, the man was cuffed and taken away. The group said he disobeyed orders by leading the militiamen away from the military encampment. A chill went down William's spine when he saw his old friend get carted away by these people he was told to trust. It was Snoddy's rifle he carried with him at that very moment, and that man first told him about the militia's efforts back in Mound City. Snoddy offered a saving hand when he and Lucinda first arrived in town. Now? He had to watch him get hauled off, helpless. He had to do something.

Discussing this with his comrades from Mound City, they left it to the military officers to weigh judgment. Snoddy did nothing wrong but try to help his city. Surely, they'd see the justification of his actions. He tried to talk with him, but two guards were always present, preventing anyone from getting too close. William grew frustrated but had to relent, or he'd get arrested, too. He shared a sad smile with Snoddy, who nodded at him in appreciation.

About an hour after this happened, William's camp received word they'd brought a new leader for the men from Linn County: General James Montgomery. General Blunt and Colonel Blair were both pleased that the legend accepted his command of the 6th Kansas because he'd already led colored soldiers back in South Carolina. As far as they were concerned, it was a natural fit. Montgomery immediately placed Samuel Doolittle as regiment captain of the 66 colored men.

Doolittle had been in the 7th Cavalry earlier but did not have anywhere near the glowing reputation Montgomery did. With little experience, the white man was forced to accept the captaincy of the colored militiamen. The other officers were all colored. Nonetheless, Doolittle tried his best to do right by the men there, and the first action taken was to conduct an inventory of weapons and ammo to see what was needed. They formed a company and inspected their supplies. When the captain neared William, he raised his rifle for inspection.

"Rifle?" Captain Doolittle barked, gesturing to his weapon. William complied, raising it higher. The old rifle shone in the daylight, polished, even though the wood showed age. The captain accepted the weapon and cocked it, checking the sights.

"How much ammunition do you have?"

"Ten rounds, sir," William replied.

"You use this thing before? You look a little young."

"Thank you, sir. It's my wife. Keeps me young." The men around chuckled before William continued. "But, sir, been out huntin' and practicin' with the other men here. We trained for weeks before comin' out."

Satisfied, the captain nodded and handed the weapon back to him before moving to the next in line. William sighed, relieved to know he'd passed the test.

They settled into camp for another two days, now a little restless. The others milled about the campsite as the officers walked by. They'd check each time to see if someone new came. Finally, Montgomery led his men out of camp and through Westport, where they could get better weapons, ammo, blankets, and other essentials. After stocking up, they headed to the Big Blue River to defend its western bank against Pap Price. Once there, Montgomery ordered the men to dismount and sent the horses back to Kansas City, safely away from the thunder of war. Without the horses, the troops would be more agile in the coming fight.

Now on foot, William stood tall with the men from Mound City, positioning themselves on the north side of the Independence Road, west of the Big Blue River. Perched on the river's bank, the young militiaman spied several companies of colored men, all gathering to fight for Kansas and freedom.

More support poured in from Wyandotte and Leavenworth, led by Lieutenant Patrick Minor, who'd been amongst the 1st Kansas Colored Volunteers. William was happy to see him again. Minor brought ten-pound parrot guns with him, handy for the coming battle.

October 22nd came soon enough, and Pap Price's men lined up behind him, posturing for an attack. William and his comrades waited on their side of the Big Blue River, hearts pounding and hands gripping rifles. The colored militiamen locked their gazes firmly on the adversaries preparing to march, but they didn't advance. Minutes passed with no movement until the troops across the river finally turned south, marching fast toward Byram's Ford. William later discovered that movement and attack were a tactical attempt to outflank the federal armies.

As clouds moved across the sky, General Blunt repositioned their forces, both Blair's and Montgomery's, lining them up east and west along the north side of Brush Creek. William followed their orders, marching swiftly to take his place amongst the others, now a mile south of Westport. That same night, people saw General Curtis pull officers into his tent for more plans. After the staff of officers heard news from Major General Alfred Pleasonton, orders were sent out. Their forces had taken Independence and were pressing Pap's rebels back. Jumping on this news, the officers set up to press south of Brush Creek at daylight. If they succeeded in the maneuver, they'd push Pap's troops from both east and north.

This news made it hard for William to sleep. He tossed and turned in his blanket, the only thing separating his body from the hard ground. Lucinda had packed it for him, a silent gift wishing him well. She hadn't said anything, maintaining a steely distance before he left, but he caught her preparing safety rituals, praying to her gods for protection and guidance. Separate from his wife and child, William felt an anxiety seep in, as if that may have been the last time he would see them. Lucinda barely said a word. When he got back, he'd work out something.

Starting to shiver, the cold leeched even more from him. Other men in the night groaned, trying to settle in. It wasn't only William finding it hard to sleep. Mere hours sat between him and his first battle. As he drifted off, he muttered a fervent prayer, asking God to watch over him so he could return to Lucinda and Rebecca with the world a safer place. If God saved him from a snakebite, wasn't it for this moment? He finally had a place to channel all the rage, all the sadness, all the pain—and he didn't need a statewide decree to get him there.

God, if you listenin', spare my body and mind. Protect me and my brothers in this battle. If it's your will I fall to a Confederate bullet, make it a sacrifice that'll make the world a better place for my baby and the love of my life. He squeezed his hands together, slipping into a fitful sleep.

October 23rd found him cold, awake, but ready.

General James Montgomery rode through the camps, rousing the men around 4 o'clock to ready themselves for battle. They'd need to get up, armed, and march in place before the sun rose over the horizon. A cold fog rolled across the field overnight, beading chilly drops on their militia coats and reducing visibility. After some delays, the federal troops crossed Brush Creek.

Waiting across the fields, Pap Price's men were already dismounted—about thirteen thousand men. If William heard correctly, they brought about eighteen thousand altogether: four thousand volunteers, ten thousand militiamen, and another four thousand cavalry from Pleasanton, circling quietly behind the rebel lines. Under General Curtis, the first orders to attack were spread.

Fifteen hundred men in blue coats surged forward and southward along the prairie and farmland. Boots hit the ground, smashing through grass and collecting dew from the fog. Confederate General Shelby's division and General Fagan's men, over six thousand strong, launched their counterattack from the opposite side. Bullets whizzed through the air, and the battle commenced.

Artillery boomed, driving the federals back across Brush Creek. William crouched low as dark shapes flew overhead, blowing huge gouts into the earth and sending out clouds of blood and smoke. Unbelievably, the Confederates did not press their advantage from the high ground. William guessed they were low on ammunition as the bombardment slowed down. Stinging from the bullets, General Curtis organized his own counter with the troops, pulling together all men from the 4th, 5th, 6th, 10th, and 19th Kansas State Militias, plus their artillery. William fought to keep up, returning fire at the enemy.

Hours rolled by, and William could see the sun cresting to what looked like 11 a.m. Colonel Blair sent orders to dismount and leave horses on the north side of the creek. Pants quickly soaked, he waded alongside the others in the creek, the cold, October waters sapping all heat from his body.

That day in the barn rushed back faster than he could push it from his mind. Master Thomas lashed him, yelling at him in the memory, right before Buck's swift kick when the horse ran past him out of the barn. His old master beat him, but now, it clicked. He didn't deserve it. A hot, white wrath filled him in defense of his childhood self. Little William, at twelve years old, didn't deserve to be beaten for voicing a truth: he was better than anyone with horses. How dare anyone try to punish him for that? The rage flushed away any leftover nerves he had, replacing it with steely conviction. He was right to be here, and they deserved to die.

Cutting into the memory, he pressed forward with the rest of his colored brigade and pulled into a line to face south. A shout "ready" echoed over the battlefield, and William raised his rifle butt to his waist.

"Aim."

The rifle butt rested solidly against his shoulder.

"Fire!"

He pulled the trigger, and a swarm of angry bullets tore into the morning toward the rebels. Return bullets whizzed by, taking a man in the chest and dropping him to the ground next to William. The blood drained from his face, and he tucked and rolled to avoid the next volley. A sharp fear rose in him as adrenaline flooded his veins. His body shook hard, but he kept a grip on Snoddy's rifle and fired back. His knee ached fiercely, but he ignored the pain as best he could.

"Fire at will!"

William reloaded and fired, a thrill of freedom rushing through him, lending speed to his fingers. His borrowed rifle grew warm in his hands from the rounds blowing through it.

Their second engagement came hard as they fired back, pressing the Confederates into a nearby Bent House orchard and cornfield. Montgomery rallied the men, signaling a hard push, and William reacted, throwing himself into the fray. While his training in Mound City was minimal, it was enough to channel the pent-up aggression toward a common enemy. He swung his rifle butt at a man, knocking him over with a swift crack. Edward came swiftly behind him, reloading to cover William. Alongside those they had trained with, they worked together to keep the enemy busy with their fury.

A command rang out, halting their advance. William lowered his rifle, looking toward the officer who was shouting. While listening, he shifted the muzzleloader down to his shoulder, placing it between his feet to load more black powder. Another shout, and he raised it again, loaded and ready. As rebel soldiers came into sight, he aimed at the closest one, a white man with a grizzled face and an angry scar, training his sights on him.

"Fire!"

A red stain bloomed on the rebel's chest as the bullet blew him backward. He didn't get up.

Stunned, a weight settled onto William, and anger blended with a deep sadness. Mechanically, the young man pushed through, loading a second round. While the death was sad, hope and pride swelled to mix in, enough emotions that he felt like he would burst. That was one less man to hurt his family—his first kill.

Henry's voice rang in his head. *Never kill or hurt a white man.* Well, now, he was a fighter in the militia, and it was his job. All around him, more colored men took down white lives, each defending their homes and families. Maybe it wasn't right to kill, but at that moment, they were all equal. Those white men wearing uniforms were trying to kill him and his comrades just as much.

By the time the fighting was over, William knew he'd watched the life leave the bodies of five men, but with all his wild shots, he probably had killed more. The swirl of emotions from earlier pulled him through the battle, giving him energy, but they'd left now. Instead of pride, anger, and sadness, William felt hollowed out, like someone had taken a carving knife into his chest and pulled out all his insides. He hadn't felt like this since the day he'd left Ole Ben to travel to Arkansas.

But they'd won. No matter what, he saw now that actions brought results. He wasn't just reacting to life anymore—he'd taken it into his hands.

Afterward, news spread that on General Curtis' left flank, General Pleasonton had defeated Confederate General Marmaduke at the Big Blue—more to celebrate. From the recounts, Marmaduke had the high ground like the rebels did there near Brush Creek, but

Pleasonton's tenacity won the day. His troops broke through and drove Marmaduke from the high ground, breaking Confederate lines and sending them into full retreat. Soon, General Curtis' forces, the Army of the Border, surged forward and southward, driving Pap Price and his troops back.

The officers guessed at that point that Pap knew he would not take Westport or Kansas City. His concerns would've had to be his wagons and supply lines. So, instead, they saw his forces turn toward Fort Scott. Spies brought news that the next few movements were from Pap Price ordering General Shelby to guard their wagon train as they hurriedly moved south.

The militiamen, including William, acted on this, moving forward rapidly. The young man barely had time to reload his muzzle. Pressing hard to keep the advantage, they marched till sundown. Pap Price had been routed.

For all that time, the freed men of the militia had fought hard, but seeing the rout unfold before them, they felt a wave of vindication sweep through them. Grim smiles broke out amongst his comrades, and William spotted the smoke from the gunfire. "We see the white elephant," he yelled out. They could hear roaring guns for miles, and somewhere amid the rebels, William knew those despicable men, Frank and Jesse James, were running for their lives.

The regiment near William's was known as the "Red Legs," belonging to General James Lane. Between breaks, William met another man of the same name, but his surname was Hickok. He confessed he was also seventeen. He and Hickok's friend, William Cody, were serving as spies for the federals for months, bringing back this crucial info for their troops to achieve victory. However, now they fought alongside them with rifles. The colored soldiers and the federal army defeated the rebel invasion of Missouri. In the process, it validated the hard work all those men put together those long weeks, risking life and limb to protect their people. Just like many previous battles with colored men fighting alongside their white counterparts, they'd fought proudly and fiercely, coordinating well with their officers. It wasn't just good information and luck—they brought true mastery to the battlefield. Hopefully, this would carry weight in the coming decisions for Kansas.

Between the celebrations, concerns whispered through the camp. Even though they were routed, Pap Price's men were moving southward. That direction went close to Mound City. William fought through his battle fatigue, but with a strong anxiety mounting within the group, they mounted up anyway, moving south to track Pap and his troops before they got too far.

Thankfully, the tracking efforts were easy. Broken down wagons and other battle debris littered their trail, strewn up and down the border area. William's thoughts turned to Lucinda, who was back at home with Rebecca. If they didn't get there in time ...

They had to.

Pushing through their exhaustion, the Mound City militia tracked Price's movements through Linn County. The brooding rebels took out their frustrations on the unsuspecting citizens in their path. With most of their men gone to the war effort, that meant only defenseless women and children were left. William passed in horror, more burned buildings and devastated lives. People gathered the broken bits of their homes, families, and even their own bodies from the depraved assaults. Every field was plundered for potatoes, corn, cabbage, fruit, or anything edible the soldiers could get their hands on. As they drew closer to Mound City, the devastation continued. William prayed that word got to Lucinda and Rebecca before Price's men did.

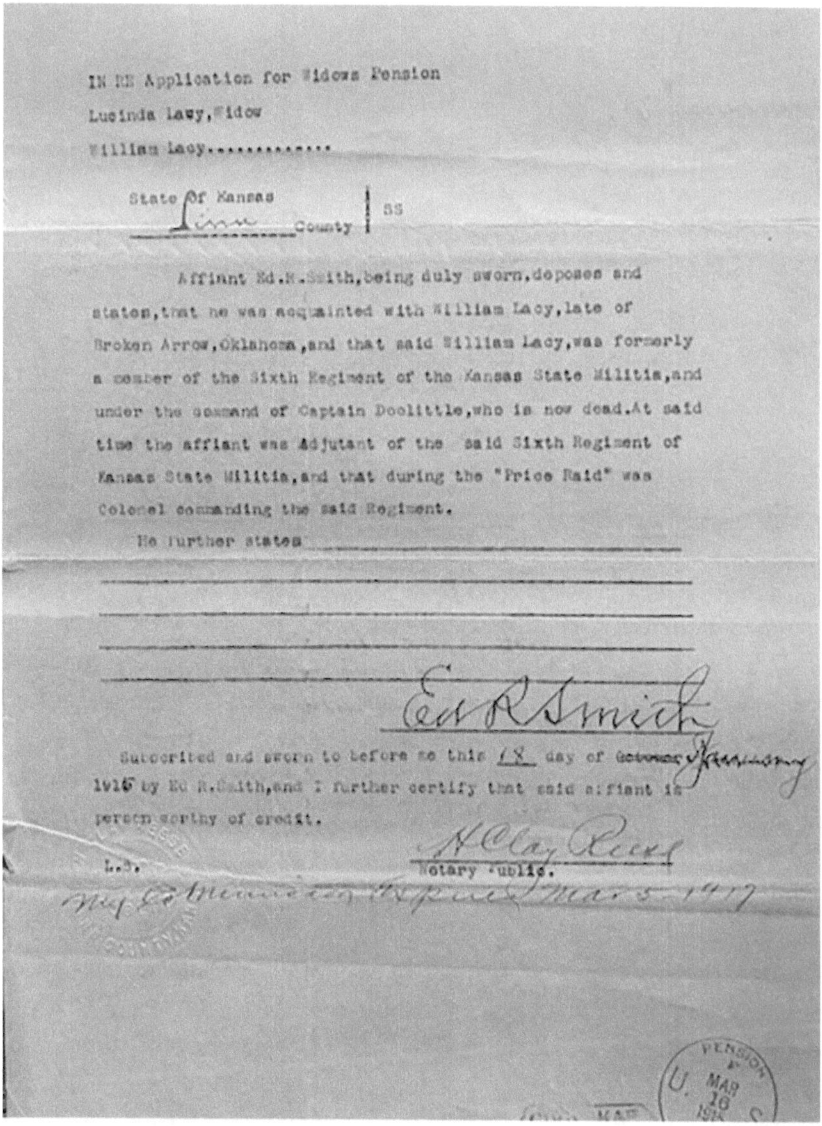

IN RE Application for Widows Pension

Lucinda Lacy, Widow

William Lacy..............

State of Kansas
Linn County | SS

Affiant Ed.R.Smith, being duly sworn, deposes and states, that he was acquainted with William Lacy, late of Broken Arrow, Oklahoma, and that said William Lacy, was formerly a member of the Sixth Regiment of the Kansas State Militia, and under the command of Captain Doolittle, who is now dead. At said time the affiant was Adjutant of the said Sixth Regiment of Kansas State Militia, and that during the "Price Raid" was Colonel commanding the said Regiment.

He further states

Ed R Smith

Subscribed and sworn to before me this 18 day of January 1916 by Ed R.Smith, and I further certify that said affiant is person worthy of credit.

H Clay Rees
Notary Public.

L.S.

Figure 21 – 1: Lucinda Lacy's affidavit, displaying William's military role in the 6th Kansas Militia during Price's raid

CHAPTER 22

What We Treasure

Mound City, Kansas—October 1864

A faint odor of blood and gunpowder reached Lucinda. She inhaled deeply, trying to place the troubling scent. Before her mind could find the words, her body knew: danger was coming.

She had already packed her bag, hid their food stores under the floorboards, and had Rebecca swaddled up tightly before the neighbors came by to share the news. They arrived at the Lacys' cabin to find Lucinda exiting the porch with her baby strapped and a knife sliding into her leg holster. With grim determination, she promised to alert the next two homes before she joined the steady stream of Mound City residents to the courthouse.

Oh, Will. A flood of shame, hot and tiresome, bubbled up in her throat. *Why didn't I even say bye? I thought my prayers were enough, but if you die and leave me here ...*

He made her so angry, acting all stupid by joining the militia. Now, why would he go and do a thing like that when so many people get themselves killed? Or worse, men come back broken and changed from war.

Still, he left without saying anything to him. Regardless of how afraid the war made her, she regretted those actions. Rebecca gurgled behind her, and she adjusted the sling to give her a comforting pat. "Don't worry, baby, Daddy's gonna come home. He has to."

Many worried, haunted faces passed her, and she met up with others near the courthouse. Some of the church ladies were directing the residents to flee. Word had come that Pap Price's troops would be there any minute, flooded with a need for revenge. Lucinda traveled light, paring down her life to the absolute essentials—travel-ready food and her baby—while others piled everything they could on their horses. Wagons passed by, trudging slowly. People plodded along, staggering under heavy luggage.

"Y'all need to drop that," Lucinda said. The people nearby looked at her. "Is anythin' in that bag worth your life?"

Sharing a weary look, her neighbors agreed with her wisdom and shed their heavy burdens, speeding up to move with the other fleeing people. All the Mound City folks looked to each other, some families offering room in their wagons to people fleeing on foot. Elizabeth's wagon rocked by.

"Lucinda? That you?"

She nodded, rushing to catch up. Elizabeth held a hand out. "Get in here. We ain't leavin' you behind." Grateful, the young lady took the hand and swung up into the wagon, taking a small place in the back. A cluster of other neighbors shifted to make room.

They all rode westward, and a whole day passed before they stopped to rest.

While Pap Price's cavalry tore across the countryside, the Kansas defenders were in hot pursuit. Colonel Thomas Moonlight's mounted brigade raced for a day and a half to reach them, thinking they were heading to Fort Scott. Moonlight's brigade met the tail of Pap's cavalry with General Shelby, covering their crossing at Mine Creek.

A thunderous battle ensued where the forces met. Feeling another creeping defeat hot on the heels of the last one, Pap Price turned the rebels eastward, now skipping Fort Scott. Instead, he ordered his forces to move back into Missouri and then down into Arkansas. Colonel Moonlight's timely arrival deflected Price's momentum, thus sparing Mound City from his violent war trail. Because of Moonlight's timely arrival to deflect Price's momentum, Mound City was saved.

William and the 6th Kansas arrived to see the aftermath of their clash. It had ended before they could help, but still, his brigade came to a rousing victory cheer, and the men mingled to share news and celebrate.

William couldn't shake the tumult of feelings alongside relief. His family and home were saved, but the destruction held his attention. Dead horses and men littered the field along the creek. People cried out in pain; some were still on the battlefield. In his haste to retreat, Price left some men behind to die. Those in a condition to walk were forced to carry their wounded companions and were all grouped up as prisoners. William thought he'd want to execute them himself, but when he saw them, broken and bloody, all he felt was a numb sense of sadness.

The officers didn't order their execution. Nurses, most of the women who rode with the troops, attended to them as best they could, but they were arrested. Shortly after the battle's aftermath was tidied up, those same officers mustered William and his comrades forward again. They needed to confirm the safety of their homes. Even with the rout, only the sight of Lucinda, holding Rebecca alive and well, could ease William's anxious mind.

They arrived on the outskirts of Mound City to find it unburned but empty. The entire town was vacant, and at first, William panicked, thinking they'd been taken. He parted from the others, driving his horse hard back to his tiny cabin.

When he arrived, he hopped off and studied the place, his heart beating furiously. The garden was still intact. Most of his belongings were safe, and there was no sign of anyone breaking in. The emergency stores were also safe under the floorboards. If Lucinda had enough time to pack that, she must've had enough time to escape. It stifled his anxiety a little, but in a frantic state, he left the house to climb back onto his horse.

When he reached the courthouse, the officers were already sharing a note found inside: the people of Mound City had escaped to their safe location but gave no hints where it'd be. William felt a pull to the west. He couldn't explain it, but when the officers allowed them to return home, he went to the western side of town to keep watch.

A day later, William hadn't slept or washed, maintaining his position at the edge of town. Sure enough, his tired eyes spotted a trail of people in familiar wagons heading back to Mound City. Clusters of people trickled back in, and with his hopes climbing, William ran toward them, talking to everyone he knew and asking if they knew where Lucinda and Rebecca were.

A steady stream of pats, hugs, and gently pointing fingers navigated them back together. A trail of colored folk walked as a group, and Lucinda rode in the back of a wagon, holding a swaddled Rebecca close to her chest. Around the wagon walked more children, safe in the center with other neighbors trudging nearby. William got close enough to catch Lucinda's attention. Her expression instantly melted from worry to staggering relief. The young man passed through the current of people walking back, shouldering through them gently to reach his wife.

Holding Rebecca close, Lucinda hopped off the Smiths' wagon, and William caught them. He squeezed them both firmly as a tightness in his chest finally released. Lucinda squeezed him closer, burying her face in his neck. "You back. I should've said goodbye better. Should've given you somethin' to bring you back home safely."

"I'll always make it back, 'Cinda."

She pulled back, studying his face with her tired, worried eyes. One hand came up, and she brushed his forehead, smoothing down his cheek. "Most of you is back. I see a lot of pain behind them eyes now. C'mon, let's get back home."

The townspeople, including William, Lucinda, and Rebecca Lacy, who could return safely to their tiny home, clustered next to their neighbors, both soldier and farmer alike. General James Montgomery also returned home to his farm.

It took a few weeks to get back into a semi-normal routine. For a while, William stood outside on the porch, sometimes for the entire night, keeping watch for anything to return. He'd meet with neighbors, exchanging advice, analyzing incoming news, and meeting with Edward in town. Together, they'd leave with other militiamen to bury their dead. William made sure every fallen soldier they came across got a decent burial. Even with help, it took weeks.

After those weeks passed with no incident, it felt like they could let their guard down. Thankfully, hard work in their crop fields helped focus some attention. Under their care, they had enough food not only to eat and fill their stores but also to share with others.

The terrifying month leading up to Pap Price's attack was seemingly over. Their army of marauders missed the town, and they could breathe easily—a big-chested inhale. William sighed, leaning against the doorjamb before walking over to put Snoddy's rifle back on the wall. Lucinda also took a sigh of relief. Things had been, understandably, tense as they filtered back into everyday life. She kept reminding him they weren't in Lawrence, and a healthy military presence was nearby.

It also helped that the evacuation gathered them even closer as a community. Lucinda had practiced more herbal medicine on the road, helping care for the sick and needy in their dire straits, and that had earned her a newfound role in the community. People came by often to ask for help—a cough here, a worrisome wart there—and Lucinda had an answer for it, balancing Rebecca on her knee while she did it. William couldn't have been prouder.

He had his own surprising following. Edward and more men from the brigade still met to discuss their plans and the next steps. Their community was one thing, but they were part of a bigger message sent from the state of Kansas: no more slaves.

On one of these trips, William brought a crop of potatoes and a few choice cuts of fresh thyme from Lucinda's garden. As people recovered, just like they learned in Lawrence, sometimes having something fresh and fragrant for dinner could make all the difference. Once there, a few neighbors stopped by to accept the extras gratefully, one promising to deliver a pail of milk to the Lacys' cabin once he had enough.

Flyers appeared again across the courthouse, another hint that life was returning to normal. He'd need to get more work soon, so he stopped by, retrieving one flyer that stood out from the others. The paper flapped in the wind, displaying a familiar government symbol. More fluttered across the ground of the same size and shape. He waved at Edward to come over and read the letter aloud.

"I don't have to read far," Edward said. He grimaced at the paper in disapproval. "It's tellin' us 'bout the election next week. We all need to vote for Abraham Lincoln, anyway."

"Right," another man chimed in from the crowd. "Most of us 'round here will too. Definitely not votin' for George McClellan. Hell, Lincoln had to fire him 'cause he was the only general who wouldn't fight. He just wanted to be a politician all along."

The election? The news hit William like a runaway cart. Of course, everything would run along as usual outside of the trouble in Kansas. After such a long month, they received little news about it, but after training, stressing, fighting, and settling back into life, something as important as the election seemed entirely foreign. Even knowing about it was hard to visualize in his head. How did these political things work?

People I talk to say Lincoln's a friend of the colored folks, so that's enough for me, he thought. Regardless, he'd support the man however he could. He thanked Edward and the other men around the courthouse and returned to discuss the news with Lucinda at home. When he got back, Lucinda had a cluster of neighbors nearby. People must've come for advice and medicine. Since it was getting colder, he dug a fire pit for his neighbors to have a better area to congregate. He split wood and made benches to expand the space where people could sit. He knew no one else would recognize it, but he tried to make them look as close to Ole Ben's church pews as possible.

William brought up the coming election around this fire pit, sitting on comfortable benches.

"What'd you think the white folks will do this election?" John Ewer, their nearest neighbor, asked. He'd come to see what the gathering was for.

William just shrugged. "Ain't never seen no election. I expect it'll go like the previous ones."

Another neighbor asked, "Is Lincoln now wantin' slaves to be free or just win the war?"

"Lincoln wants everybody to be free, not just save the United States," replied William. Either way, he'd take him as Commander-in-Chief with the war won or the slaves freed. That said, talk turned toward rebuilding efforts as the crackling fire highlighted their faces.

Days later, every white man in the county streamed to the courthouse to cast a vote. Eager to see the tally, William went along to bear witness to the event. Seeing so many white men gathered there in Mound City made him nervous, so he kept his distance from the courthouse. Even after the battles and training efforts, his fugitive slave past felt heavy around these crowds, and he couldn't afford negative attention.

Throughout the previous months, Lincoln had suffered several military defeats, including Cold Harbor and the Battle of the Crater in Virginia. He'd heard through rumors that Lincoln himself thought he had a slim chance of success in the election. However, nearly 75% of soldiers in the war voted for their Commander-in-Chief.

One by one, each man from the crowd mounted the steps to walk inside the courthouse. Each one would cast their vote for either Abraham Lincoln or George McClellan. It took a long time, but William waited out the voting process. It was fascinating to imagine what went on within those walls as men gathered to take part in selecting their next leader. Politics, even this close, seemed like an ocean away.

Hours passed until a general buzzing crowd had gathered later that afternoon. Inching forward, William found other colored folks like him waiting around the plaza. In the crowd, he spotted Mr. Smith, who waved him forward. "William," he called out. "Come over here and join us." Some other white men gave him a strange look, but he said nothing. Grateful, William jogged over to stand at his side.

"Any news yet?" William asked.

"Any minute now," Mr. Smith said just as a man exited the courthouse.

"The results are in," he waved some paper at the crowd. "Lincoln's won our county and in Kansas!"

The celebratory people excitedly discussed the details of his prevailing victory. Lincoln had seventeen thousand votes in Kansas, whereas McClellan had little over three thousand. After this, Lincoln ultimately defeated McClellan with a fifty-five percent popular vote and an electoral count of two hundred and twelve to twenty-one. Only twenty-five states could vote in the election because the southern states had seceded, giving up their ability to do so. McClellan won only three states: Kentucky, Delaware, and his home state of New Jersey.

After hearing all these results telegraphed, William and the others in Mound City joined people around the country, celebrating well into the night. Feeling elated, the young man rushed home to share the news with Lucinda, starting another fire in the pit to gather the neighbors. He invited everyone he talked to over to share in the happy festivities. Lucinda broke out some of their stores of sugar to make some sweet cakes, and the neighbors brought jugs of liquor. Regardless of what happened tomorrow, this day was a momentous win. They'd have Abraham Lincoln for four years.

For the next month, William continued to look for jobs in Mound City, now with a lighter heart and more optimism. This didn't reflect his luck. While he worked odd jobs, like making deliveries and helping on other farms, it produced very little money, and he was usually paid in food. After all, the war effort continued to march on, even through these small bouts of celebration. Resources continued to be scarce.

Word blew through Mound City via the Border Sentinel that the white men who served in the 6th Kansas were to receive payment for their service in the militia for the month. William let Lucinda know he didn't hear anything about pay for the colored men, but he'd ask anyhow. Her demeanor immediately became icy. "William Lacy, if they don't give you any pay for everythin' you did …" She didn't finish the statement.

When he got to the throng of other colored men, he spotted Edward, who broke the terrible news. The state of Kansas had stiffed its colored troops. No colored militiamen were to receive payment. He asked for proof, unable to read himself, no matter who he questioned—white soldiers nearby and clerks—the story was always the same. Despite their fierce efforts in defending their homes and risking life and limb, they fought for free.

He dragged himself home to deliver the unhappy news to Lucinda. He'd never seen her so angry. She grabbed a pot and swung it around the house. William dodged, ducking the arcing metal. "Don't you never trust no damn government again, you hear me? All that work and pain and loss, and they ain't givin' you the dignity of payment like they doin' for the white folk? This ain't a household where no gov'ment official is welcome anymore. You mark my words."

However, she calmed down a bit the next day, at least not swinging pots or cursing people. When she went into town, she pulled the ladies' group together, speaking with Elizabeth about the travesty and asking if she could do anything about it.

"We gotta protest this," she explained. "This is what your church is here for, right? Rightin' wrongs and correctin' injustice? Well, my husband is severely wronged. Can y'all address the army for this? William relies on y'all to provide. He came here to y'all's side for community and support. Now, we in need. My family was almost torn apart by the militia's efforts. I ain't askin' for me—William was nothin' but here for the church, so I'm askin' for him."

As much as they could, the church members explained to Lucinda that they had no power to demand anything. They offered some spiritual counseling, but Lucinda rebuffed them, her anger becoming icy toward the others.

"Out of great respect, I won't say nothin' more than what do you expect us to do now? We be a runnin' slave couple you done helped—not no further than this very room—to start us a life. Then we was asked to help defend these homes instead of fleein' ourselves. So what's next? If Kansas gov'ment ain't gonna treat us like people when we willin' to lay our lives down, then what does that make us? What does anythin' mean anymore?"

With a final glance, Lucinda closed the church doors to a silent, stunned group.

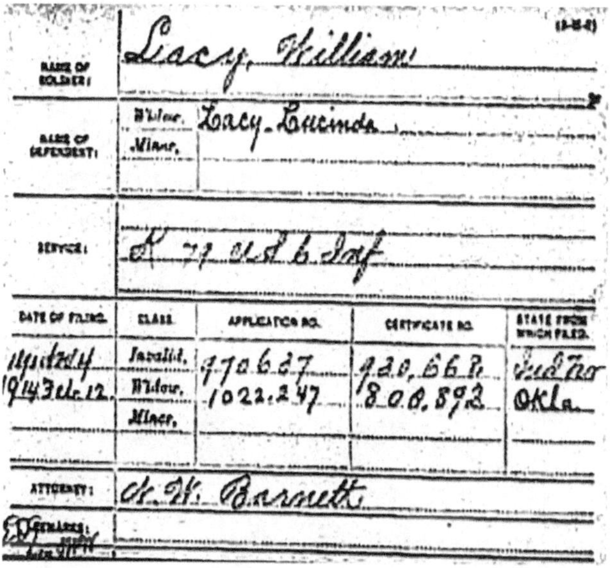

Figure 22 – 1: William Lacy's draft registration into the 1st Kansas Colored Troops

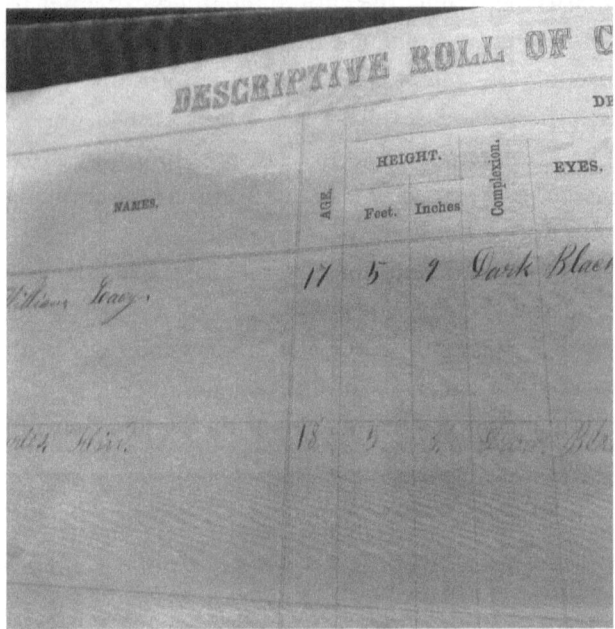

Figure 22 – 2: William Lacy's military record and description

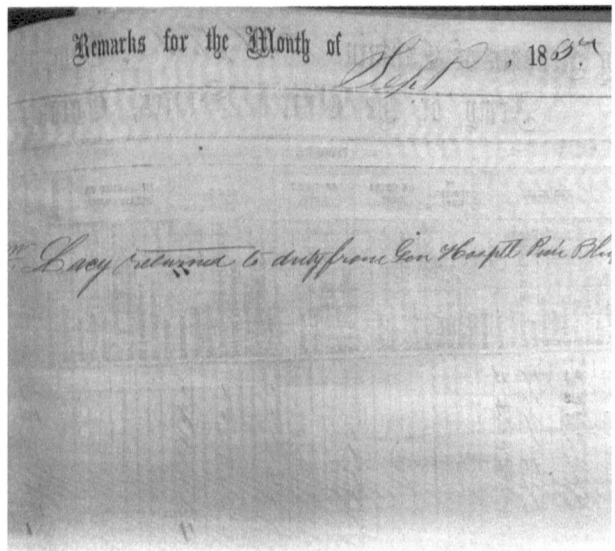

Figure 22 – 3: William Lacy's return from the hospital record

CHAPTER 23

Joining the 1st Kansas

Mound City, Kansas—January 1865

A brutal winter fell on the people of Mound City, and the Lacy family was not spared. Food stores dwindled and emptied until Lucinda scraped their barrels to keep grain in their cooking pot. Rebecca continued to grow, and as grateful as her parents were, it still meant new clothes. Thankfully, Elizabeth and their church friends came through.

By the end of January 1865, William spotted more military recruiters on his usual route into town. They spoke with people in the plaza about needing more men to join the effort. The 1st Kansas Colored Volunteers were asking for more warriors to join their ranks down in Arkansas. The news felt strangely timed, almost wistful and prophetic. He'd been around them for so long, and now the fighting force was in Arkansas, his old home. All this together sparked an idea.

He spoke to Lucinda when he got home. "I know what you're gonna say before you say it. I know what just happened to us, and I can't explain it, but I gotta go."

William entered his small living space to break the news, checking on his old rifle. It had stayed on the wall since the previous battle. Lucinda stood up and walked to stand in front of it.

"No."

"'Cinda ..."

"Don't "Cinda' me, Will. When you gonna get it? How many times we gotta dance this dance? No white folks are ever gonna have your back. You just keep askin' for it now. We barely have our life together here, and now you wanna go gallopin' off again? For what? Money? They ain't payin' you. Honor? They don't treat you with no dignity. So for what?"

"It was for protectin' you—you and Rebecca. I had to go fight then, and that's the same now."

Lucinda scoffed. "No it ain't, William. We ain't in danger now, 'cept maybe for starvin' to death. We need you here to help work and get food in our bellies. We don't need no protection now. Every time you go is more chances to die. You want that? Leavin' us alone in this world?"

"I survived once, and I can do it again. Plus, they offerin' a bonus for signups before you even leave."

"Oh, well, now that's settled," Lucinda said, taking a step forward. "You listen to me, Will. I stood by you when you started all that fool-hardy trainin' instead of runnin' with me. When we together, nothin' stoppin' us, and we made it all the way here from Coweta with just us two. And you 'bout to throw it all away for people who don't respect you enough to pay you. Again. I need a reason good enough not to see this as you bein' just as foolish as Daddy was with Momma because I ain't my momma. I ain't standin' by no foolishness."

Those words struck William hard in the chest. All this time, knowing his wife was a fighter, but it never got turned on him. In the corner of his eye, he caught their larder door open and empty. They wouldn't survive without some money coming in. Lucinda continued, stepping forward.

"You wanted to join the church, and I warned you they only care 'bout themselves. They helpin' us, but only so far as they grant it to us. You wanted to move to Quindaro. We had a good time, I'll admit, but how many steps back did that take us when we could've stayed here and worked our land? Now, you not steppin' out once, but twice for people who already done showed you who they were. Why?"

William stared directly at Lucinda, loving her more fiercely while she stood there, panting, sweating, angry, afraid. Her chest rose and fell in short bursts, waiting for his reply. Behind them, Rebecca stirred in her sleep, even though they both spoke in quiet hisses.

"You right about all that. But the church folks what got us set up here. We owe them our lives. And yeah, we had some bad times in Lawrence and Quindaro, but we gotta do somethin' with our lives. Take chances. We did runnin' here, and I didn't want to stop." He stepped forward and gently cupped her shoulders. "I know you makin' a fuss because you scared, but I felt somethin' on the battlefield. It made me realize I can protect folks and make a difference. It gave me a feeling I couldn't find anywhere else. And I'm doin' it for you. I love you more than anything, 'Cinda."

"How you gon' love me when you don't even know who you are, William Lacy?"

Without another word, she pulled herself free of his grasp and stalked to the front door, grabbing a gardening trowel. As she stepped out on the porch halfway, she turned and pointed it at him. "When you left last time, I grieved for someone I didn't know was comin' back. I didn't know if I'd be left a widow before I even turned twenty. And now I'm tellin' you if you walk out this town to fight—knowin' what you put me through—don't expect me to wait around for you. I'll do what I must to survive."

On the 25th of January, William Lacy rode his horse out of Mound City, traveling to a small village called Paris, Kansas. Once there, he signed up to join the 1st Kansas Colored Volunteers. For the second time, he left his home with a heavy heart but grim determination. He'd rather Lucinda be angry and alive than watch her die.

As he grew acquainted with the people there, he discovered hundreds of Black men from all over the nation had joined forces to help fight in the war. They had undergone a name change, and people called them the 79th United States Colored Volunteers.

He signed the allotment papers at the tent, looking the man dead in the eye. "Now, my wife is back home. She gon' need this money to live. This my second time comin' to fight and third time not bein' paid. I need assurance my family's taken care of and done right."

The man showed him he'd be mailing a certificate with "Lucinda Lacy" back to Mound City. She could retrieve the signing bonus he just earned once she received it. She'd need to present her allotment ticket and papers to the army monthly for payment. The army official would acknowledge those papers and have her take the proof to the Kansas state treasury. The only thing she'd have to do besides the travel is to make an "X" to sign the document. Their agents in Mound City would give her the pay. Even with the explanation, William watched each step until the certificate was in the courier's saddlebag.

His pay was thirteen dollars, and he had to see how much could be allocated to Lucinda and Rebecca back home. If he subtracted three dollars for clothing, he wouldn't need much more since the army would take care of food and lodging. He'd send everything back home to her. It'd be cumbersome for her to do all those steps each month, but it'd ensure she and Rebecca were cared for. Because she didn't know how to read or write, he knew Elizabeth or one of the other church ladies would help her.

William said a prayer while watching the mail courier ride off toward Mound City. He hoped God would soften her heart when she had money in hand.

With everything set up the best he could, he set off for Fort Smith with the others, traveling down through Kansas to the Arkansas fort. He never thought he'd be returning to that place again, let alone the state of Arkansas, but this was important. He was now a part of the regular army. Along with other recruits, William made his way down the river by steamboat.

When he arrived, the 1st Kansas was in charge of the town and had successfully driven off Confederate soldiers. The whole place was safe, including the surrounding cities. Once there, the officials directed the new recruits to where they'd be training, even assigning

William to Company K. The man pointed to their section of the barracks down the road.

When he got there, he ran into none other than Ralph. Running to his old friend, he cheerfully caught up with him, happy to be an official part of the fighting force. Ralph got him set up with everything.

He finally got something he'd never owned before: a uniform. Company K assigned him a standard blue coat and light blue trousers. The jacket was made from coarse wool and designed to be hardy and protective rather than comfortable. The deep, dark blue looked great to William, shrugging out of his ragged brown jacket, but he soon discovered it was mighty uncomfortable under the hot prairie sun. Coats like that seemed impractical in that weather.

He also received a kepi hat, which Ralph handed over. It had a flat top that extended forward to help shield his eyes. This was all standard issue from the Quartermaster, including the best Lorenz Austrian-made musket they had left. He received this solemnly, thankful for this newer weapon. He'd given his previous rifle back to Snoddy before he left. Ralph nodded at the new firearm, proudly stating it'd been imported at the beginning of the war as it ramped up.

As luck would have it, both sides used the same imported guns, which made it easier when they seized stockpiles. The gun William held, Ralph explained, had been cast aside by white regiments who had received newer Springfields made just a few years earlier. Like similar models, that rifle was a muzzleloader, and Ralph showed him the ins and outs. He warned him that some were poorly constructed and to be careful. One in five misfired, which made them inefficient. William took this all in stride; he'd already made peace with the lack of efficiency from his militia days. In the Western theatre of war, the colored troops were treated as less important.

Ralph continued to explain that some of the weapons were for show anyway. Many military personnel expected their company to be used for manual labor. This initially made William angry, as he'd come down to fight for his values. The politics were murky. Ralph admitted the white soldiers could experience the same issues with their weapons. All in all, they at least had rifles to defend themselves with.

As winter dragged on, the 1st Kansas, Company K members received half the food rations they'd normally need. William frequently felt hungry, but this also wasn't anything new. While it sorely tested the patience of other soldiers, he kept a positive attitude that more supplies would arrive.

Soon enough, boat whistles sounded from the river, and he happily went with other Company K men to unload the cargo from four vessels. Included with the crates were the much-needed supplies.

To his surprise, drafted reinforcements—fresh soldiers from around, gathering for the cause—were walking on the boat. As he returned with the new recruits and cargo, he saw more of the 1st Kansas Regiment. The men sprawled out amongst buildings in Fort Smith, and soon, he recognized others from that small group he had met in Fort Scott. How small was the world? After so much traveling, only a boat ride stood between him and long-lost friends sitting in the alleys he grew up in.

He stopped in front of the general store, on the same street he and Henry were beaten by the angry mob. Henry, he thought. Papa. Eliza. Everyone in Van Buren. What're you doin' right now? What would you think of me in a U.S. military uniform?

His heart ached with his lost family so close by, but he didn't dare seek them out or leave the fort very far. Besides the discomfort of being recognized as a former slave, the army had specific orders for him at their campsite.

When he finally returned after unloading and helping the newer recruits find their spaces, he could tell other soldiers were ill from various ailments. The men around the camp clutched at different parts of their bodies, complaining of aches. Dysentery, malarial diarrhea, ulcers, jaundice, dropsy, influenza, and chronic liver and kidney conditions ran rampant through the soldiers. A few even more unfortunate men suffered from smallpox and measles, according to warning signs posted outside their tents.

Even the officers of the 1st Kansas didn't fare much better. Without a well-rounded diet, everyone was getting sick. William didn't know much about health, but he knew you had to eat more than just one thing every day and at least one vegetable or fruit.

Despite the apparent suffering, disorganization, and faulty equipment, William felt he was right where he needed to be. Present there, he had finally joined the 1st Kansas he'd dreamed about so long ago. Talking with Ralph, their illustrious victory record kept him in high spirits. They'd won many battles by that January, and it made sense to William that going through all that would leave some scars.

In any case, Lucinda was back home—safe and now paid.

Figure 23 – 1: A historical marker for the battle at Poison Springs

CHAPTER 24

Endings More Bitter than Sweet

Fort Smith, Arkansas—Late 1865

Working around camp, William had only a few days of learning his brothers-in-arms' names before marching orders came. One whirlwind of movement and travel, under new officers in Company K, the young soldier found himself back outside Little Rock.

Another revisit to the past. Now a grown man, William took in the city with fresh eyes. Much had changed along with him. War had ravaged the city, draining it of color and shape.

William's captain ensured his garrison was fully equipped before joining more men for specific duties in the city. He was assigned to keep the peace with Ralph and other Company K members. They walked around the streets in a group, keeping a watchful eye for any violent outbreaks. While they walked, Ralph updated William on recent events and pointed out various notable soldiers.

The 1st Kansas had overtaken Confederate regiments outside the city's perimeter, winning battles throughout Arkansas. Since they left Fort Scott, the colored volunteers fought and claimed victory at Sherwood, Missouri, Cabin Creek, Honey Springs, and Timber Creek in the Indian Territory. William felt a mixture of pride and sourness. Of course, he was happy they gathered so much victory for the cause, but with all of this, didn't they recognize the missed payments for all of his and Lucinda's work?

Ralph droned on, gesturing at the encampment outside the city. "We also fought at Poison Springs and Flat Rock Creek here in Arkansas. Sad to say, we got pushed back mighty hard by a wave of rebels at Poison Springs. Lost a lot of good men that day. I'm blamin' the officers. We can only do so much without good equipment and strategy. We got spread out with no safe place to regroup.

"Several hundred of us died. I remember seein' a whole mess of my brothers with the scalps missin'. Them Choctaw rebels cut into 'em, led by General Stan Waite. It took a while and more pushin' hard from our end, but we gained the upper hand all across this area. We more ready than ever for more battles, and they cain't ignore us no more, even if we colored. Now, we just gotta keep the peace here in Little Rock."

When they returned from their shift, their lieutenant split them up again, having William move to guard near a row of businesses, each desperate to get back on their feet after the waves of Confederate attacks. William got some shady looks from the owners. He found out the Union soldiers also took advantage of them, commandeering supplies for "protection." In a gesture of goodwill, William respectfully tipped his hat to the store owners. He knew how hard they'd had it, and how hard it'd be to keep going through this war. There was no sense in adding to their misery.

Even with the necessary security and his efforts at respect, the young soldier and his group were harried. Many townspeople weren't used to being protected by colored men and expressed this displeasure with threats, usually followed by comments like "nigger soldiers" or simply being spat on before running. It reminded William of Fort Scott. Now, if people threatened him or threw rocks, he'd cart them off to prison. It was grim work, but he gave each aggressor several chances before arresting them. Others in his company just executed them on the street if they became too violent. After surviving so many battles, unarmed townspeople were barely a threat.

This was life for months. William did his best to keep his head above water, but he missed his family and home. He wished he'd learned to read and write so he could connect with Lucinda. On patrols, he'd wonder what she was up to and if Rebecca had learned to walk yet.

His attempts at respect paid off, and some businessmen grew to recognize the young soldier when he came by. Since William persisted in his efforts to talk, his listening ear won him a shared drink in some spots and at least less aggressive looks in others.

He also ran into familiar military faces. Captain Graton was one face he remembered from working in Fort Scott. The man asked about Lucinda, and the two spoke about their wives, who were safely at home.

Another was Sergeant Joseph Carris, who showed them a rare kindness when they were new fugitives. Carris immediately spotted William when he stopped to admire the cavalry's stables. Now, two years later, William looked more like an eighteen-year-old, mature enough to carry a weapon and fight in the war. He was thankful his participation at Westport earned him enough of a reputation that no one looked any further at his age.

Working hard, he made the ranks of infantry. While on garrison duty, he had to break up soldiers' fights when they became too rowdy, usually in the evening or on weekends. With that many men stuffed into one place and with alcohol present, it became a common occurrence. William used his friendly demeanor and rapport to de-escalate most fights before they started. He could sniff out tension with the gamblers and knew when some people were just plain ornery.

William stood outside a makeshift jail full of Confederate prisoners of war when a signal from another Company K member got his attention. Soldiers walked behind the First Sergeant, who waved his hand for more of them to cluster. William glanced back at the jail before walking into earshot, wanting to at least stay at his post.

"A telegram has come in for our commanding officer. All of you need to hear this," the First Sergeant shouted. Everyone quieted down as Colonel James Williams exited the nearby building, pulling the telegram from his pocket. Ralph had explained how the general rose to command the 1st Kansas after they left Fort Scott in October 1862. Under his leadership, they'd put down a rebel presence at Island Mound, Missouri. William had barely seen the man, so he gave him his full attention.

In a booming voice, the general read aloud to his troops: "By order of Major General Ulysses S. Grant of the Army of the Potomac, I hereby inform all who may read or hear these words that the war between the United States of America and the Confederate States of America is now ended."

In disbelief, it took William a few seconds of a rousing cheer before he joined in himself. People hooted and hollered, jumping and hugging each other. Hats were thrown into the air, causing such a commotion that nearby townspeople exited their shops to see what the fuss was about. Word spread quickly as the folks in Little Rock came to ask questions. General Robert E. Lee had surrendered two days earlier in Appomattox, Virginia.

The war was effectively over.

The 1st Kansas let food and music flow freely for the next two days. Soldiers danced to instruments played by their comrades, and the townspeople joined in with the merriment. Word passed along to the colored townsfolk, and they took to the streets alongside the 1st Kansas. Everyone celebrated the end of a very long, very bloody war.

William let the elation carry him for the first day, but soon, even the dancing around town couldn't settle him. He wanted to return home to Lucinda. Since the busyness died down, anxiety over what his reception would be back home settled over him as he worried about what he would say. Hopefully, the money sent back for his work would smooth things over. Not only that but with the war over, they'd surely lose their fugitive slave status. Regardless of how long it'd take for others to catch up, he knew they were on the side of truth. With the fighting done, freedom had won.

The army let the celebrations go on but slowly recouped over the next few days, reminding the troops of their continued work until further notice. Despite the spreading message, the southern sympathizers in Little Rock continued to make mischief, channeling their depression and exasperation at the festivities. This meant the 1st Kansas was still duty-bound to keep the peace. Some even claimed that the telegram was a hoax and they would wait for word from the Confederacy itself before giving up their support.

It took longer for the call back home to come for the rebels. General Lee had surrendered with the condition that Confederate soldiers could return home unpunished as long as they swore allegiance to the United States.

Uncertainty spun its wiry head up in Little Rock when the general celebrations died down as an immense amount of news finally caught up to the colored army. Although it wasn't anything new, word came from Captain Sholes that Congress had passed a law abolishing slavery in the entire United States. The states would need to ratify this into a new law.

In January, Missouri, where so many of the colored men in the 1st Kansas hailed from, ratified this, abolishing slavery in the state. Following this, Captain Sholes' wife told him Governor Thomas Fletches had issued his own proclamation. Not too much later, in March, Congress passed another law allowing retroactive pay to the colored soldiers who joined the war effort by 1863 to compensate for the inequalities in income between the Black and white troops.

William knew there'd be a catch, and sure enough, there was. Ralph brought news that month involving the 1st Kansas Regiment's status. Because Congress didn't authorize them, they wouldn't be receiving retroactive pay. Senator James Lane had made a hasty mistake recruiting them, and they would pay for it now.

William decided to accept the treatment since it was nothing new, and he was still being paid now. There wasn't more he could do about it anyhow, and he threw himself back into the mundane work, patrolling Little Rock and guarding the Confederate prisoners of war.

All the bells in Little Rock rang out at once, causing a stir in the city. William glanced at the nearest ringing tower, thinking some Christmas miracle must be taking place. He was quickly roused from this reverie by Ralph running up to him and grabbing his coat.

"He been shot," Ralph shouted as he shook William's shoulders. "He been assassinated!"

"Who been shot?" William said as shock settled in. "We under attack? The war's over."

"Lincoln!" Ralph clutched his forehead. "He dead now."

In Washington, President Lincoln had been assassinated. The soldiers of the 1st Kansas collectively hung their heads in respectful silence. All around him, William saw the same emotions mirrored in how he felt: mortified, shocked, saddened. Grown men, hardened soldiers—some he knew who had no problem killing another man—all broke down, weeping like babies. Ralph sobbed so hard and fell to his knees in the dirt.

Silent, William walked in reverse, step by step, until his back hit a wall. He slumped down and put his head between his legs, breathing in and out slowly. *How can so much pain exist? Why cain't people just let each other alone?*

He tried to think about how anyone could survive these constant fights, constant failing, and unrelenting cruelty. Grief was like ocean waves, rolling over the citizens of the United States, suffocating them all in a salty tide. He wondered what Lucinda was doing at that moment, and his heart ached for her so intensely that he thought he might split in two. Would the folks in Mound City cry along with him?

Pulling his hands up, he clutched them tightly in prayer. *God, please watch over the souls of Abraham Lincoln and his family. Watch over my brothers here in the 1st Kansas. Watch over my family, who are so close over in Van Buren. Watch over the good people of Mound City. My wife. My baby. Keep all the people in your holy light when they get this news. I don't know why, in your worldly presence, you could let things like this happen. Is you listening? Is you there at all?*

His hand ached, right where two puncture marks scarred his skin. He rubbed it absently.

The officers had a difficult time fielding requests to execute all the prisoners of war in retribution for what happened to their President, but they stood firm. No matter what, they wouldn't sink to the rebels' underhanded level. William knew why. If they did this, it would only lead to more bloodshed and keep the war going on even longer.

Holding strong through the next several weeks, the last rebel armies surrendered or quit in the field to go home. As the war's practical force was over, William guessed they'd also be winding down their presence in Little Rock.

But no such luck came for the men of the 1st Kansas.

Back on unending garrison duty, William received orders from Colonel James Williams to clear out the towns near Little Rock of all slaveholders illegally holding people. Thankful to make a difference, William grabbed his coat and rifle, joining others in the growing group of soldiers.

Captain Sholes assigned William to duty with a squad to move west of the city to alert more people that the war had ended. Many small towns, villages, and farms nearby were so insulated that word took forever to reach them. They wouldn't have heard of Lincoln's death, the new laws, or even the war itself ending. Their job was to march out in all directions and deliver this news.

William's squad of two men headed out, and their first stop was a small farm, miles outside of Little Rock. Quiet and unassuming, they rode in together on horseback. The cabin looked like it was barely standing up, the walls leaning together and the roof full of holes. A man appeared in the doorway. It took William and his comrades precious seconds to recognize the shotgun in his hands until it was leveled at them.

"Stop right there, lest you die right now," the man grumbled out, hands shaking to hold his weapon steady.

William's lieutenant, riding in front, held his hand up for the squad to stop. Once they'd reined in the horses, he yelled back, "The war's over, and the Union won. Now if you don't set your weapon down now and come out, we'll burn what's left of your shithole to the ground and then still kill you."

Outnumbered and outgunned, the man spat, then slowly stepped out of the doorway and onto his porch, placing the shotgun down.

While studying the woods, William returned his focus to the man as more sunlight hit him. To his surprise, the young soldier recognized him. A flood of memories hit him so strongly that William was off his horse and across the field before he knew his body was moving.

Years ago, a white man cornered Henry and him in front of the shop, causing a scene about supplies before beating his own two slaves. William remembered every detail crystal clear. At the feed store, the two slave boys with Mr. Barling were so tiny, desperate, and confused, just like he'd been. He wasn't a slave anymore—he was a trained fighter in the 1st Kansas, and they'd won the war.

On the porch, William slammed his rifle into the man's head, fully recognizing him as the man who had humiliated Henry on the porch. A bloody arc sailed across the ramshackle wood. In one swift movement, he had the rifle's barrel under the man's chin and backed him up into his house with a loud bang. The frightened man's back hit the wall, and he pissed himself.

"Wait, wait! I surrendered! What're you doin'?"

William slowly cocked the gun. He heard footsteps running behind him. His finger ached to pull the trigger. At Westport, he'd killed several men, hurting more with the butt of his rifle. The iron slid across his right index finger as the white-hot rage burned his chest. It'd be so easy.

In the doorway, two young colored boys exited the house with wide, fearful eyes and their hands up.

As the other soldiers hit the porch, William removed the rifle from under the man's chin. Shaking with relief, he collapsed onto his porch. The young soldier gazed down at him icily before addressing the two kids.

"You free now. The war's over. Ain't no more slavery in the United States. If y'all want to come with us now, you can. Nobody can tell a freed person otherwise. We'll find you a spot in Little Rock to get you settled."

The boys looked at each other, then at the man, shaking in a pile on the floor and weeping. "This our home. What else we goin' do?"

Sadly, William knew that exact predicament. Without any help, what would they do in the city? Who'd give two freed slaves this young work and a place to stay? The army couldn't. The rage left as quickly as it came, replaced by a deep sadness. He placed a hand on each of their heads.

"Remember, you free now, and you choosin' to stay. Nothin' wrong with wantin' to be home," he said, angrily pointing a finger at the man. "But you don't ever let that man tell you otherwise."

The soldiers walked back silently with William as they remounted and left the farm for the next one. They didn't ask William anything, only let him stay back as they delivered the news. It took them several months, crossing counties adjacent to Little Rock before the 1st Kansas Colored Volunteers made a name for themselves beyond the war effort.

As fall approached, William's company made a short trip to Pine Bluff. Once there, word came that the 1st Kansas was to be mustered out of service in the United States Army. Pine Bluff held his last moments as a soldier in the war, serving with the historic colored troops. Once he received the paperwork, his duty to the United States was over.

CHAPTER 25

A Parade Fit for Soldiers

Fort Leavenworth, Kansas—October 1865

After walking, riding, and eventually, steamboating, the men of the 1st Kansas Colored Volunteers arrived in Fort Leavenworth, Kansas. They spent most of the time reminiscing over their time together in Little Rock, but some conversation turned to what they'd do once they were back home.

Ralph feared nothing would change; only more jeers would be waiting. The man had taken Lincoln's assassination hard, now reticent toward any news, especially on the backs of not being paid for their service.

William grew quiet along with him, a building anxiety present when he thought about his reunion with Lucinda. Would she even be there for him? The depression was infectious, silencing the troops in the boat.

Once the steamboat pulled into the docks, he disembarked with everyone else. Rumors spread on the docks that a parade had been organized for their return. From Fort Scott memories, this seemed like an odd joke at best and a trap at worst. At least the people of Leavenworth were more friendly to the colored soldiers.

Just in case, the regiment decided to bivouac in a large field just off the Missouri River, creating company streets with their tents and keeping their leather hanging nearby for safekeeping. They hoped they wouldn't need any of it while they waited.

According to comrades, when they went into the town, not enough people in Fort Leavenworth wanted to celebrate the return of the war's most famous colored fighting force. William figured the townspeople were exhausted, even with their more favorable views of the negro soldiers. The thought of colored men trained to fight did not engender fond feelings among whites, even here, where they had abolitionists close at hand.

Soon enough, the Leavenworth Times newspaper made it into the camp. The article reported, "It's a shame that our soldiers, after four years of hard service, hard fare, and hard fighting, are permitted to return to their homes without any public demonstration or recognition." The Leavenworth Times continued, "We are ashamed that while other cities and villages in the state had given the soldiers some token of regard, the city of Leavenworth has offered nothing."

Another writer later commented on these failed efforts, comparing them to a similar city and homecoming up north when the 54th Massachusetts returned to their home state. The article claimed, "Massachusetts has honored herself in giving a suitable reception to her world-famous 54th Colored Regiment. The example is a safe one for Kansas to follow. The men of the 1st Kansas have displayed equal heroism on the battlefield and equal discipline in camp, on the march, and in bivouac."

Despite this, the colored citizens from Fort Leavenworth prioritized visiting the camp, bringing tokens of appreciation for the soldiers. They formed a committee to raise the necessary funds to hold at least one evening of entertainment and dinner for them. John Morris and Lieutenant William D. Matthews were placed in charge of this committee, and they called on the somewhat shamed citizens of the area to chip in what they could for the welcome feast.

It turned out they'd have a celebration after all. The parade's launch was scheduled for the colored Methodist church on Kiowa Street, and the procession would form with the regiment out in front, followed by the colored Sunday school classes, then the townspeople, with various tradesmen bringing up the rear. The route would circle before returning to the church grounds, where a hearty meal would be served.

The day came, and the skies opened up to a steady drizzle, not quite a downpour, but just enough to halt any outdoor activity. Thankfully, news spread quickly that it'd be postponed to the following day. The troops, William included, gathered up their leather and polished their brass buttons to prepare for their celebration, and the next day, they received what they had hoped for.

William and his comrades hiked to the church grounds, and the parade kicked off that morning. The streets were lined five deep with people to view their victorious soldiers, now famous colored fighting men with the white officers who led them. Out of the fifteen hundred people who left Fort Scott years earlier, only five hundred remained to see that parade.

Bursting with pride, the young war hero marched beside his file mates, and even Ralph smiled for the cheery event. Their navy-blue sack coats and light blue trousers were all clean, and they each nestled their rifles between their waist and armpit. Chest forward, the proud group accepted hearty cheers from the people of Leavenworth.

William felt the gravity of this occasion, however happy it was. He'd marched all over the state, ridden with these men to war, and traveled with them by boat. He felt a significant part of himself belonged to the 1st Kansas Colored Volunteers, and once this parade was done, it'd be his last march as a soldier with them. Amidst this, he crowded in close with Ralph and the others in the street and held them close, arms around their shoulders.

Parading through the streets, they finally arrived at their feast, and William happily ate that last meal with his friends. The excited townsfolk made it easier to slip back into the festive atmosphere. After years of being treated like a burden or a threat, the heroic treatment induced a heady euphoria. The same went for the food. After so much hard tack, coffee, and meat rations, a home-cooked meal was heaven.

Many figures delivered speeches during their meal, including C.M. Langston, Colonel James Williams, D.R. Anthony, and William D. Matthews. The Leavenworth Times recorded these proceedings, writing that "... several mottoes suited for the times for which we do not have the space ... The whole affair was a success. It was a proud day for the colored men of Leavenworth and Kansas and will long be remembered by the prejudiced of the race."

Stuffed to bursting, William could only remember being this happy when he married Lucinda and then at the birth of his daughter. The evening ended at Turner's Hall nearby to discuss the rights of the colored men to the elective franchise. William made sure he kept up with their election talks.

The next morning, the 1st Kansas Colored Volunteers disbanded, vanishing like a ripple in a pond. William said tearful goodbyes to his best friends, sending them off with well wishes. He promised Ralph that if he ever got back to the area, he'd stop by his place to visit.

Climbing into a wagon, William headed south toward Mound City and Fort Scott. As he rode, the wagon passed Quindaro and Kansas City. He wondered if Robinson Coach Line was back on track or if they'd moved to greener pastures. He also passed the last vestiges of the war: old, broken-down wagons, picked clean of any good, shattered wheels, dead horses, and greedy, gluttonous buzzards. Some items strewn nearby marked the same route Pap Price took as he beat a hasty retreat south toward Kansas City. Each marker settled William's heart. The land was marked by what happened, which connected him to it.

After several days' worth of travel, he hopped off the wagon, paying the driver for the ride back to his home. On the outskirts, he saw the familiar edges of Mound City: its clusters of houses and rolling farmland. It all led back to where his family lived.

Since he got to keep his uniform and rifle, he passed through the town as a war hero. Many townspeople smiled and waved, happy to see the young soldier alive again. No doubt, they'd kept Lucinda company, weathering these long months of mixed news as the war wound down. William moved forward, his feet growing heavy until he broke free of the town and spied his home. Outside, working in the garden as always, was Lucinda.

William stopped on the outskirts, his breath stolen again. How, after all this time, did she have such a hold on him?

Lucinda sat back after another day working in the garden. She wiped her forehead, sweeping sweat back, beading even in the fall's coolness. It'd been such a long, hard time, with enough difficulties to test anyone to their limits. Through it all, like clockwork, William's name came attached to life-giving money. She used this each month to ration and bolster their home, growing what she could and bartering for what she needed.

Through these long months, Lucinda prayed, clutching at the empty bedside. Her chest ached each night, slipping into the empty bed. Despite her best efforts to dismiss her husband as another foolish man, she knew, in her soul, that it wasn't true. *Breath Maker*, she prayed. *I know what I did was wrong, but what else could I have done to stop William from runnin' off and gettin' himself killed? He know my people been killed off in wars. He know my family got destroyed by them soldiers. Then he wanna be one?*

Even with her angry prayers, she set her trowel down and leaned over, sweat dripping into the rich, dark earth. "I miss my husband," she whispered. Tears joined her sweat, mixing into the garden's soil. "Been waitin' for so long. Don't never wanna see him again now. That fool broke my heart for the last time."

"Momma?"

She jolted back to the garden and looked back to see Rebecca, now toddling and walking. Their baby girl had her first steps and words without her daddy, but she was safe and well-fed. Her tiny hands pointed past their property's fence toward the city. "Who's that comin' up the road?"

Lucinda stood up to see above the wooden planks and caught sight of William turning the corner of their neighbor's house. A flood of memories opened up. She saw a tiny boy, not much older than her, ducking behind a wagon. That same boy, appearing like magic but older, was in another wagon outside her father's house. Again, that same boy, older with a wiser smile, caught her hand and ran into the woods, holding her in cavernous darkness, then covered in blood on a dirt floor as smoke from burning buildings leaked through the window.

That boy, through all his foolish decisions, was now a man. And his face lit up, a smile breaking over it as he sprinted toward their home.

"Lucinda!"

That young man, now her husband, had come back to her.

"William!"

Months of stress melted away as she ran to meet him, tears streaming down her cheeks. Behind her, Rebecca ran to catch up, yelling, "Daddy!" They crashed into each other, falling on the floor as he kissed her all over her face.

"Baby, it's over now. It's all over. The war's done. We don't never have to worry about slave catchers again. No more lookin' over our shoulders."

"Thank you for keeping us afloat. I know I said some things before you left …"

"Shh, I know," William stroked the back of her head. "We both had to do what we thought was best. Important thing will always be that we show up for each other, for Rebecca, and keep tryin'."

"I know who you are, Will. You're the best husband anyone could ask for and the best father. You've always been there for me, even if I didn't understand how. You're the love of my life."

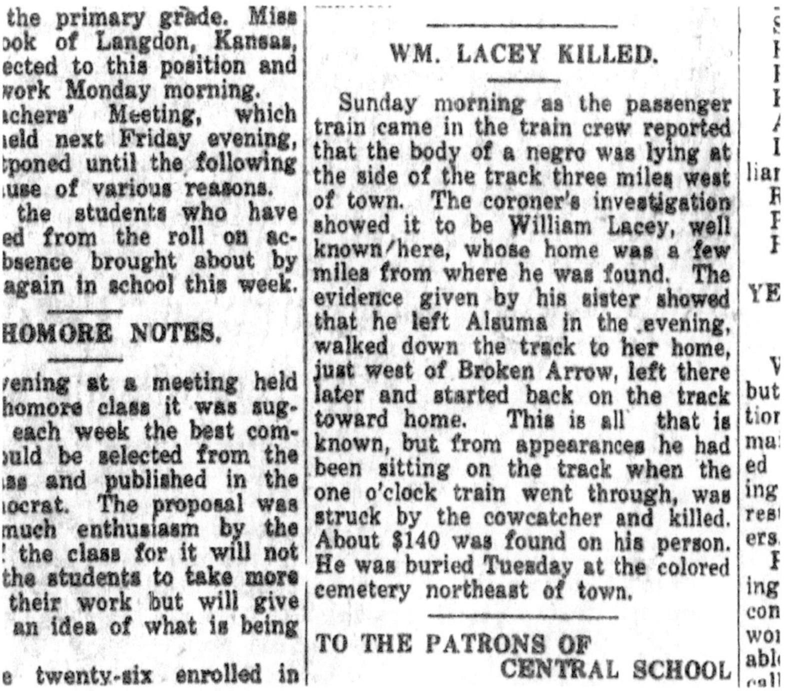

the primary grade. Miss
ook of Langdon, Kansas,
ected to this position and
work Monday morning.
ichers' Meeting, which
ield next Friday evening,
tponed until the following
use of various reasons.
the students who have
ed from the roll on ac-
bsence brought about by
again in school this week.

HOMORE NOTES.

vening at a meeting held
homore class it was sug-
each week the best com-
ould be selected from the
ss and published in the
ocrat. The proposal was
much enthusiasm by the
the class for it will not
the students to take more
their work but will give
an idea of what is being

e twenty-six enrolled in

WM. LACEY KILLED.

Sunday morning as the passenger train came in the train crew reported that the body of a negro was lying at the side of the track three miles west of town. The coroner's investigation showed it to be William Lacey, well known here, whose home was a few miles from where he was found. The evidence given by his sister showed that he left Alsuma in the evening, walked down the track to her home, just west of Broken Arrow, left there later and started back on the track toward home. This is all that is known, but from appearances he had been sitting on the track when the one o'clock train went through, was struck by the cowcatcher and killed. About $140 was found on his person. He was buried Tuesday at the colored cemetery northeast of town.

TO THE PATRONS OF
CENTRAL SCHOOL

Figure 25 – 1: An obituary for the son of William Lacy, recorded by the *Broken Arrow Ledger*

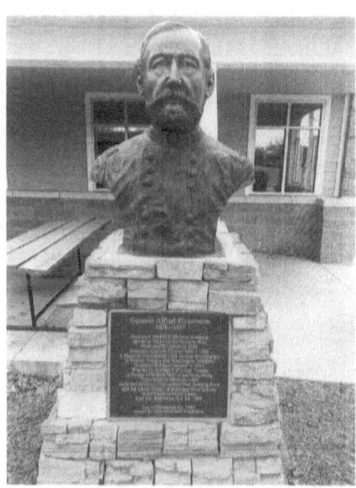

Figure 25 – 2: A statue of General Alfred Pleasonton, namesake of Pleasanton, Kansas

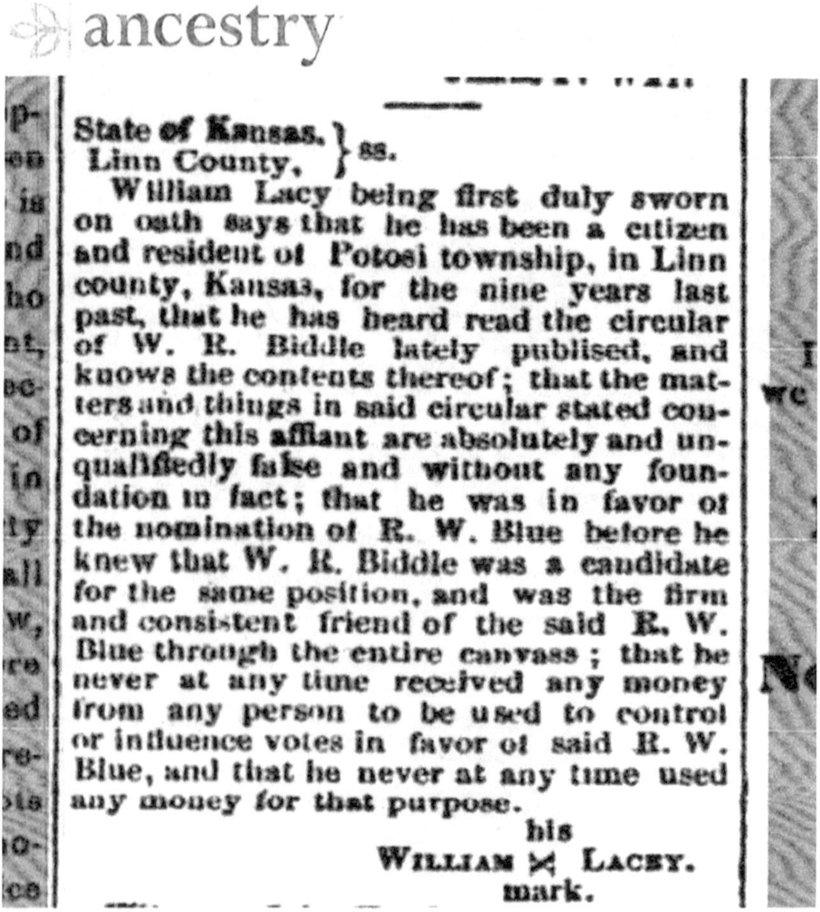

State of Kansas,　}　ss.
Linn County,

William Lacy being first duly sworn on oath says that he has been a citizen and resident of Potosi township, in Linn county, Kansas, for the nine years last past, that he has heard read the circular of W. R. Biddle lately publised, and knows the contents thereof; that the matters and things in said circular stated concerning this affiant are absolutely and unqualifiedly false and without any foundation in fact; that he was in favor of the nomination of R. W. Blue before he knew that W. R. Biddle was a candidate for the same position, and was the firm and consistent friend of the said R. W. Blue through the entire canvass; that he never at any time received any money from any person to be used to control or influence votes in favor of said R. W. Blue, and that he never at any time used any money for that purpose.

　　　　　　　　　　　his
　　　　　WILLIAM ✕ LACEY.
　　　　　　　　　　　mark.

Figure 25 – 3: William Lacy's dispute for buying votes, supported by R.W. Blue

The livery stable lately purchased by R. W. Blue from George R. Page has been repaired and refitted throughout, and is now one of the most complete institutions of the kind in Southern Kansas. It has stabling for about seventy-five head of horses and shelter for buggies and wagons besides. Messrs. Cross & Blue have put in a full stock of buggies, spring wagons and harness of the latest and best styles. Everything is bright and new. The horses are all fresh and have been carefully selected for the business. No better teams, figs and harness are to be found in Southern Kansas. William Lacy, an old and experienced livery man does the feeding and currying with promptness and in fine style, while Mr. Cross is always on hand to accomodate the public. Price for buggy and team to Mound City and return $1.50. Rates to other points in proportion.

Figure 25 – 4: R.W. Blue's livery stable with William Lacy as a livery man

Publication Notice.

William Lacy, Plaintiff, }
vs.
Margeret Tole, Defendant. }

In the District Court of Linn County and State of Kansas.

SAID DEFENDANT, MARGERET TOLE, IS hereby notified that she has been sued by the said plaintiff in the above entitled action. That the said plaintiff filed his petition in this action in the clerk's office of said court on the 12th day of May, 1882. That she must answer or demur to the petition of the said plaintiff filed in said action on or before the 26th day of June, 1882, or said petition will be taken as true and judgment rendered accordingly quieting the title of said plaintiff to lot No. (10) ten, block (152) of the city of Pleasanton, Linn county, Kansas, and forever barring said defendant, her heirs and assigns, of all right, title and interest in or to the same, or in any way making, setting up or prosecuting any interest or claim to said lot.

BLUE AND RICH,
49   Attorneys for Plaintiff.

Figure 25 – 5: Lawsuit brought by William Lacy over a land dispute. He prevailed.

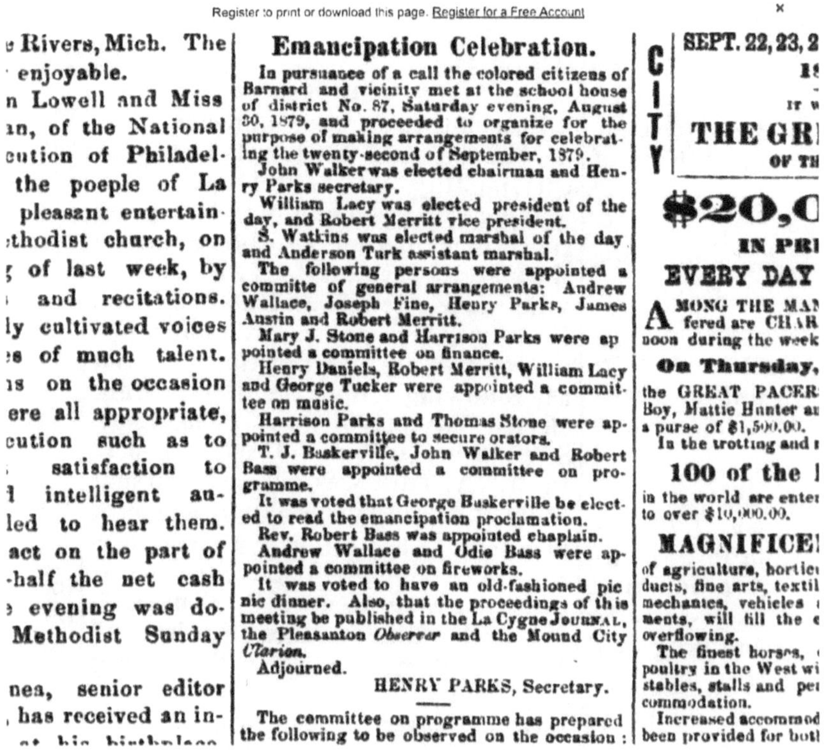

Figure 25 – 6: An Emancipation Day celebration with William Lacy as the president

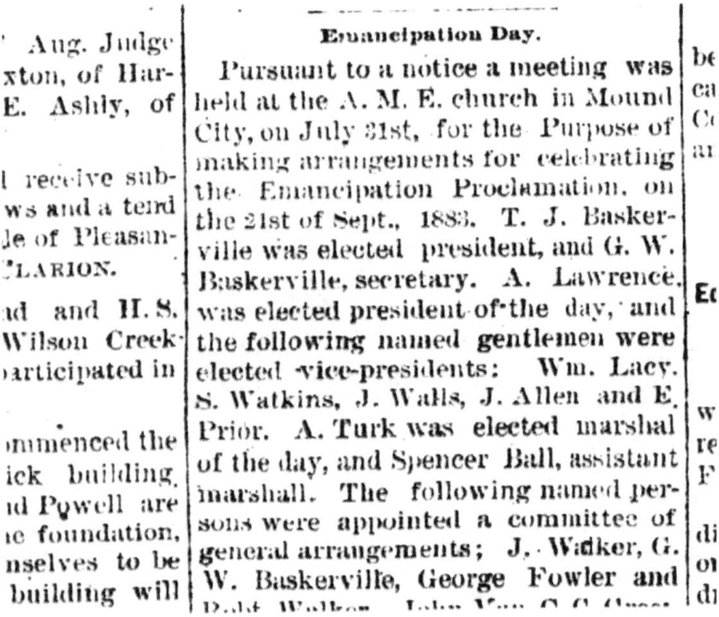

Emancipation Day.

Pursuant to a notice a meeting was held at the A. M. E. church in Mound City, on July 31st, for the Purpose of making arrangements for celebrating the Emancipation Proclamation, on the 21st of Sept., 1883. T. J. Baskerville was elected president, and G. W. Baskerville, secretary. A. Lawrence was elected president of the day, and the following named gentlemen were elected vice-presidents: Wm. Lacy, S. Watkins, J. Walls, J. Allen and E. Prior. A. Turk was elected marshal of the day, and Spencer Ball, assistant marshall. The following named persons were appointed a committee of general arrangements; J. Walker, G. W. Baskerville, George Fowler and

Figure 25 – 7: Another Emancipation Day in Mound City, William Lacy as vice-president

CHAPTER 26

Peace and Family

Mound City, Kansas—Mid 1800s

With the war won, the couple had to turn toward a more normal routine. William still had to tangle with the army for past payments owed, but he could do it from home, with his wife at his side. All across the area, changes dripped out from the state of Kansas abolishing slavery—the abolitionists had won the long fight. Citizens could no longer attempt to catch and drag fugitive slaves back for a reward to Missouri. Even if slave catchers caught them, there wouldn't be any payment, as no laws supported their return from Indian Territory or otherwise. The 13th Amendment protected them across all states now.

Finally back together again, William and Lucinda set out to invest everything in their life together. With the war behind them and no reason to look over their shoulders, more opportunities opened up to improve their lives. They'd made do with the tiny homestead, but a real farm would solve most of their problems, and more space meant they could grow their family. Rebecca wouldn't stay a tot forever. The questions that followed were naturally about how to accomplish this.

Two days later, William was back at the courthouse, now familiar ground and much friendlier since they saw him in uniform. The farmers nearby were glad for the help again, happy to see William's smiling face. He helped so much before with harvesting and repairs. A sawmill close by on Little Sugar Creek needed more help, and he was all too ready to provide it.

Between sawmill jobs, where other soldiers found work after the war, William would visit the courthouse area to find odd jobs. Studying the latest flyers, movement caught his eye. A man was posting a fresh flyer, and he asked what the job was for.

The man explained that the 1866 elections were around the corner, and he wanted to be ready. Someday, William would be allowed to vote, too. With a broad smile, the man invited William to a meeting to discuss how the people of Mound City would vote moving forward.

When he arrived, he found many other people, colored and white, voicing unanimous approval for Sidney Clarke as their representative in Congress and then reaffirming support for the current senator, James Lane.

Shortly after, the meeting thoughts came to fruition as both won their respective elections. William watched all the election results, hoping the white men who voted did so with the dream of equality for all men. Senator James Lane was also popular for his idea of colored soldiers joining the war effort and supporting Colonel William's leadership of the 1st Kansas. This solidified William's support of whether he could vote or not. However, sad tidings came swiftly afterward with news of his death and subsequent replacement with Edmund Ross. It was the season for replacements, and President Andrew Johnson did his best to fill Lincoln's shoes. Throughout the season, William kept up with the campaigning man who ran into him with the flyer.

The young man continued his work as usual. With the war ending and everyone freed, he hoped this would put his family in a better position. Feeling sentimental, William paused his work at Snoddy's place to ask him for another favor. Would he pen a letter for him back to the Lacys in Van Buren, asking for information about his family? In the letter, Snoddy added that William would like to know if Henry, Eliza, and Joe would like to live in Kansas near them. The two walked to the post office to mail the letter. William said a silent prayer it'd reach them alive and well.

Two months later, William heard the postmaster calling his name and walked across the plaza to chat. Isaac Stockton, the postmaster, had become acquainted with Lucinda through all the months of delivering his payments. Now, they regularly spoke on days William visited the area while he looked for work.

"Got a letter from Arkansas today," Stockton said, passing a large brown envelope with a wax seal.

"Thank you! From Arkansas? Been hopin' for word back home. Maybe they finally sent a reply." William nodded and eagerly accepted the letter. Stockton turned to leave, but William tapped on his shoulder.

"Oh, right, sorry about that," he said before reading the letter aloud to the young man. "Seems like your family from Arkansas is coming to see you here in Mound City. They've accepted your offer for them to come live with you. Sounds like good news! Congratulations, son."

Overjoyed, the young man hugged the postmaster before sprinting home to share the news with Lucinda. Almost breaking the door open, he waved the letter in the air.

"'Cinda, got the best news! My family's alive, and they're comin' here to meet you!"

"You don't say," Lucinda said, rubbing her belly, now swollen with a second child. "Goodness knows we could use the help around here." She paused as William approached to hold her, placing his hand on her stomach. "You think … you think my daddy and momma are still alive, too?"

"Of course they are. You want me to send 'em a letter? I'll go get Mr. Stockton right now."

"No," she said softly. "No, I think we'll wait on that." She stared off into space. "We'll have enough on our hands with your folks. I can wait to contact mine."

This worried William, but he knew Lucinda would ask when she was ready. He kissed her before swinging Rebecca in the air. "You're gonna meet your grandaddy!"

For nearly a decade, William and Lucinda poured their hearts and souls into their family, which swelled. They continued their hard work, shaping the land and pulling what money they could from helping around Mound City. Meanwhile, they welcomed more children to the homestead. Another baby girl arrived, whom they named after Eliza.

Days lazily rolled by in a calm rhythm of growing, harvesting, preserving, and celebrating. William fell gratefully into this pattern, knowing in his heart that good things were coming. Then, one day, out of the blue, this was confirmed.

Henry filled in some gaps since William fled with Lucinda. The Lacy family freed them without protest, understanding the law was the law. Theo Lacy was the one who did it. However, since the times continued to be hard, their former master couldn't pay them either. The once proud plantation owners from North Carolina, Virginia, Alabama, and Arkansas were whittled down to no more than common working-class people.

Eliza also added that their Van Buren farm fell into disrepair during the hard times. When they left, the place was overgrown with weeds, with no hands to work the fields anymore. Lacking leadership and few resources, the family couldn't dig themselves out of the mess. After all, they'd been taken care of their entire lives by the slaves.

Over a tearful reunion, they explained that their journey started in Morgan County at an Alabama plantation. Fighting Joe Wheeler, their former master, kept them there while he fought in the Mexican War, gaining him his nickname.

Together in Mound City, they had a renewed sense of vigor and determination. Of course, William and Lucinda's smaller home wouldn't be able to sustain their growing family forever, but now, they had more hands to work, and all their work went as an investment into their own well-being. While Henry and William went to work jobs around town, Eliza and Lucinda cared for the home and garden, sharing the work gratefully between all family members.

A massive rebuilding effort swept the nation, and Mound City became a part of this, thriving alongside the young family. With more time and growing stature in the community, William invited more neighbors to his fire pit to spread hope and support. Riding on this tide and meeting with the campaigning man, he visited various community offices. As a war hero who fought to save Kansas and Mound City, people trusted him, especially other freed slaves who were finding their place in the world. It was common for the Lacys to help the lost and confused newly freed colored people get on their feet in Mound City.

Joining the Grand Army of the Republic in Linn County, William celebrated and memorialized the Civil War, as they now were calling it. The organization celebrated the Union victory annually in honor of those lost and the immense sacrifices. During these celebrations, William emphasized September 22nd each year, paying special homage to Emancipation Day. His colored brethren were now American citizens thanks to that momentous occasion when Lincoln signed the Emancipation Proclamation.

With his celebratory efforts and cheerful attitude, the locals elected William as the "President of the Day" for festivities, a title and role he threw himself into with gusto. Food, drinks, games, contests, and other events were his responsibility, and he always made sure to have a grand guest read the proclamation to everyone, reminding them of what he often found too good to be true: they were a free people. More often than not, he'd be president of the event again when it came around.

William also threw himself into supporting political candidates. With his upbeat attitude and tireless optimism, folks sought him as a surrogate speaker for politicians. He found more work handing out flyers and shaking hands, delivering needed information to change people's hearts. His ability to listen made him so trustworthy and helped people feel heard. Besides this, he found a genuine passion in speeding along the reconstruction efforts. He saw what happened in Lawrence and vowed to make it easier for others.

To help with this, he studied speeches and listened to great orators when they came to speak at the local church. When the time came for him to vote, he felt a grave sense of purpose, like the weight of his decisions substantially mattered. Using his position and knowledge, he informed others, including Henry, of who was the most trustworthy and who didn't have the people's interests in mind.

On each Election Day, William would gather a host of neighbors, riding with them into town to encourage their civic participation. Lucinda would wait at home, thankful her husband listened to good sense when she added hers to the mix. While unable to vote herself, she trusted the fine men of Mound City to vote for their wives' well-being.

As the peaceful time rolled by, the Lacys were blessed with more children: Georgia, Gussie, and Roxie—all healthy babies born with Carolyn coming by and engaging in a good-natured argument with Lucinda. Then, after a few more years, they added two boys, William Jr., whom they called John, and Billy.

All across the nation, freed colored folks were making political and economic strides to balance the scales—even if socially challenging. Mound City boasted a healthy stock of open-minded people, regardless of skin color, and stood out as an exceptional place of acceptance.

One-room schoolhouses across Linn County featured a new integration of the people. Growing up in a new world, the Lacy children entered school alongside white kids from the abolitionist community, a truly unusual sight to the adults but one they were grateful for. Some folks still griped about the change but were quickly silenced with more practical notions. Besides social strides, the world had fewer resources, and kids needed school. The Lacy children excelled in grammar, rhetoric, and arithmetic. The only failure they met was trying to teach their parents to read.

Luck changed when William met a lawyer named R.W. Blue, a prominent lawman in Mound City and an avid Republican and abolitionist. The two took to each other immediately, recognizing a kindred spirit in helping their community and rebuilding their broken country.

Through their friendship, William also returned to his love of horses by managing Mr. Blue's livery stable in the neighboring town of Pleasanton. A large brick structure, the stable was massive, with enough room for 75 horses, and needed two offices to manage it. When people arrived in town, this was the perfect place to rub elbows, as they'd need a horse to get around. Even if they had their own horses, R.W. Blue livery stable was the only place to board them. It was a match made in heaven, as William got to talk with new people while using his natural talent to care for the horses.

Together, they helped provide a backbone for the colored community, with Mr. Blue representing many locals in various legal matters, especially real estate issues. William provided a handy go-between for the white man and the somewhat shy, newly freed slaves. He understood how hard it was to trust at that time.

Besides that, the two put their heads together to improve things beyond merely legal matters. Mr. Blue ran for office, leaning on William's savvy campaign support. In turn, Mr. Blue supported William when he ran for Sheriff of Linn County. While unsuccessful, the two accomplished much together in improving the lives of others in the community.

His luck changed once more when tampering charges were brought against William. Without validity, some folks took offense to his help, accusing him of buying votes in another race for a county official. Surprised, the honest man turned to R.W. Blue's law firm to defend him against the disrespectful allegations.

With his help, he was acquitted of all charges, and after the verdict was rendered, William took Mr. Blue out celebrating for a few drinks at a local restaurant.

Finally arriving home to his family, he kissed Lucinda on the cheek and ruffled Billy's hair, gazing at his many blessings. Together, they made the purchase, becoming proud landowners. William was now a real farmer, with land only a few miles down the road from Mound City in Pleasanton, Kansas. One primary reason he decided to settle here was to learn more about how the town's namesake,

General Pleasonton, whose cavalry chased down Pap Price after Westport. The man was proud to own land with the name of a war hero whose exploits helped save Mound City by driving Pap Price's troops directly into the 6th Kansas State Militia's waiting grasp. With a tract of land, a large family, and room for horses, all was well in Linn County—and with the world.

Cozy in the new house, Lucinda placed a hand on William's during dinner, pausing the conversation regarding the livery stable.

"Will, it's time. I wanna know what happened to my momma," she said. "We in a good spot now, and I just need to know if she's alive or dead. With no slavery, even in Indian Territory, it's safer to travel. I'd like to go see about her."

William fell deep in thought. It seemed like it was time, and since it worked out so well with Henry and Eliza being there, maybe Luvinia could be saved, too. He remembered the sour Billy Postoak and knew it'd be a fight they'd walk into if they didn't play their cards right.

"When the weather's good, let's head out," he said. "I'm sure Eliza and Henry can watch the children while we gone."

With that settled, William requested some time off from the stables and borrowed a wagon for the long ride back to Coweta. The trip took them several weeks on foot, but now, with a solid wagon, a powerful team of horses, and the ability to walk in broad daylight, the trip whittled down to days. They could even view the scenery without looking over their shoulders for slave catchers, sleeping peacefully at night by a fire.

The familiar treeline around the cozy village came into view, and so did the houses of Coweta. It was quiet as always, with barely any movement visible from the road, almost like a ghost town. It looked like the village hadn't recovered from the war yet, but that didn't surprise William. The place only had a flow of trade coming in, and without it for so long, what foundation did they have to build from?

Rolling through it, the couple brought their wagon to a stop near the small house Lucinda used to live in. The house had seen better days, falling farther into overgrowth as the years passed. Lucinda's hands shook as she stepped off the wagon, and William hopped off to support her.

"Just strange bein' back here after we left," she said. "You think either of them'll be happy to see me?"

"They'd be crazy not to," he replied, rubbing her shoulders. "And if they crazy, we'll just leave. We both free now. Simple as that."

Nodding and drawing in a shaky breath, Lucinda walked with her husband over to her old home. Everything looked pretty much the way she remembered. With her father's alcohol issues, he was never much help in keeping the house clean and tidy, spending most of his time in a drunken stupor.

The door opened as Lucinda neared the porch, revealing Luvinia, wearing a long blue dress. Her face was careworn from the passing years, but it broke into a huge smile when she sighted her daughter. Lucinda called out, "Momma!" With arms wide open, her mother sank to the floor when they crashed together, Lucinda squeezing her mother tightly.

"I thought you was dead," Luvinia said between sobs. "When we woke up with you gone, I thought you'd been taken or worse. Oh, my baby! My sweet baby girl's come back to me."

"I'm sorry, Momma. I had to go, though. Every day, you tried to be his wife, and he only saw you as a slave. I couldn't just be another slave in the house. I was dyin' here, and I couldn't watch Daddy kill you neither."

"He couldn't kill me if he tried."

William gave them their space, putting up the horses nearby and only approaching when Lucinda waved him over. Drying her tears, she stood and helped her mother up. "The priest in the next village over helped us escape. And now? You wouldn't believe the stories of what happened. We livin' up in Mound City, Kansas, over in a farm of our own. We got enough space for you. For …" she paused and looked at William. "Where's Daddy?"

Silent now, Luvinia creaked the front door behind her open so more light could fall into the house. The couple looked in to see Billy Postoak—a wasted, thin corpse of a man. He lay on a bed, eyes barely open, with only a weak rise and fall in his chest.

"I don't know if I can leave your father like this, Lucinda," Luvinia said. "He'll die if I go. Ain't nobody around to care for him. He was my master and my husband. I know he'll die if I leave."

"What happened?" William asked. He remembered a wiry, tall, predatory, bird-like man. But now? The intimidating Creek man had withered away.

"He took ill. Doctor said it's his liver on account of all that drinkin'. He cain't move no more, and all I can do is bring some food, hopin' he'll recover again."

Lucinda looked at William as her mother walked over to Postoak, kneeling at his side to wipe his brow. Her eyes held all the years of torment at the hands of her father but were also the eyes of a daughter who found out her father was dying.

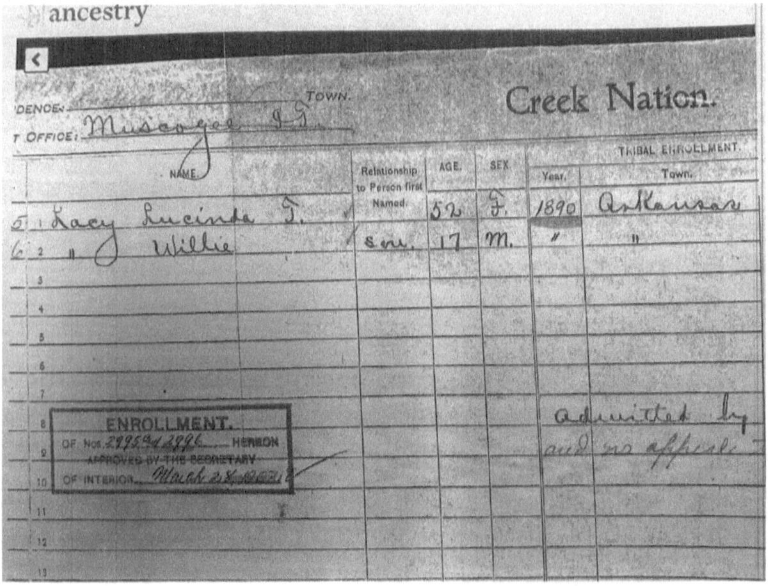
ancestry

Creek Nation.

DENCE: TOWN.

T OFFICE: Muscogee I.T.

	Name	Relationship to Person first Named.	Age.	Sex.	Tribal Enrollment. Year.	Tribal Enrollment. Town.
5 1	Lacy Lucinda T.		52	F.	1890	Arkansas
6 2	" Willie	Son.	17	M.	"	"

ENROLLMENT.
OF Nos. 2995 and 2996 HEREON
APPROVED BY THE SECRETARY
OF INTERIOR March 28, 1902

admitted by
and no appeal.

Figure 26 – 1: Lucinda Lacy's enrollment in the Creek Nation

CHAPTER 27

A Most Unusual Letter

Mound City, Kansas—Summer 1865

Staying for another day, both William and Lucinda tried their best to fix up what Luvinia couldn't get to, trying to get things as comfortable for her as possible. Lucinda helped weed her garden while William made house repairs. After this, they packed up for the return journey. They'd brought a few packages as gifts, wrapped up for Luvinia to keep.

Lucinda said a tearful goodbye to her mother, who refused to leave their home while Billy was still clinging to life. She vowed to travel to nearby Van Buren at least once a month to keep in written communication. After making the promise, the couple left.

William admired the passage of time along the road out of the town. This was the same road the 1st Kansas had acquitted themselves in the Battle of Honey Springs some twenty years earlier. Now, two former fugitive slaves, who'd avoided being so open in travel, were in a carriage in broad daylight. The moment gave William a light thrill.

Once they lost sight of Coweta, Lucinda broke down, clinging to William as sobs rocked her body. "I feel like we abandonin' her to die there with Daddy. We should turn back 'round and pull her in the wagon."

"I see where you get your stubborn streak from," William said calmly. He reined in the horses and pulled her into a tight hug. "Thought it was from Billy, but no. It's from your momma. It's a strength to move through everything in life. Your momma made her mind up, and there's no use tryin' to change it. But you did get her to write. She gon' do just that. You can trust it. You know she's alive, and we can come back to pick her up once your daddy's passed."

Lucinda dried her tears and sat back. "Right. I wish I felt more bad for him, but he's gettin' exactly what he deserved. Just wish Momma didn't feel so beholden to him."

The man took the reins again, clicking to the horses as he nudged them forward, and they were off back to Pleasanton.

It was a simple trip back after that, and they slipped back into daily life at Pleasanton. Now that she had time to process it, Lucinda thought the trip was worth it. She confirmed her family wasn't lost to time, and she could look forward to letters from her mother each month. Luvinia could honor what she needed, and there was hope for more in the future.

No one else knew about her past like William and her parents did. Although some more fearful memories faded or felt unreal, Lucinda felt like her time as a young woman had built her into the matriarch she was now. She still had a connection to her past. With the solid memory of returning to Coweta as a mother and wife herself, and comparing this to her own family's failures in raising her, she felt like she'd won. William came to her side, and she could stand tall, riding in broad daylight as a free person. Coweta, in memory, had some good attachments now.

It also solidified the insurmountable odds they overcame. Like a heavy weight was lifted, Lucinda could see their courageous flight and how stupid it was. How could anyone make such a terrible trip again? They quickly put it behind them, but now, in space and safety, she ran through all the dangerous times they shared. William discussed these with her, holding her hand gently as she told him what she remembered. It was like she'd saved up all the fear from then, and it was coming up in waves now. Some nights, she screamed and woke William, who gently held her while the pain leaked out from her body. The fears of killing, whipping, or just being forced to return to her abusive father all roared back strong.

Through it all, William held her, gently reminding her she was safe and her family would care for her. They'd made it through all the terrors alive and well. Now, they had nothing but good years to look forward to together.

The first letter from Luvinia arrived with news that her father had passed. The cirrhosis overtook him, and the villagers came together to bury him in the field behind their house. Luvinia also wrote that she was grateful for their offer but felt tied to the land. She couldn't leave Coweta any more than she could've left her father. She'd been there so long that it felt like her roots had grown deep into the soil.

Lucinda discussed it with William, and the two decided they'd visit her back in Indian Territory.

On one such trip, Lucinda arrived to find her mother pale and withdrawn. After talking with a doctor, they discovered she was dying of a kidney disease. Lucinda sent William and the family a letter, letting them know she was staying in Coweta to care for her mother in her final days.

In those months, Lucinda reconnected with the last vestiges of her family as they came in, one by one, to pay respects to her mother. The little cabin was filled with light and laughter in those final weeks, and Luvinia always kept a blissful smile on her face, saying she couldn't have asked for a better daughter.

She buried her mother next to her father in the field behind their house only a few months into her stay.

The villagers helped and then traveled with her back to the nearest postmaster. She sent William a letter, explaining the depressing news and asking him to come and retrieve her. Waiting for her husband, now alone in a sad house, Lucinda kept her spirits up by tending to the garden.

It took William less time on a speedy journey, and he arrived in Coweta just as the mail courier did, bearing another sealed envelope.

Overwhelmed, Lucinda handed it to William, who tucked it under his arm before helping his wife into the wagon. Glad to be back, she spent one more tearful minute looking back at her childhood home, now empty except for memories.

The two made the trip home, mostly silent, with William hugging her gently as she cried.

Once they arrived back in Pleasanton, Lucinda felt steadier and asked William to open the letter, gathering a neighbor to help them read:

Dear Lucinda,

> *The Creek Nation of the Indian Territory recognizes your service to our nation. For many years, you were not compensated for your membership in the Creek Nation of the Indian Territory. Pursuant to the Creek Nation Treaty of 1866, we are hereby allotting 160 acres of land in the Creek Nation for your ownership. Please make an application to the Creek Nation if you intend to obtain an allotment of land from the Creek Nation.*

In shock, the couple set the letter down and looked at each other. They couldn't believe what they heard and went to Snoddy's house to ask him to reread it to ensure it was correct. It was true.

Snoddy explained that the Dawes Act allotted them property in the Creek Nation for the years of servitude that Lucinda incurred. He detailed that Henry Dawes introduced this law to Congress, which would partition land in the Indian Territory and allot it to Indians individually instead of to whole tribes. The law also specified that Indians who accepted this allotment would become American citizens. The purpose of the Dawes Act was to force the Indians to live as farmers and ranchers like the whites in America. This applied to people enslaved by the tribes in the Creek Nation.

To accept this, Lucinda would be required to sign up as a member of the Creek Nation with the Office of Indian Affairs. Doing so would make her eligible for the allotment as a daughter of a Creek father and enslaved mother. After talking about it, Lucinda went with William and Snoddy (to interpret the writing) and signed up to receive the 160-acre allotment as head of household. This was in exchange for her sixteen years as a slave to her father. Many heavy questions arose, but the least they could do was verify the land ownership first.

All they needed to do now was bring the deed to the land they rightfully owned and claim it for themselves.

> **FORT SMITH.**
>
> **Prisoners Brought in by the United States Marshal—Dropped Dead.**
>
> Special to Arkansas Democrat.
>
> FORT SMITH, ARK., Sept. 2.— Deputy Marshal Bass Reeves and posse came in to-day from the Seminole Nation with fifteen United States prisoners, charged with various offenses. Among them were two murderers—Geo. Washington, a white man, and Chub Moore, an Indian. The latter resisted arrest and was shot in the thigh, but will recover.

Figure 27 – 1: Clipping of Deputy Marshal Bass Reeves and his investigation

> —Wm. Lacy and family went to Muscogee, Indian Territory, last Sunday, where they will hereafter make their home, his wife having a head right in the Creek nation. We hope William will have better health down there than he has had for a long time.

Figure 27 – 2: The Lacy family moves to Indian Territory, record by the *Pleasanton Observer*

CHAPTER 28

Storm for the Ages

Pleasanton, Kansas—Spring 1893

One pleasant spring day, with a warm, calm breeze, William and Lucinda placed heavy packs in their wagon. Several children helped load half-heartedly: Gussie, Roxie, Will Jr., and Billy. The remainder of their furniture and belongings were placed between the travel sacks. They had amassed enough that two wagons were needed to carry all their belongings, plus the family, from Kansas into Indian Territory.

The Texas Road was now a familiar travel route since they'd made so many trips down to Coweta. These landowners would visit them in Pleasanton, too. Thankfully, this meant a trail of cherished memories and friendly stops along the way, providing food, water, and refreshments for the horses. They made a longer stop in Coweta and returned to the house that Lucinda's parents used to own. They'd need a temporary place while they waited for Lucinda to receive her land allotment.

With the children to help, it was easier to get it back into a serviceable shape as a house. This meant replacing some logs in the cabin and sprucing it up. They also added a wooden floor so they wouldn't cough with so much kicked-up dust. William widened the porch outside so the whole family could sit together.

Within a few days, the kids felt more at home, exploring the area and discovering the gravestones of their maternal grandparents out back. The couple had a brief, sad conversation, with Lucinda feeling like she should've done more to have them at least know their grandmother. The crosses outside were weathered but still present, so Lucinda took extra time with the kids to repaint them and clear the brush. They placed a path around the graves and the house, making it easier to walk and play outside.

All the work and changes drew attention, and William created another fire pit, just like the one in Mound City that their tiny home had. This became a gathering area for the folks in Coweta, who would come to say hello to the family. Lucinda reconnected with her neighbors. Some she hadn't seen since her mother passed earlier. Since then, more people moved back to the tiny village.

Each Sunday, like clockwork, they would take their kids to a little church on top of a hill, only half a mile from the log home. They'd wait to see what the Lord had in store for them.

A hot summer day found the couple startled by a loud rap at their front door. William stood, placing a hand on Lucinda's shoulder, and walked to their door, reminding himself it was sorely in need of repair. Worried who would knock so angrily, the man grabbed his 1883 Winchester pistol, grateful he purchased it in Pleasanton before traveling. While the states were safer with the war winding down, it didn't mean thieves and other ne'er-do-wells weren't prowling for scraps.

With the pistol ready, he slowly opened the door, concealing it behind the wood. Peering out, he spotted a tall Black man a few steps off the porch. Lanky and lean, the man sported a long tan overcoat that hung off his body, a big hat, and a thick mustache.

"Hello, sir," the man said, tipping his hat. "Sorry to bother you and your family. I'm Bass Reeves, a lawman from Fort Smith." As he said this, Reeves pulled his coat back to expose the shiny sheriff's badge. William had never seen a colored lawman before, but the sheriff's badge looked real enough. Memories of his own run for sheriff flickered before he noticed the man was waiting for a reply.

"Mr. Reeves, no bother at all. What can I do for you today, sir?"

"Just came by to ask if you've seen any unusual Indians 'round these parts as of late. Any new faces in Coweta?"

Lucinda appeared in the doorway and spoke to the man in Creek. "We haven't been here long ourselves, so people might be sayin' we the ones with unusual faces. But we ain't no outlaws if that's what you came to see. Just a family with kids keepin' to ourselves."

"I can see that," Sheriff Reeves chuckled. "Well, I won't keep ya then. Good to meet you, folks." With that, he tipped his hat again and backed away. When he reached his horse, William noticed another man half-hidden behind it. He'd been watching the whole thing play out. Sheriff Reeves' traveling companion, a short man, must've been a Seminole Indian, but he never introduced himself. The two left to talk to their neighbors.

"Who was that?" Lucinda asked when they were inside again with the door closed.

"I think that was the famous gunslinger, Bass Reeves. He'd been responsible for killing most of the outlaws 'round here in Indian Territory all by himself. From what I heard, he was a U.S. Marshall, made by Judge Parker in Fort Smith. As a boy, I'd heard rumors he chased bad men all up and down these parts. Never would've dreamed he was still workin'."

When they questioned their neighbors, they mentioned they only discovered he was based in a larger town twenty-five miles south called Muscogee. William and Lucinda had made a few trips there for supplies but rarely stopped to spend time. Occasionally, they'd buy a newspaper to bring to their kids, and that's how they learned about Bass Reeves and any other news of the Indian allotment process.

More hot southern weeks passed before Lucinda received another letter from the Office of Indian Affairs. In the latest one, she was requested to appear at the office to see where her land was located. She was happy to discover the 160 acres were just north of Coweta and prime farmland.

Excited, the couple rushed to see it for themselves, and the sight took their breath away. The land was primarily flat but rolled out into hills, perfect for building new homes as they'd allow rainwater to flow away. Lucinda remembered this was important since flooding was a constant problem. The silver lining was that no river was nearby to swell in the summer, but it would mean digging a well for their water needs.

Their family back in Pleasanton came to help with the construction of their new home, barns, and chicken coops. Within a year of hard work, they had a thriving farm with corn, wheat, cabbage, peas, potatoes, carrots, and onions. William refused to grow cotton. Even though it was handy, he vowed a Lacy hand would never have to pick it again.

The food gave them all they could eat. Each year, they planted and harvested pecan trees and peaches, too. Since they had everything and more, William reaffirmed his commitment to God, promising to follow his teachings. He felt so blessed with the plenty they enjoyed that he felt called to share it with their friends in Pleasanton and Mound City. Lucinda was thrilled to help plan trips to bring goods and other supplies back to share with friends and family.

While times were easy, they weren't free from difficulties. William and Lucinda, now established on their acreage, woke up May 12th to find a brisk breeze rustling leaves outside. The sun never rose, and a heavily clouded sky kept the area dark as winds grew stronger.

Outside of Coweta, the couple and their children lived in a rural area of the Creek Nation, settling about a mile away from any neighbor. Everyone gathered inside as the wind's strength picked up enough to rock the house. They could see trees bent way over through the windows and their wheat field thrashing around in the storm. A terrible noise sounded. Animals bellowed outside in fear, and church bells rang loudly.

Startled, Lucinda recalled memories of similar occurrences. As a little girl, winds this fierce accompanied by warning bells meant a tornado had been sighted—and it was coming for them.

"Everybody," she shouted over the wind. "C'mon, y'all, we gotta get to the ditch outside." While there was no surefire way to survive a tornado, getting low to the ground would lower their chances of being blown away or struck by anything.

Frightened, her children clustered around her as William took their hands, following her lead. His strong arms kept them from leaving the ground, and the family inched their way to the ditch.

"Momma, what're we gonna do?"

"Hush now! Just keep ahold of your daddy, and we'll make it through this. I promise!"

The group settled into a ditch near the house to avoid trees and flying debris. William stood up, yelling about the horses before running to the barn. He ducked, avoiding flying fence posts while Lucinda screamed for him to come back. Quickly, the man loosed his horses to run for their lives before joining his family again in the ditch.

"Alright, everybody, hold on tight!"

Hunkering down, William used all his strength to protect his family from the tearing wind. Beside him, Lucinda cradled their children in the ditch, her hair flying wildly in the storm. Seconds passed, and the wind only seemed to get stronger, tearing at their faces if they raised them to check on their surroundings. The tornado sounded like a train whistle, a continuous hellish sound, louder than a train.

Lucinda had seen tornadoes as a child, but none like this one. This one came directly over her house. Trees uprooted around them, limbs popping and breaking from the pressure. The barn and coops also broke under the wind, and the wood and shrapnel whirled like angry hornets. Their chickens flapped, clucking overhead while being whisked away into their fields. William watched the roof of their house get ripped apart—the house they had just built earlier with his family.

Ten minutes passed in reality, but it seemed like hours. Slowly, the terrible winds died down, and Lucinda risked a peek to see if it was safe to get up. Still holding hands, the entire family climbed to their feet once their mother did. Only one piece of their home was left. Everything else—the barn, coops, and fields—was destroyed. It was almost like they'd never built anything in the first place.

Yet they had each other, alive and well for now, if not scared out of their minds. William and Lucinda reminded themselves that as long as they were alive, they could recover. So much more could have gone wrong for them, but thankfully, her quick thinking had saved their lives. She clutched her family to her tightly, crying in relief. They all stayed in the ditch as William sent up grateful prayers to God for sparing their lives.

The recovery afterward came in shaky footsteps and sobs. Each family member gathered what they could, finding their scattered livelihood. Most of their crops had been destroyed, and Lucinda feared the worst for their neighbors.

William looked for their horses again as they all split up to use up the rest of their day. Lucinda kept the children close to the house, asking them to stay within eyesight and bring whatever they found back to where their porch was. When William returned with the horses, she took one to go check on their neighbors. They'd built a friendship with Nell Crocker, a seventy-five-year-old Creek woman who lived nearby with her husband, Joe Crocker.

When she came to their neighbor's house, it was completely destroyed. She hopped off the horse and ran to check, praying they'd had the good sense to get out in time. Unfortunately, they hadn't. She cried for them. Their broken bodies were caught in the wooden debris of their falling home. Since they couldn't be helped, she decided to head to the church to see who else survived. After all, whoever rang those bells saved their lives, too.

Weeping, she rode to the church, discovering it had also been blown to bits. No bell or steeple rose above the building anymore, now shattered across the ground thirty yards away. Beneath the steeple were the legs of Miss Esther, the woman who must've rung those bells once the tornado was in sight. Lucinda's heart broke when she saw the ultimate sacrifice that woman made for her community.

Shaken and exhausted, more people poured in from the nearby villages to find others. William joined Lucinda at the church to help organize rescue efforts. The community had to gather bodies and save who they could. In all, across the area, nine people were killed in that tornado. No one in their family had so much as a scratch compared to the broken, injured people whom they helped care for.

William later whispered that God protected them, and he vowed to keep Him in their home, always, from that day forward.

Miss Esther had lived in a small house adjacent to the church, sadly alone after her husband had died a few years earlier. She threw everything into the congregation. Joe and Nell Crocker, found killed by the storm as well, would be remembered as Creeks who tried their best to farm like white settlers rather than lose everything. William helped the community bury Miss Esther, the Crockers, and other neighbors, digging graves in the small cemetery.

With neighborly help and their family support from Pleasanton, slowly but surely, William and Lucinda rebuilt their lives, cultivating everything from only debris and scattered pieces. More and more families moved to the area, often following the same path they took or what the Crockers hoped for. Like Lucinda, these new people were slaves to the Creeks.

The Lacys welcomed the Landrums, Cooks, Pegues, and Breedloves, all with the same background, to help populate the devastated area. Pretty soon, out of the ashes, grew a close-knit group of Creeks and former slaves to Creeks, all living together in a quiet, harmonious community.

Through periods of drought, they would gather and dig wells for water, looking for other ways to bring it back from the Arkansas and Verdigris Rivers. The droughts took their toll on the barnyard animals. Sometimes, they had to be slaughtered to avoid dying of thirst. Meat would be sold or given to neighbors to prevent spoiling.

Broken Arrow Man Pensioned.
Congressman Davenport has been informed that a pension of $13.50 a month has been granted to William Lacy, of Broken Arrow, Okla.

Figure 28 – 1: William Lacy's pension granted to him

Mound City, Kansas · Fri, May 25, 1888
Page 5

The death of Henry Lacy, which occurred in this township last Monday, at the residence of his step-son, Joe Wheeler, removes one of the oldest and most honored colored men in this township. Uncle Lacy was born in Rockingham county, North Carolina, but taken later to Alabama as a slave; from thence he was taken to Arkansas, Morgan county where he remained until '64 when he arrived in Kansas where he has since lived, and most of the time in Mound City township. At the time of his death he was 93 years of age. He was among the number who first organized the Second Baptist cuurch here, and a consistent member of that church up to the time of his death. His remains were buried at the cemetery, here, Tuesday.

Article clipped from Linn County Republic

More Clippings by tags, date and location

Figure 28 – 2: Obituary for Henry Lacy

CHAPTER 29

The Scars We Bear

(*Lacy Homestead—April 1889*)

A letter showed up for the Lacys from Joe Wheeler up in Pleasanton, advising them to visit as soon as possible. The kids, now literate, shared what they could make from the letter's contents. Thankfully, since the school systems were set up, the kids helped maintain a postal connection between the Lacy homestead in the Indian Territory and their family in Pleasanton. Each time they visited Coweta, the kids would make a game, pointing out signs and words to help teach their parents how to recognize them. It worked, and the aging couple felt a new world opening for them.

However, the letter was difficult to understand, and even with the kids' help, it was vague, only conveying a sense of urgency. Confused, the couple bid a hasty goodbye to their kids, grown enough to care for the farm in their absence, and hit the road back up into Kansas.

When they arrived at their old home, they were expecting the worst. Letters that dire don't usually summon people for good news. After they walked through the door, their older children greeted them, sharing the sad news that both Eliza and Henry had taken ill.

Eliza was the worst off, succumbing slowly to a respiratory illness they believed was tuberculosis. Henry was also ill but still able to stand and move about. Soon after saying their goodbyes, William held Eliza's hand as she sighed, moving to be with the Lord.

They held a simple funeral in the local cemetery, and after a few days to make sure everyone was handling it as best they could, they left to return home. William said his goodbyes to Henry, even though a thought in the back of his mind whispered this was the last time he'd see him. Colder and distant, Henry accepted a longer hug from William before he hopped back in the wagon. Lucinda said nothing but placed a hand on his leg in support.

A month after they returned home, they received another letter from Pleasanton. Henry died, too. Having just returned, William and Lucinda sent a reply with condolences but didn't have the time to return again. In his will, Henry left his property, twenty acres of land, to William.

William carried this with him but knew there wasn't much to be done. With their short, intensely traumatic life together, Henry gave him the best gift he could: space to become himself. While the whole family loved each other, the torturous circumstances of slavery left deep scars in each of them, creating a tense distance between the older generation. It was hard, if not impossible, to build those deep bonds a family needs when your sibling or parent could be sold off or beaten to death at a moment's notice.

Similar to the news of Ole Ben's death, William felt a tug in his heart, saddened more by his lack of capacity to grieve than by the death itself.

As the oldest male in the family, that letter made him the patriarch. Even while stretched across the state, he was now the lynchpin holding them all together.

In this strange and scary time, a land rush pressured the community sorely. Over fifty thousand people lined up to snatch what land they could with the open, unused lots west of the Indian Territory. This was after Congress passed the Indian Appropriations Act, which brought twelve thousand tracts of land in one hundred sixty-acre allotments to Americans.

According to the proceedings, a person could stake a claim to a lot and then work on it to improve it for several years, thus receiving a homestead. Many people raced to stake their claims but were dismayed to arrive and realized some folks got there sooner. Many were nearby or knew beforehand, and they snatched up the land first, leading to land fights. While challenging, most of these were settled at the local level.

Families rode horses and Conestoga wagons, while others ran on foot to claim any part of the two million acres of land. Located mostly west of where the Lacy family lived, this still significantly interrupted their daily lives as hundreds of people raced across their land, moving westward. With that many people, it brought many frightening occurrences.

The tiny village boasted all the hardworking folk, like the Lacys, who had settled in the area, recovering from the major tornado years earlier. Most travelers shared in this ethos, coming to join in with the other simple farmers. However, not all were like this. Vandals and thieves running from law enforcement also took advantage of the rush to find new opportunities.

William and Lucinda and their neighbors northwest of Coweta were not the only ones to suffer from this. Even before the land rush, Black families struggled with establishing their own communities in the area, often from slavery or escaping racism. The Indian Territory provided a space where that would all be less of a worry. The five civilized tribes had agreed with the U.S. government that they wouldn't practice slavery.

Working in her garden, Lucinda spotted a man coming up the road. She called to William, and together, they greeted him at the edge of their property. The man introduced himself as an agent from the Oklahoma Immigration Organization, or the "OIO." He explained how the organization was trying to make the Indian Territory a Black state. He requested that William and Lucinda move westward near the towns of Kingfisher or Guthrie. With more people around, they could establish a safer place where racism wasn't an issue in their local communities.

They took the pamphlet from him, skimming the front to see colored folks moving from the Indian Territory to Oklahoma. William knew from his travels that many colored families had made similar decisions, but looking at his wife and all the work they put into their farm, he knew it wasn't for them. Around their homestead, they'd already cultivated close friendships with their Creek neighbors, especially in the reconstruction efforts after the tornado. William's 1st Kansas Colored Volunteers fought in the area, making friends and settling family members up and down the Texas Road. While attractive, their home was familiar.

Just before the turn of the century, a movement started to create another town. William and Lucinda's land lay between the new village and Coweta, stretching further northwest. Townspeople excitedly talked about it, calling it "Tulasi," a Creek word for "old town."

The Tulasi village was established in the early 1800s when the Creeks first came to the Indian Territory after the Trail of Tears. This was long before the couple settled in the area, but it'd been mostly quiet, with a few Creeks as its citizens. Its central location kept its primary purpose as the site for the Creek Council.

Since the land rush, the town swelled in size with mostly white settlers, drawing tens of thousands of people to the Indian and Oklahoma territories. Its central location wasn't just for the council. These settlers had commandeered it as a base of operations to expand into the eastern and northern regions. Changing its name to Tulsa was acceptable to the white settlers, who needed a place for businesses and a government. By then, a move for statehood had begun.

William took notice of all these people, thinking maybe this fierce influx could be a good thing. Since more people were close, it meant more buyers for his crops and more businesses to rely upon.

Since selling his inherited land from his late father, he was doing much better, now boasting a robust bank account with money to swing at investments.

Simultaneously, their children were blossoming into their own. Roxie seemed to have sprouted into a young lady overnight, and a young man named Gabriel McIntosh came calling on her. With Eliza and Rebecca already married in Kansas, seeing Gussie or Roxie moving away with new husbands was harder. Not to mention, with fewer people on the farm, it'd be much harder to work the land each year.

When they spoke to him, Gabriel was a strong, fine gentleman who brought his knowledge through reading and writing. Both his parents were slaves to Creeks, and this was something he bonded with Lucinda over. Like William, he took voting seriously, and they discussed elections together. With their blessing, Gabriel married Roxie right away, and soon, the couple was blessed with a baby girl named Georgia, after her sister.

Flourishing with the marriage and happy to be a part of the family, Gabriel established a school for freed children in the Coweta area. Joining forces with William Sr. and Jr. and his son, Gabriel, ensured they'd research and cast their votes responsibly.

In September 1907, the trio rode their carriage to Coweta's center, excited about the increase in business and their family's influence. They came to cast their vote for statehood and became bricks in history by creating the state of Oklahoma.

Settling onto their porch one lazy evening, William and Lucinda rocked back and forth together, gazing out across their lush farmland. Unfortunately, as time passed, the large farm was eaten up as folks moved closer to Tulsa, seeking work and entertainment. Fearing that their baby boy, John William, would soon want to leave the nest, they decided to give him some land to care for. This would reduce their fears about hiring someone to help them, which would be difficult without a fair salary.

About forty acres were parceled out and handed to him adjacent to their farm. They secretly hoped the land would keep him closer as they aged. Seeing each child striking out on their own was difficult. Farming was a good idea, but it became more challenging without a large family to help.

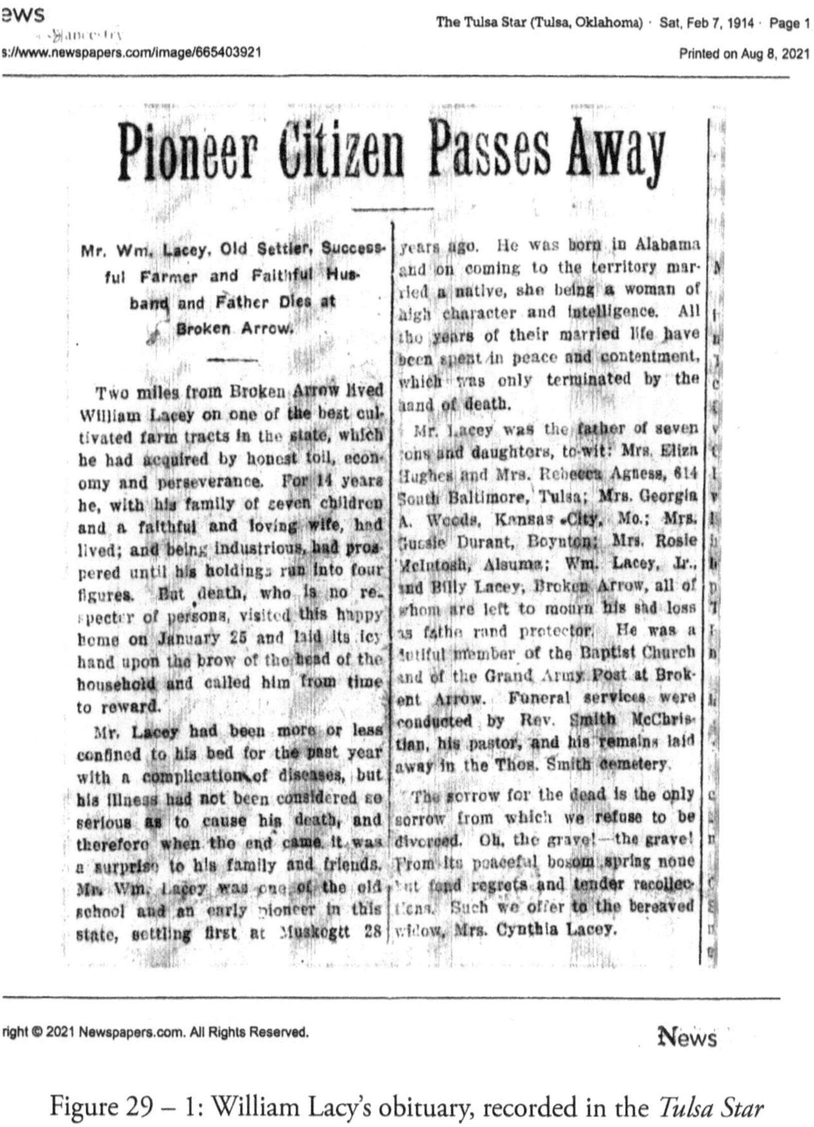

Pioneer Citizen Passes Away

Mr. Wm. Lacey, Old Settler, Successful Farmer and Faithful Husband and Father Dies at Broken Arrow.

Two miles from Broken Arrow lived William Lacey on one of the best cultivated farm tracts in the state, which he had acquired by honest toil, economy and perseverance. For 14 years he, with his family of seven children and a faithful and loving wife, had lived; and being industrious, had prospered until his holdings ran into four figures. But death, who is no respecter of persons, visited this happy home on January 25 and laid its icy hand upon the brow of the head of the household and called him from time to reward.

Mr. Lacey had been more or less confined to his bed for the past year with a complication of diseases, but his illness had not been considered so serious as to cause his death, and therefore when the end came it was a surprise to his family and friends. Mr. Wm. Lacey was one of the old school and an early pioneer in this state, settling first at Muskogee 28 years ago. He was born in Alabama and on coming to the territory married a native, she being a woman of high character and intelligence. All the years of their married life have been spent in peace and contentment, which was only terminated by the hand of death.

Mr. Lacey was the father of seven sons and daughters, to-wit: Mrs. Eliza Hughes and Mrs. Rebecca Agness, 614 South Baltimore, Tulsa; Mrs. Georgia A. Woods, Kansas City, Mo.; Mrs. Gussie Durant, Boynton; Mrs. Rosie McIntosh, Alsuma; Wm. Lacey, Jr., and Billy Lacey, Broken Arrow, all of whom are left to mourn his sad loss as father and protector. He was a dutiful member of the Baptist Church and of the Grand Army Post at Broken Arrow. Funeral services were conducted by Rev. Smith McChristian, his pastor, and his remains laid away in the Thos. Smith cemetery.

The sorrow for the dead is the only sorrow from which we refuse to be divorced. Oh, the grave!—the grave! From its peaceful bosom spring none but fond regrets and tender recollections. Such we offer to the bereaved widow, Mrs. Cynthia Lacey.

Figure 29 – 1: William Lacy's obituary, recorded in the *Tulsa Star*

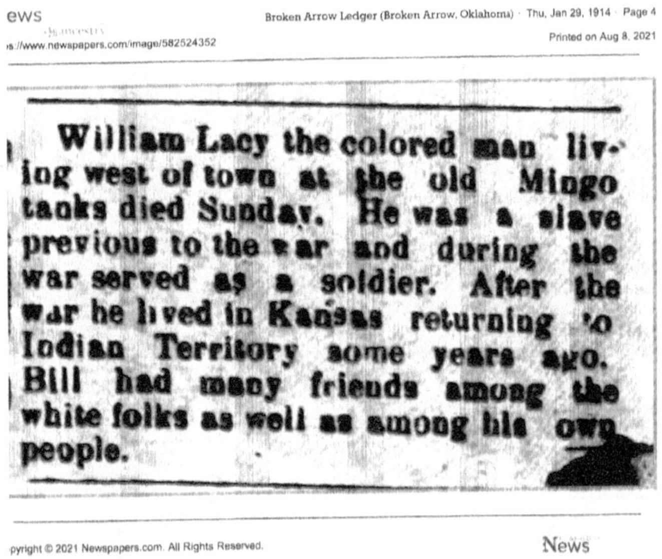

ews

s://www.newspapers.com/image/582524352

Broken Arrow Ledger (Broken Arrow, Oklahoma) · Thu, Jan 29, 1914 · Page 4

Printed on Aug 8, 2021

William Lacy the colored man living west of town at the old Mingo tanks died Sunday. He was a slave previous to the war and during the war served as a soldier. After the war he lived in Kansas returning to Indian Territory some years ago. Bill had many friends among the white folks as well as among his own people.

News

Figure 29 – 2: William Lacy's obituary, recorded in the *Broken Arrow Ledger*

CHAPTER 30

Passing the Torch

Lacy Homestead—Turn of the Century

Giving the land to John William kept the farm working, but it was only a temporary fix for the larger problem.

While one hundred and sixty acres were life-changing, William and Lucinda discovered that owning a large amount of land came with both issues and blessings. Remembering their former lives as slaves, they knew it took finesse and many skilled hands to properly work and care for an extensive property. Each crop needed special care, timing, and time invested to prepare it for sale or consumption.

The huge Lacy homestead also differed from the ones William grew up with—his Lacy Springs childhood and the Van Buren property. Emerging from adolescence, he daydreamed about the power and respect owning a farm would bring, but that contrasted with the stressful reality. His body never fully recovered from past injuries, and with age advancing, it became harder to enjoy life with the strenuous work it took to maintain the land.

So, bit by bit, they sold pieces of it.

First, twenty acres went to the Peques, then fifty to the Landrums. They were grateful for the money these sales provided, sustaining them for a long time. As William and Lucinda moved into their twilight years, they turned to more social activity in their community.

Each weekend, they'd attend a party at a neighbor's home. Sometimes, they took one of their grown children with them to socialize. With the expanding area between Muskogee and Tulsa, many towns popped up as small groups searched for opportunities in the West. This meant more people were around to meet and rub elbows with. The cities of Porter, Haskell, and Bixby, all populated by colored folk and their Creek neighbors, searched for a better place than the slavery and racism they left behind.

The Lacys created their own social circle of friends. It was easier since they learned how to provide a strong, welcoming space for people, just like they did in Mound City. While the white abolitionist presence was not as strong as their memories in Kansas, the same feeling of goodwill and community support grew around them.

They spent this time attending church and events as people gathered in the pillar of the community. William's powerful presence sometimes equated him to their preacher, but he never fully learned to read or write. Sunday school was also a common occurrence, as were Wednesday prayer sessions. Lucinda grew fond of the church members, relying on them like her ladies' group back in Mound City. Ice cream socials, weddings, and funerals, while sad, were all causes to gather and support each other. This extended to Christmas parties at local businesses with dancing, food, gifts, and carols. Easter came around annually, as did Emancipation Day, and they were all causes for worship and gratitude. They even rebuilt the church after the tornado—the same design, with two columns and a short steeple.

More than anything, William threw himself into his membership with the Grand Army of the Republic or "GAR." The organization that helped him back in Pleasanton find more meaningful ways to give back was established as a social service for Union veterans. Since so much devastation happened during the war, it was only natural to help those who had sacrificed so much. William knew the cost and wanted to help where he could.

He'd regularly promote Decoration Day during GAR events, talking to men who served in the 1st Kansas. As time passed, he also reached out to Confederate veterans, bridging what felt like an impossible divide when he was a young man. Many of them returned to Indian Territory to reenter society. He'd met with these men throughout the year to organize ways to support their widows and orphans, the less fortunate members of society.

Each Decoration Day, William and Lucinda would gather their family together—grown children and grandchildren alike—and honor fallen soldiers. They'd provide food, drinks, games, and prizes for the winners. Patriotic music would float through the air well into the night, and photos were common to commemorate each time.

It was a cold October day in 1913 when the aged couple celebrated their fiftieth anniversary. By then, their granddaughter, Georgia, had taken a husband, Frank Osborne, and moved west to the neighboring town of Alsuma.

The family spread. Their grandson, Roy McIntosh, had also taken a wife, moving to Alsuma. The town had a history as rich as the family's, getting its name from the three men who established it, a combination of their wives' names: Alice, Susan, and Mary.

Besides this, the Missouri, Kansas, and Texas railroads came through these towns, establishing a depot there. Many other colored families, descendants of freedmen from Indian nations, moved to these communities. The Breedloves, Greens, and Colberts all moved to Tulsa. John William was married briefly to a woman then, but his second marriage had more promise. Then, he'd met and married a friend's daughter, Melissa Green.

Since they'd survived so much in their childhood and had grown into determined, strong-willed, optimistic adults, William and Lucinda relished the sweet days of their twilight years.

Most of their family was together for a party on Christmas after their son's marriage. A few weeks after the crowd left, William caught the flu. With the weakening effects, he decided to rest in bed for a day or two. Lucinda cared for him, sitting by his side as the fever washed over him, recounting hazy memories of their past.

William shared the earliest things he could remember with Lucinda: lazy barn days with Buck, church times with Ole Ben, and playing marbles with Catfish and Theo. She squeezed his hand, reminding him of the time he threw a stone and helped some wild Creek girl he didn't even know.

Lucinda climbed into bed and pulled her husband close, stroking his head. He had quieted now, so she kept reminiscing alone. She talked about how lucky she was that some strange, wonderful boy had shown up in her life, giving her a reason to live and hope in her troubled childhood. She reminded him of the muddy cave, how even though it was dark and scary, having each other had given her the strength to go on. She lingered on their stagecoach days in Quindaro and Lawrence, which, while brief, were shining moments of happiness for her. And, finally, when she reached back far enough to the boy who'd stood by her side all that time and had grown into a man she'd been proud to share her life with.

William Lacy died in the arms of his loving wife. Not horseboy, or Private Lacy. Not a hunter, soldier, or sinner—but a man who chose love and family over all else.

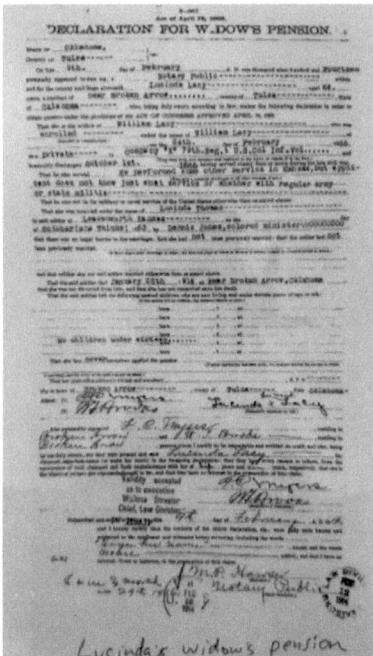

Figure 30 – 1: Lucinda Lacy's document in a fight for widow's pension

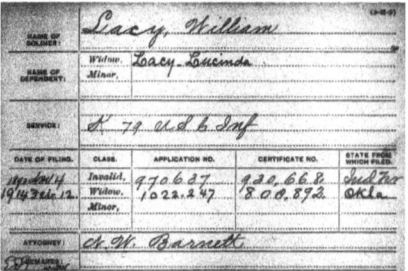

Figure 30 – 2: William Lacy's pension, post-mortem

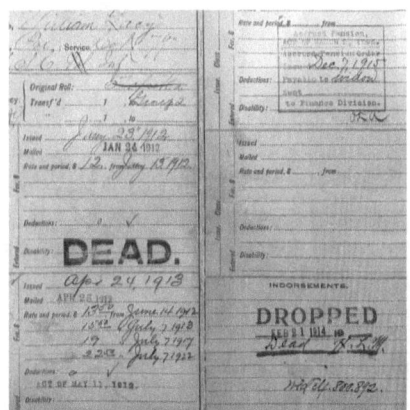

Figure 30 – 3: Pension record for William Lacy, deceased

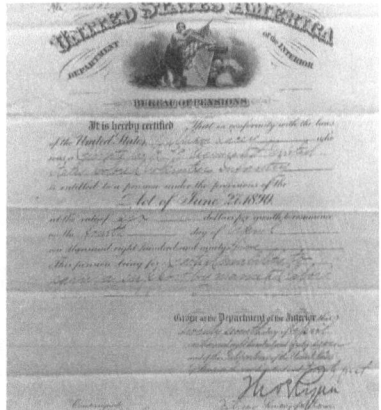

Figure 30 – 4: Pension Record

Charles Matthews Examiner.
(Write surname first plainly.)
Inv (Class.) No. 970637
Soldier William Lacy
Priv Co. K, 79 Reg't U.S.C.Vol.Inf.
Submitted Rejection Mch 1, 1892
Reviewer, 18
Re-submitted, 18
Reviewer, 18

FROM BOARD OF REVIEW TO
Medical Div.
2d charge
Examiner
2d charge
Sp. Ex. Div.
Misc. charges

REJECTED

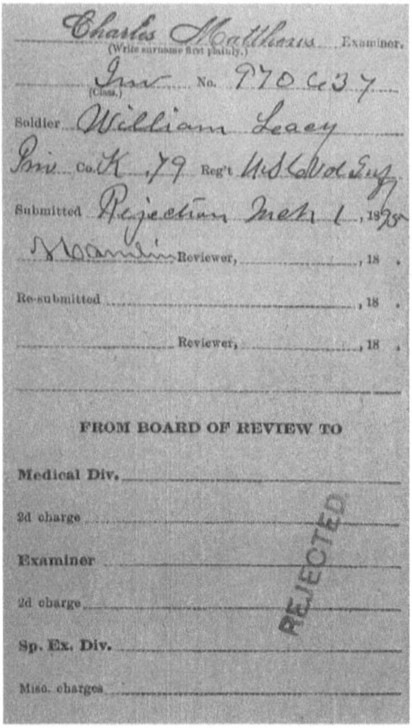

Figure 30 – 5: Pension Record

Southern. Division.
H. B. Whitney. Examiner.
(Write surname first plainly.)
Orig. Invalid. (Class.) No. 970637
Soldier William Lacy
Co. K, 79 Reg't U.S.C.Inf.
Submitted Rejection July 8, 1891.
ROBERTSON JUL 27 1892, 18
Re-submitted, 18
Reviewer, 18

FROM BOARD OF REVIEW TO
Medical Div. AUG 6 1892
2d charge
Examiner
2d charge
Sp. Ex. Div.
Misc. charges
Cert. Div.

REJECTED.

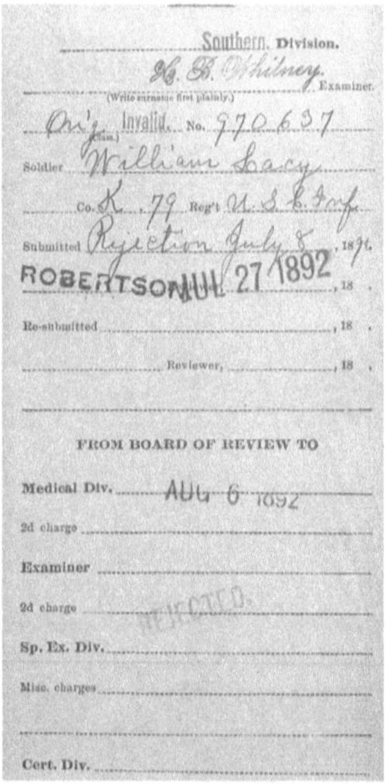

Figure 30 – 6: Pension record

BUREAU OF PENSIONS,
Washington, D.C., June 2nd, 1896
Mr William Lacy
late a Priv
Co. K, 79 Regiment U.S.C.V.Inf
an applicant for ORIGINAL
Invalid Pension, No. 970637
on account of disability from
Rheumatism
Blind or bleeding piles
and kidney disease
has been directed to report himself to you.
Very respectfully,
D. L. Murphy LOCHREN,

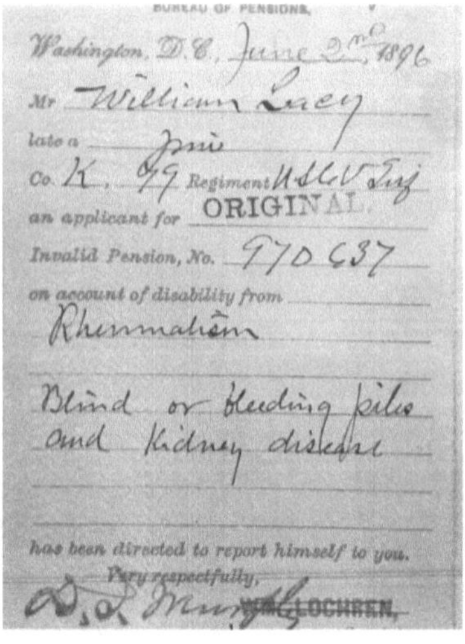

Figure 30 – 7: Pension record

So. Div.
Department of the Interior,
BUREAU OF PENSIONS.
Washington, D.C., Sept 26, 1900
Mr William Lacy
late a pri
Co. K, 79 Regiment U.S.C.Vol.Inf.
an applicant for inc.
Invalid Pension, No. Ctf. 930668
on account of disability from kidney trouble, piles, diarrhea, ... small of back, rheumatism, heart dis. injury to lt knee
has been directed to report himself to you.
Very respectfully,
H. CLAY EVANS,
Commissioner.
Dr. M. R. Chapman
Vinita
Cherokee Nat. Ind. Ter.
CLAIMANT'S POST-OFFICE ADDRESS:
Estosee
Cherokee Nation

PENSION OFFICE DEC 15 1900

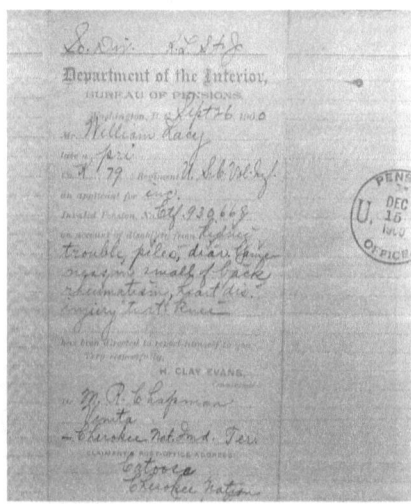

Figure 30 – 8: Pension record

Wid. orig. 1082,247
Lucinda Lacy
William Lacy
Co. K, 79th U.S.C.Inf.

May 21, 1915.

Mrs. Lucinda Lacy,
Broken Arrow,
Oklahoma.

Madam;

Your above cited claim for pension requires the sworn testimony of two credible witnesses having the requisite knowledge, other than Jennie Little and Susan Tucker, showing whether you and the soldier were known and recognized as man and wife in the community in which you resided from the date of your alleged marriage in 1863, to the date of his death, and that you always lived together, without separation or divorce, during that time.

You should furnish statements from Jennie Little and Susan Tucker, giving their ages, which they failed to state in their affidavits on file.

Very respectfully,

G. M. Saltzgaber
Commissioner.

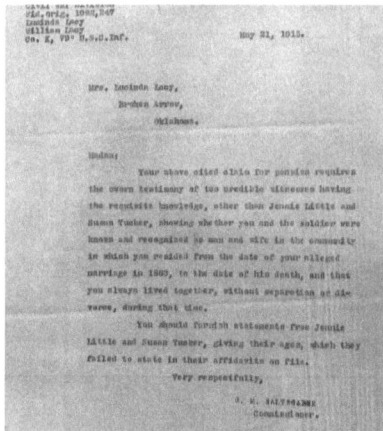

Figure 30 – 9: Pension record

June 13, 1912.

Commissioner of Pensions.

for pension under the Act of May 11, 1912,
of William Lacy of Tulsa, Okla.

Very truly yours,
James A. Davenport

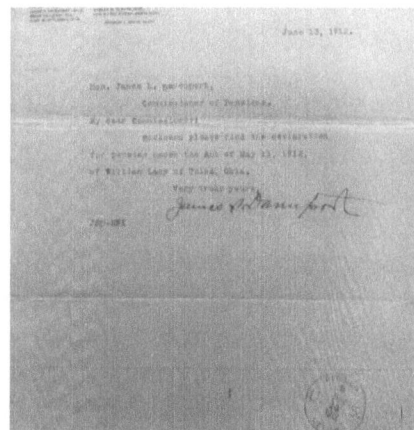

Figure 30 – 10: Pension record

BUREAU OF PENSIONS,

Washington, D. C., July 17th, 1894

Sir:

You are hereby directed to report yourself for medical examination to the **Board of Examining Surgeons** Dr. Callahan's Office
(St. and No.) Rooms 4 & 5 Bank Bldg.
Town Muscogee
County Creek Nat., State Ind. Ter.
within three months from date hereof.

The Board meets at 10 o'clock a.m. every Wednesday in each month.

Return this slip with the date of the examination indorsed hereon by the Secretary of the Board making the same.

Very respectfully,
Wm Lochren
Commissioner.

Claimant: William Lacy
P. O.: Muscogee
Creek Nation Indian Ter.
Attorney: H. S. Berlin
P. O.: City

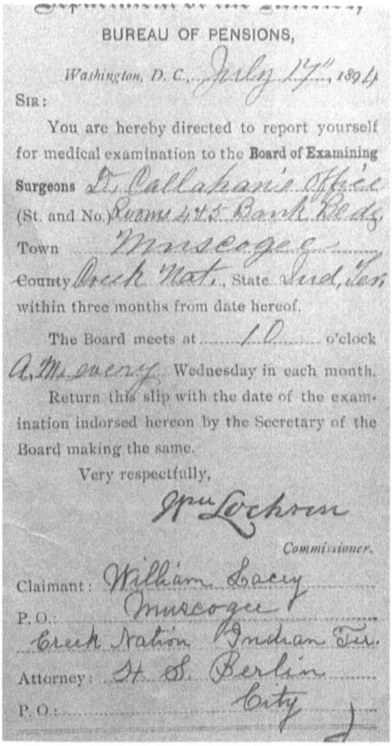

Figure 30 – 11: Pension record

CHAPTER 31

Unearthing the Past

Morgan County, Alabama—May 10, 2025

"If you ask me what I came here to do ... I will tell you I came here to live out loud."

—Emile Zola

Looking back over my life, I realize how fascinated I have always been with history. As an African American, our history and the plight of my people brought to the country in chains have always fascinated me. We struggled to overcome a repressive history of bondage in America. Then came the ensuing battle to dismantle the system of Jim Crow and segregation laws throughout the slave areas of this nation that kept away from us our wages of sweat and ties of our families. There were so many good people, Black and white, who assisted in destroying that system, and all Americans should celebrate them and that achievement.

Over the years, I have watched virtually every movie about American slavery that I have had access to. I have visited places across the nation relevant to the peculiar institution, such as the Annapolis, Maryland Harbor, where Kunta Kinte, a slave whose history was chronicled in the television series *Roots*, entered America on a slave ship. I visited the Courtland, Alabama, town square, where the slave blocks used for selling slaves still exist today. I spent time in the Charleston slave quarters, where they were also sold by the thousands to white Americans with their fists full of dollars. These are just a few of the hundreds of locations I visited to better understand the American slavery system. Each visit brings me closer to the victims and closer to the oppressors' way of thinking.

My professional endeavors brought me from the Midwest to the East Coast to live in 1992. One of the nicest things about that relocation was the proximity it offered me to Civil War battlefields throughout Maryland and Virginia. Every other weekend, I'd head out to see another battlefield or Civil War site to add to my understanding.

A few years before I came to the Washington D.C. area, I had seen *Glory* starring Denzel Washington, Morgan Freeman, Matthew Broderick, and Cary Elwes. So, when I arrived on the East Coast in 1993, I watched the movie for a second time and joined the Civil War reenacting group that made the movie as soldiers in the 54th Massachusetts Regiment. This organization was called Company B.

The organization had about fifty extremely sharp Black men from around the mid-Atlantic region. They were well-read on Civil War issues and many other parts of the soldier's life. Most of them were veterans of more recent wars, but they all had a distinct fire for preserving the history of the soldiers of the 54th Massachusetts and other Black Civil War units previously lost to time. I owe any credentials I have achieved in this area to the time, discussion, and energy given to me by these amazing men.

Additionally, some white men in Company B and other regiments portray white officers in these reenactments, and I duly recognize their efforts to educate the nation in unity with these Black soldiers—special love and appreciation to you.

Working alongside these special men, regardless of skin color, only grew my love for the Civil War and my people's history. We've reenacted some battles discussed in this text with these organizations, such as Honey Springs and Poison Springs. Earlier, I had no idea my reenactments had historical connections to my ancestors. These battles resonated emotionally with someone in my bloodline whose life was in jeopardy. Can you imagine the gravity of this?

My work has taken me to stages, platforms, and fields to discuss the United States Colored Troops and their heroism. However, there is nothing like standing on an actual battlefield beside their ghosts.

I have stood on many battlefields: the battlefield at Olustee, Florida, where the 3rd United States Colored Troops fought in February of 1864; Honey Springs battlefield, where the 1st Kansas Colored Volunteers fought so bravely; Morris Island, South Carolina, where the 54th Massachusetts fought so bravely, both on July 18, 1863. To stand at Brush Creek in Kansas City now has new meaning to me. Knowing that my great-great-grandfather, William Lacy, became a man and a person at that location is breathtaking.

Walking those locations gave me a visceral feeling like never before. My guess is that the ground there is soaked in history—it's a place where my Black fathers and grandfathers chose to sacrifice themselves to win. Their blood and sweat made our nation what it is today. These hallowed sites are just as important to me as Gettysburg, Nashville, or Shiloh.

I have visited these locations without my Civil War uniform or being involved in some organized event. Even as a spectator, the emotion is still present in me. I drove out to Island Mound, Missouri, once to see the location where the first Black men fought in the Civil War.

I arrived in a small town, Butler, about fifty miles south of Kansas City in Bates County, Missouri. The National Historic Site was a simple field with a large, wide circular pathway cut so visitors could walk out to the sites of Hogs Island and the Toothman Farm, where the first action occurred. The folks in that county have memorialized the event and showcased it in a museum. It is the most important thing that has happened in Bates County, Missouri.

When I later visited the Honey Springs Battlefield in the Indian Territory of Eastern Oklahoma, I found a vast field with slow, rolling hills, located near a roadway called the Texas Road. In 1863, just like you read in William and Lucinda's story, a battle was fought there. The Black soldiers of the 1st Kansas Colored Volunteers and Native American soldiers of the Indian Home Guard defeated the

Confederate soldiers with their own Native American Choctaw fighters. It is difficult to visualize the Native Americans fighting one another over slavery, but it happened.

I believe that twenty-eight years of Civil War reenacting prepared me to meet and know my ancestor who fought in this conflict.

So, when CNN invited me for an interview, I thought I was ready and that they would ask me about my Civil War knowledge. But when the nice woman from Ancestry, Nicka Sewell, said the name of the man who was my great-great-grandfather, William Lacy, and that he was a soldier in the 1st Kansas Colored Volunteers, tears streamed down my face because somehow and someway, a connection fell into place, stretching across time to him and his era. His pain and fear swelled in me, too. His resolve and determination strengthened me. When I looked at my own children and pictures of my parents, I saw that everything we owed was thanks to the struggles that came before us. After feeling that, I owed it to these great people to unearth everything I could to preserve their place in history. More importantly, we need to anchor them into the future they fought so hard to give to us.

My first stop was the Morgan County Archives in Alabama. A cheerful man named John Allison helped me find everything about Lacy Springs and the prominent family who lived there. Several books with information chronicled the family's lives and wills filed with the archives. They were an invaluable resource. Yet when I reviewed the documents, I saw nothing with the name of William Lacy on it. However, I found information about other slaves on the plantation, so I copied and kept the information.

A few days later, a man named Todd Mildfelt called me. He had seen the interview on CNN and reached out to me through Facebook. He said he believed he knew where William Lacy's land was located in Mound City, Kansas. I immediately went there to see the land he owned and uncover everything I could about his life.

While I was there, I took a trip to Fort Scott to see the actual fort where the 1st Kansas Colored Volunteers mustered in the Civil War and where they camped while they trained to go to the front lines. I met two men named Arnold Scoffield and Carl Brenner. They were gracious enough to invite me into the fort. Because the fort is a National Historic Site, not many events take place anymore, but I received a tour while there. These gentlemen presented me with a book called *Soldier in the Army of Freedom* by Ian Michael Spurgeon. They said it was the one book a historian had to own if he was interested in the 1st Kansas Colored Volunteers and their history. As I left the fort, Mr. Scoffield told me something that was sure to come true. He said I was about to embark on a very special journey, and truer words were never spoken.

While there, I learned that William Lacy ran a livery stable on behalf of its owners in the nearby town of Pleasanton, Kansas, after the war. Todd Mildfelt showed me the building, and some of the brick still gives hints of a livery stable today. Today, the location is owned by a wonderful man named Chad Carpenter, who uses it as a motorcycle shop.

Next, I traveled down to the Indian Territory to find the cemetery where William was buried. A website called "Find a Grave" lists cemeteries and grave locations of anyone buried there. CNN's interview gave me a short obituary for William Lacy and a clue to this location. The website hinted at the row and space where he may be buried. I wanted to see these locations so badly that I drove from Washington, D.C., to Kansas and Oklahoma during the COVID-19 pandemic to satisfy my curiosity.

It was pouring rain when I arrived in Broken Arrow, Oklahoma. However, I was determined to see the location of the former slave and soldier—my great-great-grandfather.

I had to ask for directions from everyone who entered the convenience store near the gravesite. After about thirty minutes of inquiring in the warm rain, an elderly gentleman pulled in to gas up his old pickup. He looked like he had been around here for a long time. So, I thought if he didn't know where this tiny cemetery was located, then I would go home. Sure enough, I asked him, and he pointed me to the Wagoner County water tower and said it must be that small cemetery near the tower. Armed with this information, I struck out to find William Lacy's grave.

When I found the cemetery, I felt justified. It was tiny—about the size of a common household property. The area had been a gift from the Creek Nation to the Black freedmen who needed a place to bury their dead.

The small wooden sign with "Thomas Smith Cemetery" written on it was lying on the grass beside the road, just waiting to be driven over. I placed it back on the fence and navigated inside the entrance to escape the road. The rain pelted me harder as I walked through the knee-high grass. Something inside would not allow me to quit, not even for the day. Finally, up against the western fence of the cemetery was a broken soldier's tombstone. It had the feel of all other soldiers' tombstones with white marble and rounded tops, but the top had been destroyed. It was all I could do to see the partial name and 79th USCT carved into the stone. Next to it was a larger gray-colored tombstone, but it had fallen on its face. It was very large and heavy. Fortunately, I could lift it up enough to see that it was Lucinda Lacy's tombstone.

Now, I had found them. The old slave couple who had escaped bondage just a few miles from here and made a life in Kansas, only to return to their homelands.

Next, I had to decide what to do about his tombstone that was destroyed and her tombstone that was pushed over. I reached out to the Facebook website listed on the small wooden sign on the front of the cemetery and left my name and number. A man with a silky-smooth voice called me a few days later. It was James Hardman. He explained that we were cousins and immediately struck up a friendship. As it turns out, he and I both wanted to address the tombstones. Together, we set in motion an effort to clean and refurbish the cemetery. The Veterans Administration provided a new tombstone for William Lacy, and we had Lucinda's power-washed. Next, we set a date for a memorial celebration to replace the new stone for William's grave.

After seeing the CNN segment, the CBS Morning Show called and wanted to do a segment on William Lacy, somewhat like the CNN segment. I explained that I was preparing for an event at the cemetery, and they asked if they could come to film the event. We gave them an exclusive, and they flew a film crew from New York to

Broken Arrow, Oklahoma, to interview us and see the small ceremonial event.

William and Lucinda's story was now on *CBS Mornings* with Gayle King. I would never have been able to unearth this story without the help of all the names I mentioned in this book.

After William's death, Lucinda received his pension, but not without a fight with the army to prove she was his wife. Although there is no proof, family folklore has it that Lucinda was shopping on Greenwood, better known as Black Wall Street, on May 31, 1921, when the Tulsa Race Massacre began. She was able to escape and died a few months later from kidney failure.

Thank you for reading this tale. I sincerely hope this look into the past memorializes the lives of some truly amazing people. From my family to yours, remember that we can find strength in dark times if we look to each other. Never forget that at the end of even the darkest, muddiest cave, there will always be a helping hand.

Calvin Osborne